Dynamics of Profit-Focused Accounting

Attaining Sustained Value and Bottom-Line Improvement

BY

C. LYNN NORTHRUP

CPA, CPIM

THE EDUCATIONAL SOCIETY
FOR RESOURCE MANAGEMENT

Copyright ©2004 by J. Ross Publishing, Inc.

ISBN 1-932159-22-3

Printed and bound in the U.S.A. Printed on acid-free paper
10 9 8 7 6 5 4 3 2 1

Library of Congress Cataloging-in-Publication Data

Northrup, C. Lynn, 1939-
   Dynamics of profit-focused accounting : attaining sustained value and
bottom-line improvement / C. Lynn Northrup.
      p. cm.
   ISBN 1-932159-22-3
   1. Managerial accounting   2. Activity-based costing.   3. Total
quality management. I. Title.
   HF5657.4.N677 2004
   658.15′11—dc22
                              2004003204

   This publication contains information obtained from authentic and highly regarded sources.
Reprinted material is used with permission, and sources are indicated. Reasonable effort has
been made to publish reliable data and information, but the author and the publisher cannot
assume responsibility for the validity of all materials or for the consequences of their use.
   All rights reserved. Neither this publication nor any part thereof may be reproduced,
stored in a retrieval system or transmitted in any form or by any means, electronic, me-
chanical, photocopying, recording or otherwise, without the prior written permission of the
publisher.
   The copyright owner's consent does not extend to copying for general distribution for
promotion, for creating new works, or for resale. Specific permission must be obtained from
J. Ross Publishing for such purposes.
   Direct all inquiries to J. Ross Publishing, Inc., 6501 Park of Commerce Blvd., Suite 200,
Boca Raton, Florida 33487.

Phone: (561) 869-3900
Fax: (561) 892-0700
Web: www.jrosspub.com

DEDICATION

This book is dedicated to my wife, Jessica.
Thank you for your help and support
that took this book from a dream to a reality.

TABLE OF CONTENTS

PREFACE

My original intent with *Dynamics of Profit-Focused Accounting* was to provide, in a single educational source, all of the major productivity tools and related accounting and scorekeeping applications. In the process of accomplishing that objective, the boundaries of what I originally conceived were expanded. I stretched my own learning and knowledge as new ideas and concepts emerged with the development of the manuscript. Originally, the intent was to cover lean thinking, Six Sigma, and the Theory of Constraints together with throughput accounting, activity-based analysis, and balanced scorecards. I thought it was important that financial managers and accountants have a better understanding of these concepts. On the other hand, it was equally important for operational people to gain understanding of how productivity initiatives should be measured and evaluated. These mysterious concepts needed to be discussed and described with fundamental simplicity. While these initial goals were achieved, I ended up with much more in my shopping cart than was intended.

I am pleased with these diversions because this book's purpose shifted in positive ways as it neared completion. This book should provide an educational foundation for corporate performance management in the twenty-first century. Businesspeople and educators will find that all of the elements have been touched in some fashion. Therefore, this book will be useful to the CEO, CFO, and controller down to and including employees working on the line or in a cubicle. The world of productivity and measurement has been combined with a dose of leadership, together with a look at the future of knowledge management. All the basics of the cutting-edge concepts and methodologies encompassing corporate performance management have been defined or described in this book. The book provides the basics and points the way to further exploration and learning.

We begin with a history of how productivity and accounting emerged and how they are being utilized and applied today. Next, lean manufacturing is described together with the fundamental elements of lean thinking and how to implement them. Six Sigma is explained together with its tools and applications, and the Theory of Constraints and its thinking processes are spelled out. Activity-based costing and management is then described so that fundamental understanding of its purpose and best applications can be utilized, as it might be appropriate. I explain where activity-based analysis should be used and where it should not be used, together with simplified and faster ways of applying it. Throughput accounting is revealed together with applications on overcoming the shortcomings of traditional cost management. The next tool described is the balanced scorecard so that the reader can comprehend what the scorecard does and how it should be applied.

I developed some of my own thoughts about how to apply these tools and provide a new reporting model called profit-focused accounting. This model spells out how to utilize all of the tools to build a simpler and faster accounting and financial reporting model. I show how to apply the speed of throughput accounting and explain where and how to use activity-based analysis to improve understanding and control over nonmanufacturing business processes. Nonfinancial metrics using balanced scorecard concepts are described together with mapping and measuring strategy and knowledge assets.

A chapter on value-based management and measurement is included. This leads into a discussion and description of the implications of the Sarbanes-Oxley Act. The discussion includes exploration of the "back to basics" approach needed for organizations to ensure that their financial reporting processes are reliable. The discussion also covers the merits of the economic model versus the accounting model and spells out the two concepts in understandable terms. This is followed with a chapter that explains the key metrics and measures that organizations will need to understand, together with tips on where and how to use them. Cost of quality is explained, as are the details of how to compute the cost of carrying excess inventory. Knowledge management is described as it relates to strategy and the improvement of innovation and business processes. This book would not be complete without describing the issues of great leadership, as discussed in the next chapter. All of the strategy and measurement tools are worthless without effective execution of leadership.

This book wraps up with a discussion of all the concepts that were presented together with thoughts on how to improve the impact of performance management and financial reporting. A continuous planning process is offered, in addition to describing the need for continuous training and employee empowerment.

It is my sincere desire that readers will enhance their knowledge and gain new understanding and ways to apply these tools and concepts more effectively to improve the performance management, productivity, and profitability of their organization.

THE AUTHOR

 **C. Lynn Northrup** is the principal of C. Lynn Northrup, CPA based in Wilmington, North Carolina. In addition to his CPA and consulting practice, he develops and teaches continuing professional education programs. Lynn was previously with McGladrey & Pullen's national manufacturing consulting practice, where his specialty was conducting operational and work flow assessments focused on business process improvement and performance measurement utilizing ERP systems. He also worked on the application of strategic cost management and analysis concepts.

After starting his career in public accounting with Arthur Young and PricewaterhouseCoopers, he was the Controller at Schlegel Corporation in Rochester, New York. Schlegel, a complex multinational manufacturing company, grew rapidly from $10 million in sales to $300 million from 1965 to 1984. Lynn developed and implemented the cost accounting, financial, and budget forecasting systems for this company on a worldwide basis, which included over thirty-five profit centers located in seventeen different countries.

In addition to creating his own CPA and advisory practice, Lynn has held various management and executive positions in industry including controller and vice president of finance. His experience includes working with a wide variety of manufacturing companies in diverse industries plus construction, service industries including CPA firms, mail order, hospitality, real estate, and nonprofit organizations.

Lynn received a B.B.A. from Clarkson University in 1960 and was certified in production and inventory management (CPIM) with APICS in 1999. He is licensed as a CPA in New York, North Carolina, and Oregon and is a member of the American Institute of Certified Public Accountants and the North Carolina Association of CPAs. He is also an active member of APICS. Lynn can be reached at cln@northrupcpa.com.

ABOUT APICS

APICS — The Educational Society for Resource Management is a not-for-profit international educational organization recognized as the global leader and premier provider of resource management education and information. APICS is respected throughout the world for its education and professional certification programs. With more than 60,000 individual and corporate members in 20,000 companies worldwide, APICS is dedicated to providing education to improve an organization's bottom line. No matter what your title or need, by tapping into the APICS community you will find the education necessary for success.

APICS is recognized globally as:

- The source of knowledge and expertise for manufacturing and service industries across the entire supply chain
- The leading provider of high-quality, cutting-edge educational programs that advance organizational success in a changing, competitive marketplace
- A successful developer of two internationally recognized certification programs, Certified in Production and Inventory Management (CPIM) and Certified in Integrated Resource Management (CIRM)
- A source of solutions, support, and networking for manufacturing and service professionals

For more information about APICS programs, services, or membership, visit www.apics.org or contact APICS Customer Support at (800) 444-2742 or (703) 354-8851.

™Web
Added
Value

Free value-added materials available from
the Download Resource Center at www.jrosspub.com

At J. Ross Publishing we are committed to providing today's professional with practical, hands-on tools that enhance the learning experience and give readers an opportunity to apply what they have learned. That is why we offer free ancillary materials available for download on this book and all participating Web Added Value™ publications. These on-line resources may include interactive versions of material that appears in the book or supplemental templates, worksheets, models, plans, case studies, proposals, spreadsheets and assessment tools, among other things. Whenever you see the WAV™ symbol in any of our publications, it means bonus materials accompany the book and are available from the Web Added Value Download Resource Center at www.jrosspub.com.

Downloads available for *Dynamics of Profit-Focused Accounting: Attaining Sustained Value and Bottom-Line Improvement* consist of cost of capital, EVA™ component and bridging the GAAP templates, a product/customer matrix, performance assessment scorecard, and a dashboard tutorial.

PAST, PRESENT, FUTURE

Business has been flooded with management methodologies, productivity tools, and terminology over the past half century. The rapid pace of change has been accelerated further by innovation and technology. In this age of knowledge and information, it is critical to have a thorough understanding of what tools are available and how to use them. Organizations need to understand how to measure and execute strategy and the best use of nonfinancial and financial metrics. Businesspeople will learn the best techniques to measure and account for operational excellence and how to measure and account for innovation.

In a single source, readers receive an in-depth overview of all the cutting-edge productivity methods and measurement tools used in today's business environment. From this foundation, training is provided on how to keep score and apply the scorekeeping tools. I start with an overview of the history of how these tools and methodologies were developed. Each major management methodology and philosophy is explained, followed by a comprehensive review of accounting methods and scorekeeping tools.

Suggested application techniques for using these tools are provided, together with a new accounting and reporting model. Instructions on using performance metrics and measures are provided along with tips on how to apply them. Highlights of the issues associated with the Sarbanes-Oxley Act are blended into a dialogue on value-based management and measurement. After an evaluation of leadership and thoughts on executing strategy and tactics, a summary and review bring the tool kit together with visionary thoughts for the future.

The methodologies that are reviewed include lean manufacturing, Six Sigma, the Theory of Constraints, activity-based costing and analysis, throughput accounting, balanced scorecards, and concepts for value-based management and measurement. Easy-to-understand explanations and discussions on the operational productivity concepts are provided along with details of the latest accounting and scorekeeping techniques and issues. A model and vision for the most effective techniques for using and measuring the impact of these tools are presented. I realize that all the tools will not be right for every organization. These tools should enable one another. By understanding how each tool can be utilized, managers will be equipped to determine the best combination of tools and methodologies for their organization.

Financial managers will gain a better understanding of operational and strategic issues and how to account for and measure profitability. Operational managers will gain new insights about accounting and scorekeeping techniques. By offering all the contemporary management concepts and philosophies from both a financial and operational perspective, managers will enhance their ability to deal with the speed and accountability issues required to be competitive in the twenty-first century.

THE PAST

The 1950s and 1960s

History provides many lessons on coping with the present and helps guide us into the future. Cost management techniques and accounting principles used in the 1950s and 1960s have not changed dramatically in their ability to help in managing the development and innovation in productivity and business philosophy. Understanding the evolution of management philosophies over the last few decades provides some ideas regarding the steps needed to correct the problems and imbalances to measure and account for productivity more effectively. Productivity has seen many innovations, but accounting is much the same as it was fifty years ago. It still has not become very relevant as a management tool.

Manufacturing performance over the past half century looks like a wide V as shown on the graph in Figure 1.1. Starting in the late 1950s, manufacturing productivity consistently declined until about 1975. After 1975, manufacturing companies began to learn of these innovations in addition to feeling their competitive impact. Based on this wake-up call, a period of sustained improvements in productivity started to take hold and evolve into continuous growth. The capability of operations and production people grew with this surge and they continued to innovate and use new techniques. This has not been the case with accounting tools and methods used to measure this increased productivity.

The 1950s and 1960s were a total cost world. My career in public accounting began in 1960 and I vividly remember the focus from this era. Production, not quality, was the key driver and finance numbers were motivated by efficiency and full utilization. The business environment focused on the numbers that

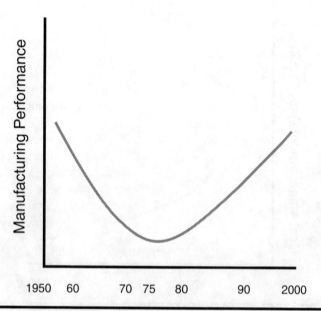

Figure 1.1. The Resurrection of Manufacturing Performance.

utilized traditional cost accounting methods and management by objective. Cost management tools of the 1960s and 1970s were characterized by standard cost systems and variance analysis from standard and budget. Product costs were loaded with allocations of overhead in an attempt to determine product line profitability and profitability by customer. Projections and budgets were based on historical costs as a predictor of the future. In almost all cases, the basis for allocating overhead to product cost and for inventory valuation purposes was direct labor. Labor efficiency was measured by department and work center with emphasis placed on making sure that the equipment and facility were being fully utilized. Purchase price variances were tracked with pressure applied to the purchasing function to purchase material from the lowest cost supplier. Cost of quality was not an issue and the voice of the customer took a back seat, if it was ever heard at all.

During the decade from 1960, the relevance of cost management data took the same downward path as manufacturing productivity. This is illustrated in Figure 1.2. During this time period, inventories increased and profitability declined as Schonberger clearly describes and documents in *World Class Manufacturing: The Next Decade*. The difference between productivity management and cost management is that productivity continued to improve and the relevance of cost management just kept decreasing.

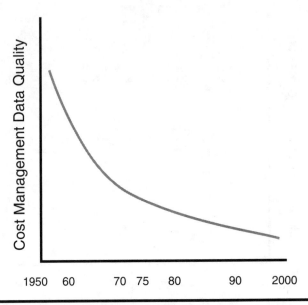

Figure 1.2.   The Declining Relevance of Cost Management.

The 1970s

The 1970s brought a surge of new innovations and tools. The Japanese utilized W. Edwards Deming, from Philadelphia, to revitalize their industrial process. Total quality control and the concepts symbolized by the Toyota Production System lifted the Japanese to industrial prominence. American manufacturing companies continued on a downward spiral until about 1975 when they started to discover the ideas taught to the Japanese by Deming and utilize them in American factories.

During this period of innovation, we started to see total quality control, just in time (JIT), and kanban being utilized. Total preventive maintenance, supplier partnerships, and quality function deployment started showing up in some of the more progressive companies. The Japanese showed us the effectiveness of employee involvement, cross-careering, and visual management. Target costing became an effective competitive weapon, which was another innovation learned from the Japanese.

Deming clearly had an impact that extended far beyond the realization of most business managers. Capturing and preserving Deming's knowledge and lessons will serve us well in the future. Deming was a statistician who started working with the Japanese in 1951 to rebuild Japan after World War II. He taught the Japanese to build and export quality, in the form of product for

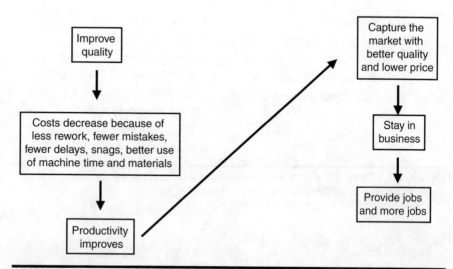

Figure 1.3. The Deming Chain Reaction. (Adapted from page 25 of *The Deming Management Method* by Mary Walton, from page 252 of *Out of the Crisis* by W. Edwards Deming.)

exporting, in turn for receiving food. He helped the Japanese factories understand the effectiveness of process controls and how to redesign products to bring them under control. Utilizing these techniques and Deming's management philosophies, the Japanese started to capture worldwide markets. Dr. Deming became a national hero in Japan, while he was virtually unheard of in America. It was not until about 1980 that American captains of industry learned the impact of Deming and his new tools. Deming created a foundation for management that is still being constructed.

One of the significant teachings from *Out of the Crisis* by Deming is "The Deming Chain Reaction," which is shown in Figure 1.3. Dr. Deming also introduced his famous Fourteen Points shown in Figure 1.4. These Fourteen Points and the Seven Deadly Diseases emit a guiding light that provides solid lessons for twenty-first century managers. The Seven Deadly Diseases are:

1. Lack of constancy of purpose
2. Emphasis on short-term profits
3. Evaluation of performance, merit rating, or annual review (Dr. Deming suggested that "management by fear" is a better name)
4. Mobility of top management
5. Running a company on visible figures alone ("counting the money")

1. Constancy of purpose	8. Drive out fear
2. Adopt the philosophy	9. Break down barriers
3. Don't rely on mass inspection	10. Eliminate slogans and exhortations (warnings)
4. Don't award business on price	
5. Constant improvement	11. Eliminate quotas
6. Training	12. Pride of workmanship
7. Leadership	13. Education and retraining
	14. Plan of action

Figure 1.4. Deming's Fourteen Points. (Adapted from pages 34 and 35 of *The Deming Management Method* by Mary Walton.)

6. Excessive medical costs — healthcare
7. Excessive costs of warranty, fueled by lawyers who work on contingency fees

The 1980s

The 1980s brought more new innovations resulting from the visibility of Dr. Deming's work. Clearly, concepts such as those designed for manufacturing and assembly, benchmarking, and the cost of quality can be traced to the Deming influence. Companies like Wal-Mart and other forward-thinking operations created point-of-sale technology, electronic data interchange, and quick-response linkages to retailers. Reengineering, digital design, rapid prototyping, and cross-docking are concepts that started in the 1980s. Activity-based costing became a trendy tool for many companies to offset the irrelevance of historically based cost management and generally accepted accounting principles (GAAP) in an attempt to help them manage and operate their businesses.

While Deming started the momentum, there were other disciples and gurus who created the JIT/TQM movement. JIT is a management philosophy that was based on simplicity with an attitude of "do it, judge it, measure it, fix it, and manage it." The philosophy worked at a pace that did not wait for reports to arrive from the accounting department. It was a "take action, get it done, and do it right the first time" approach that literality rendered the meaning of cost management obsolete.

TQM, the acronym for "total quality management," was synonymous with JIT. This philosophy became the rage for businesses during the 1980s. These philosophies evolved from the Japanese style of quality management, most notably Toyota. Disciples who followed the Deming lead then developed their own theories and teachings. The common theme was: Make the product right the first time and acquire and use resources only as you need them. For JIT and TQM to work, speed and simplicity became key elements of success. Creating simplicity established a platform for change.

TQM launched the benchmarking movement to search out, study, and implement best practices, providing the movement with far-reaching consequences. It was not just a manufacturing tool, but a philosophy of managing and a set of business practices that emphasized continuous improvement in all phases of operations and all types of organizations. An Arthur D. Little study reported that 93 of the 500 largest corporations in the United States had adapted some form of TQM by the early 1990s. It literally became a cornerstone of how organizations functioned as they entered the twenty-first century.

Predominant quality leaders included Joseph M. Juran and Philip Crosby, who felt (along with government leaders) that emphasis on quality was a necessity for doing business in a competitive world market. This led to the establishment of the Malcolm Baldrige National Quality Award in 1987. The award recognizes organizations in the United States for their achievements in quality and performance excellence.

The Juran Trilogy included:

1. Quality planning
2. Quality control
3. Quality improvement

Philip Crosby identified his own "14 Quality Steps" which have become ingrained into the quality management philosophy:

1. Management commitment
2. Quality improvement teams
3. Quality measurement
4. Cost of quality evaluation
5. Quality awareness
6. Corrective action
7. Zero defects committee
8. Supervisor training
9. Zero defects day
10. Goal setting
11. Error cause removal
12. Recognition
13. Quality councils
14. Do it over again

While TQM focuses on producing quality products and the delivery of outstanding customer service, it requires the support of all the organizational and business functions such as human resources, engineering, accounting, and information technology. TQM provides the required tools for JIT to work successfully. Based on this platform, JIT drives a company to organize the way it works and operates. The key component of JIT is to have only the required inventory when needed. The speed and acceleration of JIT demands quality that produces zero defects, reduction of lead times and setups, together with reduction to the length of queues and waiting time. It also involves improving the relationships with suppliers to ensure the highest quality and that they have the ability to deliver material exactly when it is required.

TQM led the revolution of the 1980s and forced companies to create entirely new strategies and businesses just by changing the way they managed quality. The United States was not the only country jumping on this bandwagon. It was a global event, and all the players in the global economic arena were forced to take advantage of these fundamental concepts driven by customer needs. The competitive requirements of the global economy made speed, quality, and business process control essential for survival. The acceleration of productivity and the flow of information from related systems were more than the lumbering ancient cost management and GAAP were capable of supporting. The acceleration continues and the gap gets wider. Production scheduling and logistics systems have evolved into "enterprise resource planning," known as ERP. These systems do contain accounting systems, but the accounting logic is based on the concepts that have not changed much since 1960.

New measuring tools that attempted to overcome the shortcomings of cost management and accounting measurement include activity-based costing and management in the mid-1980s and the balanced scorecard in the early 1990s. These are topics that will be addressed in greater detail in later chapters. A critical issue here is to understand the accelerated pace of development in customer service, quality, and production management. This need spawned the Theory of Constraints, lean manufacturing, and Six Sigma out of TQM and JIT, and they have evolved into their own management philosophies, concepts, and tools. Understanding this evolution is important before we explore each of the concepts in greater depth.

THE TOYOTA STORY

Toyota is a legendary example of how Japanese productivity and quality concepts led the productivity revolution. This is not meant to be misleading, since

Toyota was not the only player creating rules for the game, but it is a story worth understanding. Almost every practitioner studies the Toyota system with great scrutiny. James P. Womack and Daniel T. Jones, credited with starting the lean movement, wrote *The Machine That Changed the World* (with Daniel Roos) to document the Toyota Production System.

During the 1980s, there was no other automotive facility in the world that achieved the level of low-cost flexibility as Toyota did. The renowned Taiichi Ohno was the creator of this new model for manufacturing. They created the "kanban concept" and made it so famous that it has been copied and implemented worldwide. The kanban premise is that "if we have used inventory, replace it as it is needed." It utilizes a concept of two bins that you replenish as each bin is emptied.

Toyota's system is much more than kanban as it also utilizes cellular manufacturing to take advantage of multiskilled workers so they can provide multiple tasks at a single work cell location. This concept includes the people side of the business by incorporating hands-on training and cross-functional teamwork. The work environment contains a do-it-yourself attitude and includes preventive maintenance and tooling development.

Another key element of the Toyota system is "takt" time. This represents the time between the completion of parts or units as determined by the requirements of the schedule. Takt time relates to the German word for musical meter and was adopted by the Japanese when they were learning aircraft production from the Germans. Takt time is the link of the pace of production to customer demand. Toyota uses repetitive manufacturing schedules and develops the schedule using takt time. The experienced Toyota workers plan in detail how to design their work for next month's production. All work cycles must fit into the time window allowed by takt time. When the new schedule starts up, all production steps are triggered by kanban signals calling only for parts that are needed by the users.

The Toyota system is designed to allow flexibility of output. When a schedule changes takt time, all tasks are revised and incorporated into a new plan. Toyota plants are designed to build a wide variety of vehicles on the same production line, and since the equipment was designed with such changes in mind, the workers revise the plans for effective use of the line. The rate of production maintains assembly speeds of ±15 percent that are communicated to suppliers that learn to and are required to provide the assembly lines with JIT response.

Another unique feature of the Toyota system is that employee understanding and training are built into the organization. All employees know where they are and what is going on. This is aided by the use of visual displays to monitor the key pulse beat of the operation. This visibility helps to maintain a simplistic human system integrating everyone in the entire operational and strategic process. They maintain agility as well as speed. Understanding this concept helps to explain and understand how many American companies struggle to remain competitive.

The Toyota Production System places as much responsibility at the "lowest" level possible. John Y. Shook describes this management approach in "Bringing the Toyota Production System to the United States: A Personal Perspective (*Becoming Lean*): "Toyota managers, the good ones anyway, would rarely tell their people what to do; they would lay out a problem, ask for an analysis or a proposal, but always stop short of saying, 'Do This.'" This provides the workers with a feeling of responsibility and the ability not to worry about top management reprisal or criticism. It is interesting to see the emphasis on the top down and bottom up in *The Strategy Focused Organization* by Robert S. Kaplan and David P. Norton and its correlation to the Toyota application.

The Toyota story is significant because kanban, JIT, and one-piece flow synchronized to customer demand are now primary elements of all of the major management philosophies we will be exploring. There are large differences between the culture in Japan and other countries, including the United States. This helps to understand the challenges we face to adopt these concepts.

THE PRESENT

Today, early in the twenty-first century, we have the Sarbanes-Oxley legislation, which was enacted to keep CEOs, CFOs, and controllers on course after the scandals at Enron, WorldCom, Tyco, and a growing list of others. Executives are required to certify the accuracy of their financial statements and the existence of systems and internal controls that will support accurate and meaningful data. But amazingly, even with the significant investment in technology, most companies do not know — with any level of comfort — what products and what customers generate their profit and how much. The Fortune 1000 companies are actively pursuing lean manufacturing to go faster and Six Sigma to control how it is being done. Many balanced scorecard initiatives are also being pursued. Knowledge management and other intangible factors that drive companies to find nonfinancial metrics help overcome the shortcomings of traditional cost management and measurement driven by GAAP.

The current rage is CRM, known as "customer relationship management," together with BI, or "business intelligence" systems. These tools are in addition to ERP systems, advanced planning systems, and a host of e-commerce technology solutions being utilized at an accelerated pace. Just look at the on-line auction phenomenon created by eBay, Yahoo, and others. Companies raced to implement ERP systems in fear of Y2K problems at an accelerated rate just before the tech bubble burst in 2000. The problem was that companies hurried to implement technology without ensuring that the basic structure and internal controls supporting these systems were reliable.

One example from my consulting experience serves as an excellent representation of what typically exists in many businesses. I was engaged to create a chart of accounts for a company that was using older software to run its accounting system and now wanted to integrate its system by implementing a new accounting system that would coordinate with the order entry and production control system. The manufacturing manager and a programmer under his direction were developing their own customized software. The owner/CEO decided that the company also needed to have CRM and to initiate a Six Sigma program at the same time. This organization took over a year just to implement the chart of accounts I developed for it because the controller could not and would not change to the new system. The CPA serving this company had little expertise other than financial statement and tax return preparation. The controller was a glorified bookkeeper who processed accounts payable and collected accounts receivable. She had little or no involvement with management reports prepared for the CEO, which were nothing more than allocations of the general ledger figures developed two weeks after the end of the month. The figures had little correlation to actual activity in the production facility, except that payroll was included and reconciled with the data. Customer orders and quotations were handled manually using software that was not integrated with the accounting data.

The problems described above are typical in many other organizations. The ego of the CEO was a factor because he wanted to run before the company could even walk. The turf mentality and organizational silos were clearly evident. Even more serious was that the accounting function was not capable of providing or understanding the most basic elements of cost management. The company clearly did not have the right people to get the job done and would not spend the money needed to do the job properly.

In addition to not having personnel to get the job done, the business processes were not effective and integrated. Businesses too frequently do the wrong things because of lack of knowledge and training. Furthermore, they are looking for the Holy Grail in contrast to assessing their operation and then focusing on correcting the root causes. Efforts to do things right take time and focus to stay the course. This is just one example that repeats itself with regularity.

THE FUTURE

Taiichi Ohno created a model that businesses throughout the world are trying to emulate and integrate. We have ERP systems and are now moving to ERP II in addition to utilizing executive information systems to absorb the accelerated flood of information that technology has created. Eli Goldratt had it right when he addressed, in *The Haystack Syndrome* over a decade ago, the problem of sifting out relevant management information from an ocean of data. If anything, the situation has worsened. We appear to have created a situation where all business does is place itself in a position to make more mistakes faster. The speed has increased, but the basic solution still waits to be implemented.

We have lean to make things go faster and Six Sigma to provide the process control to make it work. Activity-based costing and management can help us direct continuous improvement and align the costs of activities with products and customers across the entire supply chain. The strategic focus of balanced scorecards will help align strategy throughout the entire organization. Then we will require a profit-focused accounting process capable of creating short-range profitability in addition to measuring the creation and building of value.

For all these tools to work, we need to provide education and understanding of how the tools work and how to apply and integrate them into the business process. A key component of our challenge is to realign, fix, and implement business processes to take advantage of our full array of capability. Perhaps it is even more critical to provide the education and understanding throughout all levels of business organizations regarding what tools are available and what effort will be needed to make them work. One thought that struck me about the Toyota Production System was the discipline and determination applied to the effort and the time devoted to making sure everyone understood the system and how it worked.

 Web Added Value™

This book has free materials available for download from the
Web Added Value™ Resource Center at www.jrosspub.com.

2

CONCEPTS OF THE LEAN ENTERPRISE

Toyota symbolizes "the lean enterprise" and the management philosophy that evolved from the principles developed regarding how they functioned and operated. From its beginnings, lean has taken on new meaning and purpose. From the Toyota story, we have observed that lean is customer oriented and focuses on simplicity, speed, flexibility, visibility, and accountability for its impact. The lean concept deals with dynamic events and it adopts the philosophy of application of continuous improvement directed to eliminating all operational and organizational waste. Most of the lean initiatives have been directed toward operational waste, with less attention directed to organizational waste. However, lean thinking can be applied anywhere waste exists.

The five key elements of lean include:

1. Manufacturing flow
2. Organization
3. Process control
4. Metrics
5. Logistics

The lean focus in most organizations is centered on streamlining the flow of materials through manufacturing. One of my associates was the plant manager of a company that was an early adapter of lean. He reduced the number of operations through which material flowed from fifty-eight down to twenty-three separate functions before ending up in finished goods inventory. While the company was successful at paring down the number of steps, it was not able to generate much excitement beyond the dramatic and dynamic changes in

13

process flow. My associate indicated that process control and logistics received some attention, but there was little focus on organization and metrics.

The purpose here will be to create an understanding of lean manufacturing and the terms commonly used in lean applications. I am not creating a detailed "how to" manual, and it must be remembered that this book is meant to provide a broad understanding of the concepts. A suggested reference for lean is *Lean Manufacturing Implementation* by Dennis P. Hobbs, CPIM.

Understanding lean and its impact requires some knowledge of the terminology used. By providing this foundation, it will be easier to grasp the application concepts for implementing and using lean tools. An overview of "the five elements" and the key steps that comprise them follows.

MANUFACTURING FLOW

Manufacturing flow, as stated, generates most of the excitement because of the physical transformation that occurs. Lean manufacturing is reliant on providing products that customers want to buy. Since lean is customer oriented, it requires an analysis of the level of demand of the products requested by customers. From this analysis, production processes must be scheduled to produce quantities of product that match customer demand and yield the high level of quality that customers expect. Takt time was introduced in Chapter 1 and is based on the units a customer demands and not producing one unit more than requested. This holds inventory at minimum levels. Takt time is determined by dividing the available time for production in a day by the designated rate of production that is needed to meet customer demand.

Workload is a process of balancing machine time, available manpower, and the time necessary to conduct machine setups and changeovers. These factors and the time they require are then correlated with takt time in order to create the best balance of all the variables and factors necessary to meet customer demand. Setup time is a critical element of lean since it can have a significant impact on total production cycle time. Accordingly, because of its significance, it also offers the most potential for accelerating cycle times. The lean process includes taking advantage of all ideas from the bottom up to balance the total workload with takt time.

"One-piece flow" means to manufacture products with no wait time, no queue, and no batches. Since most products will spend 95 percent of their time waiting either to go through an operation or in inventory, this becomes a significant issue. This is a very idealistic objective and not always practical, but by placing emphasis on setup and the amount of lead time required, it creates follow-up situations that set the tone and tendency for all other processes to flow along. The objective with one-piece flow is to attempt to produce products, one at a time, based on the rhythm of the takt time. Try to imagine the drum beat in a band and you will see that the production process is doing literally the same thing by staying with the rhythm of the beat. This approach of producing one piece at a time results in the earlier detection of defects and problems on the production line, thus producing real-time feedback.

A major component of manufacturing flow is the layout of the shop floor. Lean initiatives usually employ cellular work centers in contrast to production lines. Layout of the production cells attempts to accomplish the most efficient and effective setup for work to flow through the workstations and to take advantage of the cross-training capability of the worker being utilized. The Japanese were required to take advantage of the maximum capability of their workers and thus adopted the cellular setup out of necessity and survival. The layout utilizes process mapping to detail the steps of the process as it exists and then revises the layout by creating a "to be" vision to achieve the objectives of takt time and load balancing. There are a number of tools to accomplish this task; Microsoft Visio is one of the more common tools. This tool is also used to analyze value and nonvalue activities presented in the chapters on activity-based costing and management.

Another key element of lean is the use of kanban systems. Since product is pulled through the production process in a synchronized flow, it is necessary to have a sign or a signal for when it is necessary to supply material to the production system. This concept was a key element of the Toyota system that utilized cards to signal suppliers when additional material was required by a process. It is also known as the two-bin system. When one bin was emptied, it became the automatic signal for replenishing it with the other bin. In the lean world, kanban signals have evolved to LED indicators that note the takt time pace and also serve as a signal for replenishment. The kanban concept was the core of the just-in-time (JIT) system and is very similar to pulling material or product from a supermarket shelf as you need it. The entire model is integrated into production scheduling as part of the JIT pull concept. The size of the kanban or the quantity of material that a supplier, internal or external, needs to provide is based on applying the daily rate of production multiplied by the replenishment time and divided by the time available. This calculation provides the quantity of product used for the kanban signal or bin.

ORGANIZATION

Lean manufacturing (or lean thinking) became a fashionable technique when it was launched during the mid-1990s as companies attempted to trim the excess out of their organizations. Everyone wanted to jump on the bandwagon. New consulting practices emerged and, combined with business process reengineering, became the mandate for achieving greater profitability. Too frequently, the mandate fell on operational people to jump-start these initiatives without help from top management. Top management wanted the result on the bottom line, but not the involvement in, or understanding of, the lean initiative.

Lean manufacturing creates change and directly impacts how people work and what they do, and can frequently determine if they will even continue to have a job. Lean projects tend to be directed to the manufacturing processes without being understood fully by all the players in the organization. However, when effective organization of the lean effort occurs in conjunction with communication and training, an environment is established where success is more likely. Reflect back to the Toyota story and consider the effort that was placed on every detail of the process from a bottom-up perspective. The challenge of educating, or re-educating, an organization is monumental and will require time and patience.

Corporate and organizational culture embraces structure and social operating mechanisms influenced by the beliefs and behavior of people. People need to understand what is expected of them in order to accomplish the desired results. Lean efforts need to be planned and communicated carefully regarding the types of changes that will occur within the organization. Why are we changing what we have been doing and what are we changing? A road map for change then needs to be created so that people can understand where they are right now and what it might look like after the changes have been implemented. People also need to understand the future benefits associated with the change and how it will improve their work environment and security.

Many of the lean approaches will represent totally new concepts to people. Some people might not be capable of operating in a lean environment. Others will adapt without any problem once they understand how the changes will impact them. It is important to take the time to develop the program and then communicate it to all levels of the organization. This critical step never receives adequate attention and focus.

A critical success factor in implementing lean is to make sure that the organization's financial function is part of the planning and communication process. Finance needs to understand how the lean initiatives will change the way the organization operates and the impact on the financial results. Also, finance needs to understand how to monitor and measure the program if it is to be successful and maintain a high level of momentum and enthusiasm.

Lean manufacturing will include the use of cross-trained team members who utilize a cellular work structure as a foundation. This is a major change that needs to be understood and communicated to the organization. In addition, the entire flow of material and information will be shifted, along with those who will be responsible for maintaining its flow. Lean thinking is all about empowering employees at lower levels, resulting in a transition of organizational ownership. Consideration of these issues and their impact on all levels of leadership, together with how the business will be run, are critical factors that determine the level of lean success.

PROCESS CONTROL

All lean initiatives are based on implementing and maintaining rigid standards for controlling the manufacturing processes. Therefore, it is important that greater explanation and understanding are provided regarding some of the critical lean concepts dealing with process control. Continuous improvement provides the foundation on which the Toyota Production System was created. Lean process control is modeled after the Toyota Production System objective of one-piece flow, centered on customer demand, in order to achieve and maintain the highest level of flexibility. A key element in achieving this objective is the method used for changing setups in conjunction with takt time.

The changeover terminology was developed by Shigeo Shingo at Toyota and is called the "single minute exchange of dies" or SMED. This concept has major implications in implementing improvements to the flexibility and speed of process throughput. The faster and more efficiently these changeovers are made directly affects inventory levels throughout the operation. Significant and dramatic improvements are possible and can be achieved to reduce investment in inventories. The key components of setup include: (1) segregating the activities, (2) recategorizing the activities, and (3) reducing or eliminating the changeover steps being performed. Additionally, the procedure includes the steps of an external setup, when a machine is running, and an internal setup, when a machine is stopped. One of the procedures of the improvement process is to take a video of setup procedures in order to diagnose opportunities for making it faster. Since most companies have no idea what occurs during a changeover, this step provides visualization that operators can grasp quickly. When they can see themselves performing the procedures, they are then able to identify areas and opportunities to accelerate the process.

During a recent consulting project for a folding carton manufacturer, the issue of preventive production maintenance was suggested. After the failure of a $25 bearing that shut down the entire line for three days, management quickly decided that regular maintenance and stocking backup replacement parts was

- Machine breakdown — Functional failure of diminution
- Machine setups — Inaccurate specification
- Machine stoppage — Unexpected breakdown
- Machine speed — Actual versus planned
- Process defects and rework — Continuous and intermittent
- Process variation — Start-up yield

Figure 2.1.   Total Productive Maintenance: Six Big Losses.

a good idea. Formal total productive maintenance programs are critical to lean so the flow of a process is not disrupted other than as scheduled. Figure 2.1 identifies six typical areas where production losses occur.

Process control concepts include tools to help avoid mistakes since something inevitably is going to happen. These tools, or devices, are placed in a process to ensure that the operator performs the operation correctly or to inform the operator if a defect occurs so that corrective action can be taken. The lean tool for mistake proofing is called "poka-yoke."

A fundamental constituent of lean programs is housekeeping, which is called "5S." The English translation of the five Japanese words comprising 5S is as follows:

1. Sifting
2. Sorting
3. Sweeping
4. Standardizing
5. Sustaining

These basics represent an essential part of any lean program.

Visual controls are an important element of the shop-floor communication associated with lean programs that makes them successful. This method of communication allows workers to know how material is flowing and what job is being performed. These visual signals also indicate what job is next in the queue. Workers maintain visual measurements that represent an indication of what is happening in their area and how they are performing relative to plan. Workers take responsibility for their performance and for improving it continuously. This translates to better results than when someone else is responsible for measuring and monitoring performance. This gives true meaning to the term empowerment.

The last element of process control is the graphic work instructions used by workers in their area to guide them through steps of the operation. These instructions can be actual pictures or charts. In some instances, computer screens offer visual steps of the operation and detailed instruction on how to perform setups efficiently and line changeovers that workers can access as needed.

METRICS

Lean manufacturing is designed to improve performance through increased quality, improved customer service, and with less cost because of the operational and organizational enhancements that are designed into the process. Significant attention is given to metrics and measuring in Chapter 13, so only a minimal acknowledgment to these issues will be provided here in the discussion of the five primary elements of lean.

Lean programs have measures that, if effective, are simple and straightforward, with accountability focused on the continuous improvement effort of the team implementing the improvements. The obvious metrics include yield, number of defects, customer returns, and delivery time. Understanding the benefits and impact of a lean program frequently is not achieved because of the excessive attention given to short-term profit impacts measured using traditional cost metrics. Accordingly, this tendency often contributes to concealing the true value of the program and its cost savings.

LOGISTICS

Logistics is a critical ingredient in understanding lean and its effectiveness. It starts with customer demand and fulfilling that demand with the highest quality product or service and in synchronizing its flow throughout the fulfillment process. Logistics covers all the internal and external elements of work flow and material through the facility including the work cells and delivery to the customer. The essence of logistics can be defined as representing the total effort required to create the highest levels of customer value at the lowest total cost.

In describing a lean manufacturing environment, it is important to understand and grasp the logistical steps. At the same time, this should not be overwhelming. One of the primary objectives of lean manufacturing is to pull product through the production facility as determined by demand from the customer and to avoid producing in batches. This requires a manufacturing plan that adjusts the plant structure, cellular organization, and setup based on customer demand. Enterprise resource planning systems contain materials requirements planning modules that facilitate this plan; some companies use spreadsheets and others employ advanced planning and scheduling systems. The plan drives how the facility is structured, or restructured, and the design of production cells.

Logistics should prioritize material flow from suppliers utilizing the ABC inventory concept that focuses first on A items that have lower volume and high value for daily replenishment, then on B (medium-value materials and medium lead times for weekly delivery), and then lower value C items that can be scheduled for monthly delivery. The advantage of having material flow to meet demand and avoid buildup of inventory investment is a challenge and a critical ingredient to achieving lean objectives.

In addition to material handling plans, there likely will be extensive orientation and training of suppliers so that material is delivered not only within the time requirements of the kanban signals, but in conformance with quality specifications to prevent defects, thereby facilitating on-time delivery to the customer. Demands from customers also require logistical coordination in order to maintain effective delivery schedules. This becomes a balancing act to ensure effective communication and appropriate inventory turnover.

Kanban pull signals represent the core of lean manufacturing. Remember, kanban signals were determined based on customer demand and were developed in the planning sessions. These signals can be cards, ping-pong balls, or digital electronic messages using electronic data interchange or e-commerce Internet communication. Material flow should be first-in/first-out with the objective of maintaining a flow rate equal to production to avoid any physical buildup in queues requiring waiting time to be processed. Consistent with this objective is the necessity to level load the work and balance it with suppliers to maintain a delivery rate equal to customer demand.

One of the more logistical lean challenges is to adjust to the requirements resulting from variation in demand for different products and volume and still achieve the objective of one-piece flow. In *World Class Manufacturing: Lessons of Simplicity Applied,* Richard Schonberger describes how companies such as Harley-Davidson, Honda, Kawasaki, John Deere, and others make some of every product every day at the same pace. Synchronized flow is dependent on utilizing cells that are designed to make a family of parts. The mix-model sequencing is then designed to make close to the same buildup mix of products that are sold each day and within the same family to avoid accumulation of excess inventory.

THE LEAN ASSESSMENT

Any lean initiative needs to begin with an understanding of how the organization is currently conducting business to establish a baseline to evaluate the potential for improvement. A component of the lean definition is continuous improvement; the first step is to identify improvement opportunities. I will highlight the steps and components of what should be considered in a lean assessment.

The assessment should evaluate the company objectively in the light of the five primary elements of lean manufacturing based on an analysis of the current situation. After considering the possibilities and potential, a gap analysis should be prepared to illustrate the difference between the identified opportunities and the challenges required to implement the necessary changes.

My experience, based on conducting numerous operational assessments, indicates that organizations should allow at least five to ten days to evaluate all of the issues. After reviewing and evaluating the gap analysis, management can then decide whether or not to move forward with lean manufacturing and where to direct the lean effort. The key elements in this process are to assess the needs of the customer and consider how simplifying product design and the production processes will impact the quality and time of delivery. This analysis will provide an indication of potential cost reduction and the likely improvement of the value stream flow. The assessment should also consider the competitive forces facing the business and how to best align the company's strategy with the marketplace in terms of products, processes, and technology.

The key areas that an assessment should evaluate are the flow of information and material. Begin the assessment at the vendor or source of material used in the process and follow the flow into the facility, through the processes, then through to the customer. This assessment step should include all the major products and processes and should focus on locating the value streams (products or product families) that offer the greatest potential for savings. Always apply the 20 percent rule to make the process improvements that will yield 80 percent of the dollar benefit when identifying and selecting areas for applying lean improvements. Lean initiatives should be launched to generate the greatest impact with the least effort. Not only does this make the most use of available time and resources, but it also creates a positive response to the change initiatives. People can see the benefit and therefore get excited about sustaining the effort.

The lean assessment sets the stage for what is possible and how the organization should proceed to implement the program. In addition to obtaining management approval and buy in to the change process, it is critical that the people who will be impacted by the change be included in the assessment process. In addition to just conducting a mapping of the critical value streams, the assessment process needs to include diagnostic interviews of personnel who currently are part of the production process and of personnel who have direct contact with the customers because they will provide a source of ideas on how

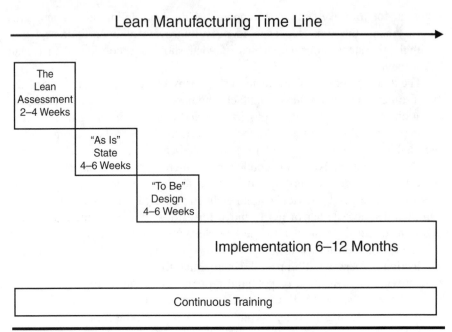

Figure 2.2. The Lean Road Map.

to "lean" the process. They will also become part of the solution. By involving them in the beginning, success is more likely assured.

The assessment is only one step along the way. Figure 2.2 shows what steps are required and how long it takes to launch a successful lean manufacturing program. Figure 2.2 illustrates not only the duration of time and the key steps, but also more importantly the continuous training that is needed to assure lasting improvement and lean success.

The lean assessment is not only a tool for engaging the lean team members and gaining their commitment, but it also represents an opportunity to confront and evaluate the level of management commitment. The potential success from making the cultural changes to accelerate process speed while enhancing customer service is a prime objective for conducting the assessment. Basically, the assessment helps to decide if the journey is worth the trip.

KAIZEN EVENTS — LEAN PROGRAMS

"Kaizen events" are the meetings of the lean team to achieve unending improvement in implementing lean concepts into the manufacturing process, identifying lean opportunities, finding solutions, and in using and applying the tools. A

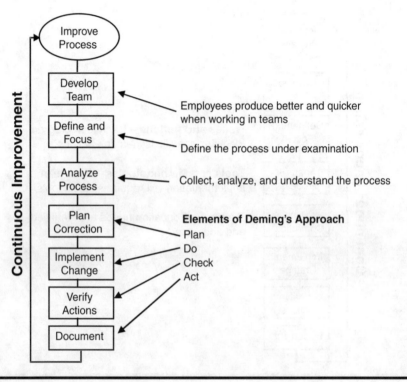

Figure 2.3. The Kaizen Cycle.

kaizen event typically takes from four to five days. These team events consist of activities carried out by the cell teams and represent the implementation component of lean manufacturing programs.

Kaizen events will occur at regular intervals throughout the transition to lean manufacturing and probably periodically after the implementation has been considered complete. It is important to understand that kaizen means "unending improvement." Teams will be assembled to conduct and maintain the continuous improvement effort. The kaizen cycle as a continuous improvement tool is presented in Figures 2.3 and 2.4. The cycle includes elements of Deming's approach and philosophies.

The overall implementation process and ongoing continuous training will drive the need for a variety of different kaizen events focused on a range of issues. They will include all of the topics discussed earlier in the chapter in the discussion of the five elements of lean manufacturing. Topics will include cell design and takt time, kanban, visual controls, housekeeping, and how to establish one-piece flow effectively.

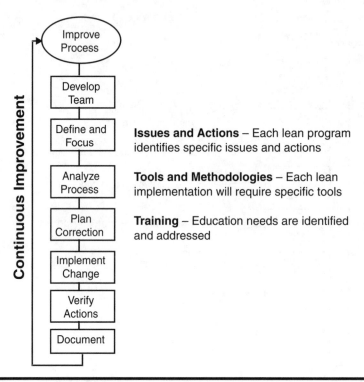

Figure 2.4. The Kaizen Cycle.

Additional topics include changeovers (SMED), mistake proofing, statistical process control, cross-training, and measurement. Other events may deal with mix-mode manufacturing, balancing the workload, or perhaps design for manufacturing and assembly, and cycle times. The list can go on as issues and challenges develop. The key here is to gain an understanding of kaizen and how it impacts the lean approach.

LEAN MEASUREMENT

Lean manufacturing emerged out of the simplicity of the Japanese/Deming efforts that started in 1951. The entire effort focused on cell workers managing and measuring their own activity to the schedule. Difficulty begins when complex financial measurements are introduced on a simple system. They are not needed and will not work very well, if they work at all.

I described the need for all members of the organization to be involved with lean manufacturing programs. Unfortunately, this does not happen very often and not very effectively when it does occur. The traditional silo management typical of many organizations and manufacturing operations has difficulty understanding the simple effectiveness of the Toyota system. They fail to grasp how the culture of Toyota workers is capable of cascading the necessary signals throughout the entire organization relative to the flow of work through the process. Toyota's ability to use its tools and techniques to produce high quality at the lowest cost has not always been replicated effectively by Western companies. This represents the challenge for understanding how all the new tools and techniques work and can be utilized today in the twenty-first century.

The measures need to be simple and easy to apply. The number of factors that are measured should also be minimized. After the speed of the manufacturing process has been accelerated, there should be a significant reduction in inventory levels. Other measurements are not going to make much of a difference because production flow will move too fast. It is important to understand the bottom-line benefit before and after the lean initiatives are under way.

Starting a lean program should be equated to doctors diagnosing patients. They will conduct a diagnosis (i.e., lean assessment) and then establish a baseline to determine what to fix and then how to fix it. Instead of performing an operation or therapy, kaizen events will occur to determine the rearrangement of cells, establish takt time, analyze setups, and balance production. In this sense, creating a simple list of what to measure should include:

- Quality
- Speed (cycle time)
- Cost
- Customer

Chapters 12 and 13 discuss the measurement of value, scorekeeping tools, and metrics, but it is also important to understand the philosophical overview of lean measurement.

Lean manufacturing and lean thinking, if implemented and applied properly, will generate profit improvement. Because the processes and the flow of product have improved, from customer wants or demand all the way through the process to delivery of the product or service to the customer, there will be fewer people and less space used to accomplish this activity. There will also be less inventory investment and more cash. The problem with measuring lean programs occurs when the quarterly financial results fail to report the perceived improvement on the bottom line. If revenue from additional sales activity does not consume the freed-up resources of people, space, and equipment, these costs will continue and the benefits of the improvement will be lost. It is critical to utilize freed or additional capacity to avoid losing the benefits of continuous improvement.

Incorporating lean thinking in the strategic vision and communicating this vision throughout the organization is crucial. Lean thinking and improvements need to be made for the long haul and not just become a quick fix to buoy quarterly earnings.

The success of lean thinking or any initiative needs to be embraced on an organization-wide basis from the beginning. All functions of the organization need to be on board from the start of the program. Consider the end in mind when beginning the lean initiative. Consider as many applications as possible for making competitive use of the success of a lean strategy. This is where an organization needs to utilize long-term measures of value as discussed in Chapter 12, in addition to the simple measures described above.

An appropriate conclusion is drawn from *Profit Beyond Measure*, written by H. Thomas Johnson and Anders Bröms in their discussion of Dr. Deming's observation on measurable circumstances. Deming observed that over 97 percent of the circumstances that affect a company's financial results are immeasurable, while less than 3 percent of what influences final results can be measured. And according to Deming, American managers tend to spend over 97 percent of their time analyzing measures, but less than 3 percent of their time is spent on what really matters — the unmeasurable. Lean techniques are based on simplicity and flexibility. It is important to keep it that way.

WAV Web
Added
Value™

This book has free materials available for download from the
Web Added Value™ Resource Center at www.jrosspub.com.

3

DIMENSIONS AND IMPACT OF SIX SIGMA

Six Sigma is commonly recognized by business managers as the killer app used by GE, Motorola, Allied Signal, and other corporate giants. Many smaller businesses perceive this is too much fire power and too costly for them to implement and manage. This potent management tool has been shrouded by an incorrect impression that has, to some extent, restricted its application. On the other hand, many companies have attempted to apply it without fully understanding it and realizing its true capability. I will explore the dimensions of Six Sigma, remove the myth, and provide a road map and an understanding of how to discover its potential impact for improving profitability.

Before digging into the details, let us first establish some basic understanding. Six Sigma is a process of asking questions that can produce tangible, quantifiable answers that translate into the creation of breakthrough profitability. It is not restricted to manufacturing, as it can be employed by any organization to improve its effectiveness by reducing the defects in operational and commercial processes. By improving processes and eliminating defects, companies create a competitive advantage in the way they do business and provide service to improve customer satisfaction. Some companies are well known for their leadership in adopting Six Sigma. Plus, there are thousands of other entities adopting and employing Six Sigma techniques that include service organizations, governmental entities, hospitals, and other healthcare providers. The tools and techniques are not restricted to a few large corporations; they are available to any organization. Six Sigma focuses on improving or changing a process so errors and defects are eliminated permanently.

SIX SIGMA AS A STRATEGY

In order to understand why Six Sigma might be considered a component of business strategy, it is first necessary to realize its purpose and application. Fundamentally, sigma represents a standard deviation or, in statistical terms, how much a process output varies from its nominal or mean average value both in a positive and a negative direction. Imagine a normal bell-shaped curve together with the range for deviation showing Six Sigma at the extremities of the curve. Understand that sigma (σ) is a measurement (see Figure 3.1) that shows defects per million for the range of 6 through 3σ and the percentage of error-free rate, expressed in percentages. Statistical process control uses this standard deviation to measure defects that occur in a business process. With the details firmly in our grasp, we can start to understand why a business strives for 6 versus 3σ and why Six Sigma methodology might become a component of business strategy.

In order to gain a sense of the potential power of Six Sigma, look again at Figure 3.1. We can see that 6σ shows a yield of only 3.4 defects per million occurrences, which is an error-free rate of 99.9997 percent. When 6σ is achieved, a virtually error-free business is created. Error-free businesses can typically expect, on average, to achieve the following magnitude of improvement:

- 20 percent margin improvement
- 12 to 18 percent increased quality
- 12 percent reduction in employees
- 10 to 30 percent capital reduction

When businesses can achieve improvements of this enormity, they have more cash, which allows them increased flexibility so they can do more with less, thus creating a greater range of investment options. Their customers receive higher quality products and better service. This creates a huge financial

	Defects per Million	Error-free Rate
• **Six Sigma** (6σ)	*3.4*	*99.9997%*
• Five Sigma (5σ)	233	99.977%
• Four Sigma (4σ)	6,210	99.4%
• Three Sigma (3σ)	66,810	93%

Figure 3.1.   Six Sigma Is a Measurement.

advantage that provides companies with an edge because of the competitive opportunities and capabilities gained from Six Sigma. Companies that operate at less than 6σ are not capable of competing with Six Sigma companies. The situation is comparable to a high-school football team trying to compete in the NFL. Companies that have not achieved this high level of process control are mismatches and cannot compete effectively with companies that have reached Six Sigma control.

The difference between 99 percent accuracy and 6σ, 99.9997 percent, does not seem like much, but it is vast. Some examples that illustrate the difference will transmit the magnitude of just how much difference I am talking about:

- Unsafe drinking water almost 1 hour each month
- No electricity, water, or heat for 8.6 hours each year
- No telephone service or television transmission for nearly 10 minutes each week

When you transfer these examples to business, it starts to become understandable why businesses operating at 99 percent, or 3 to 4σ, will not be competitive with companies that are virtually error free. The difference is a rate of 6,207 errors or defects per million occurrences. This rate of error falls straight to the bottom line in terms of lost profit and cash flow.

Consumers in the twenty-first century just will not tolerate poor quality, slow delivery, and poor service. Since the market controls the sales price, companies are not able to increase prices to cover the cost of quality and service demanded by the customer. They are required to improve their processes in order to reduce costs and improve quality, delivery, and service at the same time or go out of business. A Six Sigma approach represents a solution that enables companies to improve the value they deliver in all aspects of their business and increase their profit margins at the same time.

The ramification of adopting Six Sigma requires that the concept become a corporate or organization-wide strategy and business philosophy that is embraced by top leadership with full understanding and acceptance from top to bottom. It is not a supercharged total quality management (TQM) program delegated to the quality manager and operations team to implement and monitor. This type of approach is doomed for failure before it starts. Six Sigma initiatives not only focus on improving all business processes, product quality, and customer service, they also provide a profound impact on shareholder/stakeholder relationships, employee training and recruitment, and supplier partnerships. The entire company will change as Six Sigma is implemented because business quality will be improved dramatically. This new level of quality and discipline will also change the way products and processes are designed.

The focus of Six Sigma is much more intensive than other initiatives to improve quality. We have seen how the Deming movement created an industrial and productivity revolution as just in time (JIT) moved to TQM. Then we had, and still have, the lean thinking approach. We also learned that cost management and accounting did not help, and in fact hurt, these efforts to improve quality and productivity. Activity-based costing and management emerged, and then came balanced scorecards. *The Goal* and the Theory of Constraints became another arrow in the quiver. Six Sigma has become the latest rage. The focus required to achieve success is demanding, as illustrated by the vivid difference between 3 and 6σ variation. Six Sigma just cannot be accomplished without extreme focus and discipline. It takes more than wanting to pursue it.

One of my clients wanted to implement Six Sigma and actually started the process, which included engaging a well-known consulting firm to help. After discovering the company-wide commitment required for success, the CEO quickly realized that his processes and people could not begin to cope with the immense challenge that they faced. It is a mountain climb that requires many thousands of steps and complete organizational focus during each step upward. Companies must be committed to doing all the things that need to be done to eliminate defects in their industrial and commercial processes.

A defect can be defined as anything that fails to meet the customer's expectations or requirements. Going back to my client, they did not even have basic systems that worked. So, until they learned how to walk, they certainly were not going to run, let alone climb a mountain. The concept of Six Sigma is valid and produces results, but organizations must realize that they need to start at the beginning and climb the mountain one step at a time.

Creating a strategy and a vision that includes taking all the industrial and commercial processes to a level of zero defects, combined with realization of the commitment, communication, discipline, and focus to achieve Six Sigma, is the first step. Looking at and understanding the success of Jack Welch at GE and Larry Bossidy at Allied Signal, among others, the importance of leadership and execution becomes clear. CEOs and business owners have to understand why Six Sigma is a strategy and what it will take to make it successful. Some perceive that Six Sigma is nothing more than statistical measurement of processes. In reality, it represents all the strategic steps that an organization needs to mistake proof its processes and provides the focus needed to accomplish the continuous improvement required for success.

Understanding strategy is important to realizing how Six Sigma can provide impact to an organization. Strategy represents the vision of where the organization is going, how it will get there, and how it will sustain growth and momentum. Successful strategies require more than a planning retreat and a bound manual that documents the key components and tactics. More than anything, a successful strategy needs to be understood by the entire team for it to be effective and successful. Six Sigma has an impact on how every team member in the organization will execute all of the business processes. Application of the methodology requires more than attending a few training sessions. For Six Sigma to create profit impact, it must become a way of working to produce the highest quality products and customer service virtually free from error. From the industrial processes to commercial processes, every team member must be a part of the pulse beat of the error-free operation. A good comparison is the Toyota story. It provided the foundation for success, as the Toyota process was a model for lean manufacturing, Six Sigma, and to some extent the Theory of Constraints. Each of these philosophies embodied some elements of the Toyota system.

BENCHMARKING AND CHANGING WHAT COMPANIES MEASURE

A Six Sigma strategic process begins with establishing a baseline measurement of the existing process error rate. If the baseline metrics indicate a 3 to 4σ error rate, then the next step is to determine how other companies in similar businesses stack up. Are we better or worse than similar companies? In what areas of the operation are we better or worse? The analysis will probably show that the average competitive company operates in an error range of 3.5 to 4σ. Look at the leading companies in the industry, and by comparison, what level of error rate are they achieving?

Comparison of your operations to operations of competitive companies will show that you are likely doing better in some areas and probably not as well in other areas. These differences not only provide a road map for where to begin the Six Sigma process, but also quantify the competitive advantage that will be achieved from successfully reaching a Six Sigma level.

The benchmarking effort should not be limited to competitive companies, but should also evaluate common processes within the company and how well functional steps within a process are performing. This comparative analysis must be performed with the baseline assessment and then continued as part of the continuous improvement process. This step is seen in the Toyota story and is a critical component of its ongoing success. Employee teams at all levels of the organization perform these benchmarking comparisons and reviews. Information is then cascaded up and down to all levels of the company as part of its operating culture.

Benchmarking is an important Six Sigma tool. The following points help to spell out what benchmarking does and why it is such a good tool:

- Identifies best practices
- Guides approaches for improvement
- Helps to manage change
- Helps set and determine improvement priorities
- Identifies the best approaches
- Establishes best practices
- Typically requires a team effort
- Is not a one-time event
- Is not the same as competitive intelligence or market research

Another definition states that "benchmarking is a continuous, systematic process for evaluating the products, services, and work processes of an organization that are represented by best practices for the purpose of organizational improvement." In addition to organizational improvement, it is also important to add operational and process improvement. By utilizing benchmarking techniques in a systematic and analytical manner to evaluate and assess operations, the results of the analysis can be applied to achieve Six Sigma–level organizational and process improvements on a continuous basis. After I explain the Six Sigma tools in greater detail, the reasons for the emphasis placed on benchmarking will fit into the picture with greater clarity. For now, it is important to understand that benchmarking provides valuable information and is a process of learning that helps provide answers to the following two questions: What does this business do compared to other businesses and what doesn't this business do compared to other businesses?

How much do product and service quality cost? The answer obviously will be different for each organization depending on its size and on the soundness and ability of its processes to operate at a level of Six Sigma. Figure 3.2 provides an interesting view showing that when defects and failures increase, the associated cost of control also increases. By driving down the number of incidents and the time associated with them, organizations experience a dramatic reduction in cost. Benchmarking externally, internally, and functionally is a first step to understanding what is occurring and what is possible.

The obvious culprits are scrap and rework in the production process as well as the cost of poor-quality material received from vendors. Now consider the cost to inspect, test, and conduct quality audits in terms of equipment and personnel. In addition to inherent failures and defects, the cost of latent failure and defects is even more dramatic because of the impact it has on the customer. High risk of latent failure results in increases to warranty cost and the cost to maintain customer satisfaction. The cost of customer satisfaction includes accepting returned material, the time and expense associated with communication, and issuing refunds. The potential for lawsuits and other warranty issues pro-

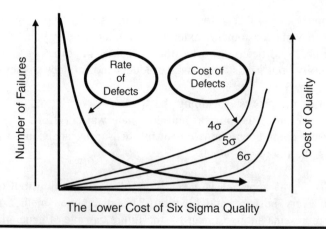

The Lower Cost of Six Sigma Quality

Figure 3.2. The Cost of Control.

vides clear logic and justification for eliminating any chance of incurring downstream failure and customer dissatisfaction.

Companies operating at a level of 4σ or worse frequently dismiss Six Sigma efforts as unachievable because they require too much effort, time, and money. Frequently, these organizations expect instant success and forget that every journey begins by taking that first step. In order to gain and sustain momentum, logical implementation efforts should begin by selecting high-priority situations to ensure success and concentrating on process improvement to eliminate errors and defects completely. One of the benefits of Six Sigma tools is that improved processes through product and process design will help to avoid the necessity for inspection and testing.

I will not be able to answer every question about Six Sigma and why it makes sense. However, understanding some of following detailed steps used by Motorola for overcoming variation problems provides helpful insights:

1. Define Six Sigma tolerances on all critical products and process parameters.
2. Minimize the total number of parts in the product.
3. Minimize the number of process steps.
4. Standardize the parts and processes used.
5. Use statistical process control (SPC) during the design and prototype design phases.

Motorola then applied the following six steps for achieving Six Sigma for nonmanufacturing functions:

1. Identify the products you create and the services you provide.
2. Identify the customers (external and internal) for your products and services and determine what they consider important.
3. Identify your needs (to provide products and services so they satisfy the customer).
4. Define the process for doing the work.
5. Mistake proof the process and eliminate wasted effort.
6. Ensure continuous improvement by measuring, analyzing, and controlling the improved process.

The Six Sigma approach is a fact-based decision-making tool that can be applied to every business and function. This disciplined method of solving problems represents an investment for the future capable of generating savings and creating breakthrough competitive advantages. The key to success is that companies must be willing to apply the focus and discipline necessary to execute the program.

SIX SIGMA ORGANIZATIONAL STRUCTURE

Understanding the Six Sigma strategy and process is not enough in itself. Realizing the organization-wide impact of a Six Sigma initiative and how it functions is imperative before learning about the tools and their application. Let us consider how organizations should manage the many process changes required, identify project priorities, and determine the special people skills that will be required to reap the benefits of the Six Sigma initiatives.

All the senior leaders of the organization must buy in to initiating a Six Sigma program. Successful initiatives will require them to take responsibility and ownership for its direction. The next steps are to ensure that all employees in the organization understand the Six Sigma vision and apply the concepts to their jobs and work areas. Empowered employees represent the core of the ultimate success of the changes and continuously improving on the processes. The organization will create deployment champions and build teams around the improvement projects deployed.

Listening to the voice of the customer to determine critical-to-quality issues and then applying value stream analysis to determine which projects have the largest financial impact typically identifies Six Sigma projects and establishes implementation priorities. Projects will range from cost reduction to quality improvements. A project sponsor is assigned and in turn reports to a member of the senior management team. The project sponsor has responsibility for implementation and accountability for the success of the project. The project team will consist of project leaders and members who have received specialized Six Sigma training.

Six Sigma competencies contain different levels of training and instruction on applying the tools. The designations provided to these levels of competency range from green belt to black belt to master black belt. Training is further broken into industrial and service specialization for black belts and design for Six Sigma (DFSS).

Master black belts are the most highly skilled in the methodologies and tools of variation reduction. After a project-based certification program, typically a year in duration, master black belts then train and mentor black belts in addition to helping in the selection and management of high-value projects. They also maintain the integrity of the Six Sigma measurement and develop Six Sigma learning materials. Black belts complete four weeks of classroom training over a period of four to six months and then demonstrate mastery of the tools by participating in a major process improvement project. Black belts also are responsible for training and mentoring green belts. Green belts complete six days of classroom training to develop a working knowledge of the methodology and tools and have also worked on a project with high-impact business results.

Project implementation utilizes a mix of team members, green belts, black belts, master black belts, and employees. Green belts and employees have part-time involvement while black belts and master black belts are assigned to projects on a full-time basis. In addition, projects can and will utilize experts in lean manufacturing, activity-based management, and total productive maintenance.

THE SIX SIGMA TOOLBOX

The Six Sigma approach uses a wide variety of tools to help bring processes under control and offers a proven logic for problem solving. The "DMAIC" method ensures that every problem will be approached in the same consistent way and is outlined as follows:

- *Define* project goals and customer deliverables.
- *Measure* the process to baseline current performance and quantify the problem.
- *Analyze* to determine the root cause(s) of problems and defects.
- *Improve* the processes by removing defects and nonvalue activities.

■ *Control* future process performance and avoid recurrence of defects and variation.

When the DMAIC method is used effectively, it provides clarity in understanding the problems in existing processes. Companies know where and how they failed to delight customers in the areas of cost, quality, and services. They can identify areas of waste and rework, what slows down the processes, and what it will take to speed them up. The term "variation" means defect or a deviation from the ideal results of a process.

Define is perhaps the most critical element of DMAIC because it provides a road map for defining and clarifying the objective. The organization has to first define the goals and objectives of the strategy from the top down. The teams that will lead the effort need to be selected and organized. Teams will then prepare a clearly documented analysis map quantifying the magnitude of all identified opportunities. At this point, all opportunities should be assigned a project priority. From the priority list, a project is selected, defined, and assigned a project leader. The project analysis includes a quantification of the expected returns together with a time line for its completion.

After the project has been approved, the team moves into the *measurement* stage of DMAIC. The teams use data collection tools, map the processes, prepare analysis developed from data gathering, and create a baseline or an "as is" statement of how the process and work are now being performed. For many companies, this is an eye-opening experience when they learn they are breaking new ground and realize that no previous documentation was ever prepared or developed.

The *analyze* stage of the project involves evaluation of the data gathered during the measurement step. The team then utilizes the DMAIC tools to highlight areas for improvement and creates a priority list of problems and the root causes for the process variation. The tool kit also contains tools and methodologies for eliminating quality defects and improving process velocity.

Following *analyze* is the *improve* phase, which is the development of solutions that are focused on confirmed causes identified during the analysis stage. Solutions evolve from design of experiments (DOE), brainstorming, benchmarking, straw models, and the development of action plans. This phase is the implementation of the best-identified solution to the problem.

Control tools are used to lock in the benefits resulting from the *improve* phase of DMAIC. The control phase validates and monitors the system against standards and procedures to ensure future performance. After establishing process capability, SPC and other tools will be applied to prevent and eliminate any chance of mistakes.

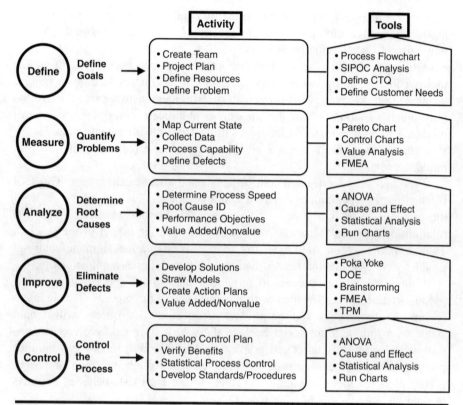

Figure 3.3. The DMAIC Tool Kit.

DMAIC TOOL KIT

The DMAIC and Six Sigma tool kit is well stocked. Knowing what the tools are and how they are used will help you understand how to get the most from Six Sigma. Figure 3.3 provides a summary of the DMAIC approach and lists the tools utilized. Some of the more common tools include the following:

- Process mapping
- Failure mode and effect analysis
- Measurement system evaluation
- Statistical tests
- DOE
- Control plans

Process mapping allows teams to identify the order of events to provide a product or service, eliminate waste, uncover problems, and compare the "ideal" work flow to what actually happens.

Failure mode and effect analysis helps to identify process failures, minimize their frequency, and provide better detection of the factors leading to failure.

Measurement system evaluation uses measurement instruments to determine how much variation within the measurement process contributes to overall process variability versus variation resulting from measurement "noise."

Statistical tests are utilized to separate significant effects of variables from random variation.

DOE helps to identify and confirm cause and effect relationships. This tool is usually used in situations where it is not completely clear as to the cause of the problem. DOE is a structured and organized method for determining the relationship between factors affecting a process and the output of the process. These experiments are used extensively as a Six Sigma tool in manufacturing, product development, marketing, and to test transactional applications.

Control plans are intended to provide a plan of the process and control product characteristics together with the variables in the process. This helps to ensure that the process, and the product produced by the process, will remain stable over time and not revert back to the way it operated before being improved. A variety of charts and graphs are maintained to record and monitor product characteristics and process variables. They might be trend graphs or scatter plots that help determine the relationship that exists between two sets of data.

Companies implementing Six Sigma universally use and apply the DMAIC methodology. However, there are adaptations of the methodology, additional tools, and areas of expertise applied to achieve maximum bottom-line impact. In order to provide an overview of understanding, some of the more common tools employed are described. The objective is to encourage companies to use all of the management tools and techniques that work best for their individual situation. Since some of these techniques are described and reviewed in later chapters, I will only touch on them briefly here.

DFSS evolved from the DMAIC tool kit and provides employees a methodology for designing products and services capable of meeting Six Sigma standards. This is typically a four-phase process of *identify, design, optimize,* and *verify* or a five-phase process of *identify, define, design, optimize,* and *verify.* By listening to what the customer wants, the first critical step is to divide this information into both customer requirements and product requirements. Tools utilized during this process include *quality function deployment,* which defines what is important to customers; *failure mode and effects analysis;* and *supplier, input, product, output,* and *customer* product maps. Products are designed and the production processes are then optimized utilizing process capability information and a statistical approach to assure that tolerances can be maintained and that performance predicted is in conjunction with the design of the process and the product. The verifying or validation phase provides feedback on sourcing, manufacturing, and design.

Activity-based management is another tool utilized with Six Sigma that helps to provide a different view of products and processes in a comprehensive and realistic fashion. This tool then helps companies manage them more effectively and ensure continuous improvement by studying the activities creating the costs. Many companies employ enterprise resource planning to integrate, accelerate, and sustain process improvements throughout the organization. The concept of lean manufacturing or lean enterprise provides a customer satisfaction–oriented approach utilizing simplicity, speed, flexibility, visibility, and accountability to improve processes and increase the acceleration of throughput. Six Sigma then provides the ongoing control of the processes that allows companies to sustain the advantages of acceleration and continuous improvement.

IMPLEMENTING AND DEPLOYING SIX SIGMA

The decision to implement Six Sigma is driven from a strategic vision that requires a company or organization to create an environment focused on its customers and free from product defects and process errors throughout its operations. From this starting point, the execution of the strategy and all of its ramifications is initiated. Where do we start, what do we focus on, what tools do we need, who will lead, and who will work on the projects? These are just a few of the many questions business leaders pursuing Six Sigma will ask, and the list goes on. There are many excellent books that document the approach and an abundance of consultants who will provide assistance, mentoring, and training.

My purpose is to provide a sense of implementation and deployment, not to detail every step of a self-directed Six Sigma launch. In addition to the many reference books, APICS, the American Society for Quality, and many Web sites offer Six Sigma support.

Sustained Six Sigma programs will have passed the recognition of needing Six Sigma and its potential impact. Mikel Harry and Richard Schroeder classify this as moving from the "discover" stage into the "decide" stage. "Decide" is when an organization approves the Six Sigma initiative and define the purpose and scope of how it will be applied in the organization. Typically, the consensus of how long the initial implementation process will take ranges from twelve to eighteen months, depending on the aggressiveness and capability of the organization.

The initial implementation phase will include an "organize" and "initialize" stage of implementation. "Organize" requires establishing the Six Sigma organizational structure that will include the following:

- Senior management
- Deployment champions
- Project sponsors
- Master black belts
- Black belts
- Green belts
- Project team members
- All employees

During the "organize" stage, organizations will establish their financial targets and create time lines for training senior management and the deployment champions, which can take up to three or four months. A key component to Six Sigma success is that organizations need to preserve continuing focus of their senior management team. Six Sigma is not a "launch" and then wait to see how it works, but a continuing process of review, involvement, and communication.

The "initialize" stage of implementation typically consists of developing deployment plans, metrics, communication, selecting and hiring appropriate human resources, training champions and black belts, and the selection and funding of projects.

After "initialize" comes "deployment or implementation" together with ongoing evolution. This phase of the initiative will involve work on selected projects in addition to training for project champions and black belts. Deciding where to concentrate the Six Sigma deployment focus will vary depending on the critical success factors that are most significant to each business. Typically, the focus will be on customers and on the processes that provide the products and services to customers. Ultimately, focus shifts to processes that need to be improved to accomplish lasting change and create impact on the bottom line. Other areas that will draw focus and attention include special problems and product and process design. Organizations will utilize DFSS to optimize processes and improve the design of products based on customer input. In order to sustain the initiative, training will be extended to green belts and process improvement team leaders.

The thrust of Six Sigma and its impact on companies vary depending on the size and complexity of the organization. Smaller companies may see noticeable change in quality and how they operate in twelve to eighteen months from the initial launch. Larger and more complex organizations will require longer periods of time to see and feel the change from the initiative. Throughout these stages, the entire organization needs to be connected and committed to pursue its Six Sigma objectives continuously.

What is needed in terms of commitment and resources to successfully sustain Six Sigma? The number of black belts within a company is usually calculated at 1 percent of the organization's total employees. This means a company with 1,000 employees will require ten black belts. Black belts are expected to generate annual savings of $150,000 to $250,000 per project. This will vary from company to company and with the training and capability of the individual black belts. Also, the actual ratio of black belts to employees will vary depending on whether their focus is industrial or commercial application.

THE POWER OF SIX SIGMA

Six Sigma is a metric that has taken on a much greater business meaning as the evolution of the productivity and the competitiveness of global markets have accelerated. The term is not understood fully and its potential is hidden under a cloud of misperception. In reality, Six Sigma is a powerful tool capable of business transformation when applied and utilized to change how people work. Its power is equally potent for use by small organizations as it is for big business. In fact, it might be easier to apply with faster results since the complexity of larger organizations provides greater challenges of implementation. The way people work determines profitability, and when properly understood, Six Sigma allows people to work more effectively.

Our focus is about tools and understanding how they can be applied to improve bottom-line profitability. Like all tools, it is important to know what they can do, how they work, and the best way to apply their capability to improve performance. Six Sigma, like every other tool described, is not a silver bullet or the Holy Grail. It takes considerable work and discipline for any tool to become effective. Big changes take time, commitment, and training to reap the potential benefits from the methodology.

One of the advantages that Six Sigma offers is its approach to structure and the definition of skills and expertise to improve processes and solve problems successfully. The creation of champions, master black belts, and black belts establishes a proven curriculum for training in DMAIC tools to eliminate variations and problems. It keeps the process of change on the same page. The organization structures of Six Sigma provide authority for people to make and execute decisions based on facts and not operate from a platform of hunches.

Injection of black belt capability into an organization, regardless of its size, can establish a new foundation of confidence and the ability to set goals without fear of failure. Karate black belts rely on power, speed, and decisiveness and therein lies the basis for Mikil Harry's development of the term in the mid-1980s. The application of focus and commitment combined with speed and decisiveness can be compared clearly to the Toyota story and how it applied these ethics and gained empowered commitment throughout the entire workforce.

Smaller organizations may need to adapt how they use Six Sigma as an effective tool. They will need to train and learn how to apply the tools. The various stages of implementation will probably change because they may lack the people resources to organize in a typical Six Sigma fashion. Furthermore, the timing of how and when waves of project implementation should occur will need to and can be modified to fit. However, the lesson of how to improve processes and to isolate and solve problems will provide companies with a competitive advantage, even for many smaller companies. Six Sigma provides a proven structure and road map that give all organizations a tool that works. The power is learning how to use it and knowing where to apply it.

This book has free materials available for download from the Web Added Value™ Resource Center at www.jrosspub.com.

4

UNDERSTANDING THE THEORY OF CONSTRAINTS

It is a management strategy, a philosophy, and a thinking tool with a wide range of capability and capacity to improve bottom-line profitability, productivity, project management, and marketing. It is a simple, yet seemingly complex, management methodology developed by Dr. Eliyahu M. Goldratt, an Israeli physicist. Reflect back on the evolution of productivity and its measurement since 1950.

During the mid-1980s, the predominance of MBA-trained managers were locked into an old paradigm of how to measure and manage. Goldratt looked at all of the traditional approaches and conceived a new revolutionary view that was written as a fast-paced novel, *The Goal,* that managers actually read and are still reading. *The Goal* was translated into thirteen languages and over two million copies were sold. Management schools started including it in their curriculum. The Theory of Constraints (TOC) has evolved into being included as part of the APICS body of knowledge and its applications have spawned consulting practices. The designation of "Jonah" led to further teaching, implementing, and practicing the thinking concepts developed by Goldratt.

The first edition of *The Goal* was published in 1984. Since then, Eli Goldratt has published five additional books that build on and enhance TOC. He has also co-authored additional books and been published in numerous journals and magazines. The AGI-Goldratt Institute was founded by Eli Goldratt and provides an ongoing source of training and learning tools to understand and implement TOC concepts ranging from audio to e-learning to videos.

THE BASIC PREMISE

TOC represents a systemic view of a company that is a system with a set of elements in an interdependent relationship. The goal of a company is to make a profit. Anything that limits a system from achieving higher performance toward its goal is a constraint. Any system has very few constraints as *The Goal* portrays and, at the same time, any system must have at least one constraint. *The Goal* was written using the Socratic method that asks questions that define the problem and which thereby are likely to produce the best solutions.

TOC has demonstrated that organizations typically focus on managing and measuring components rather than taking a global approach. Start with the question: What is the goal? You will see typical questions asked ranging from how to achieve better customer service to mere survival. The stark reality is that without earning a profit today and in the future, companies cannot survive. They may survive for a while, but in the long term, organizations that are not capable of generating profit and achieving a return on their investment in excess of the cost of that investment will not make it over the long haul. You have to be capable of driving your economic engine. When organizations realize the reality of the goal and then focus and leverage on how to achieve it effectively, the wheel of change and continuous improvement can be accelerated.

Most organizations have limited resources and have a considerable number of things that need to be accomplished at the same time. By identifying and focusing on the overriding constraint of the organization, they are then capable of making the necessary changes and achieving their goal in significantly less time than they ever thought possible. The simplicity and power of this management philosophy help to achieve breakthrough results when applied to many different situations. The initial focus was on production planning and scheduling and produced significant reductions in work-in-process inventories with corresponding increases in cash flow. These improvements resulted from shrinking lead and cycle times and cutting batch sizes. Because of these applications and enhancements, many companies saw that they had significant excess capacity and were able to take advantage of results in increased revenue and market share. Lean manufacturing initiatives might be more effective if they focused their improvement effort on the constraints rather than applying energy and funds on fixing nonconstraint areas that may not have an impact on organization-wide goals. Six Sigma initiatives also could enhance their effectiveness by focusing projects on the constraints to ensure that these processes are under control. The power of critical-chain buffer management applied to project management provides both of these initiatives with a tool to reduce the time necessary for project completion. This is especially true with product development and product design. It is important to understand the potential of TOC when used in conjunction with other methodologies such as lean and Six Sigma. Now that we realize the leverage capability and power of TOC, let us build some understanding about how it can be achieved.

TOC builds on the simplicity of fundamentally concentrating on the real barrier to ongoing continuous achievement rather than relying on the traditional methods utilized by the "cost world" for almost a century. We will build on and utilize the accounting application of TOC that is called throughput accounting. The model is based on providing organizations with an alternative model that is based on simplicity and speed with the capability to overcome the "cost world" paradigm.

Let us start by understanding that anything that limits an organization from achieving the goal is a constraint. Providing a thinking process to ask the questions required to identify the constraint of the organization is a fundamental element of the TOC management philosophy and strategy. It builds on the following fundamental questions:

- "What to change?"
- "What to change to?"
- "How to cause the change?"

Until the fundamental constraint is identified and managed, there will be no improvement. Without change, the constraint will continue to manage the organization.

Organizations, companies, and individuals are always continuously involved in a series of actions. Actions can be attached to a chain or a chain of events. The strength of the chain is only as strong as its weakest link, whatever that link might be. The chain cannot be stronger than that weakest link. If the weakest link in the chain is made stronger, then the strength of the chain is only as strong as the next weakest link. And so it goes, from link to link, from constraint to constraint.

The Goal used a Boy Scout troop on a march, which represented work to be performed, to illustrate how the concept of constraint works and can be applied in other situations. The path of the march is equivalent to inventory and the greater distance between the marching Boy Scouts represents increased investment in inventory and time to produce product. The Boy Scout troop contained a wide variety of boys of different heights, ages, and physical capabilities. As the boys marched, the older and stronger scouts would march faster, leaving gaps and holes in the line of troops. In effect, this correlates to increasing the amount of inventory investment. The troop leader finally realized that the troop could only collectively march as fast as the pace of the slowest scout. Based on this discovery, the scoutmaster put the slowest scout at the head of the line. The pace and speed of the march were then controlled by his speed, which caused the other scouts behind him to adjust their marching speed to match his pace. Based on this adjustment, the entire troop was then able to stay together and arrive at its destination as a group. This was a much better solution than having some scouts arrive early, having some get lost, and others not arrive at all. The goal was to have the entire troop arrive at its destination, together, and at a certain time. Since the constraint was the slowest Boy Scout, all the other scouts were subordinated to the slowest marcher. If his pace was to accelerate, the constraint would be elevated to the next slowest marcher, and so on. By tying a rope to connect each Boy Scout, it was possible to regulate and control the marching distance between each scout. When this parable is compared to inventory and production, one is able to see overall that the journey was more efficient and consumed less investment in inventory. This closely resembles the kanban signals and one-piece work flow utilized by the Toyota production system (discussed in Chapter 1) and lean manufacturing (Chapter 2). It provides focus on the goal and management of the constraint.

The "five focusing steps" of TOC can also be related to the Boy Scout example described in the above paragraph. Remember, the constraint is represented by the weakest link of the chain. The Boy Scout chain could only march as fast as the speed of its slowest marcher. In order to maximize the ability of the Boy Scout troop to arrive at its destination in tact, it was necessary to apply the following five steps:

1. Identify the constraint.
2. Decide how to exploit the constraint.
3. Subordinate and synchronize everything else to Step 2 to improve performance or increase the overall speed of the troop march.
4. Elevate the performance of the constraint.
5. If the constraint has shifted in any of the above steps, it is necessary to go back to Step 1.

TOC is effective based on the simplicity of its applications. Many management tools are ineffective because they are too complex. TOC becomes powerful since identifying the constraint and thinking clearly on how to exploit it and then subordinating and synchronizing are not difficult concepts. It is like "ah, so that is what we have to do," and thus becomes a simple concept of understanding. The power lies in its application and simplicity.

DRUM-BUFFER-ROPE BASICS

The most consistent and largest problem that I have encountered in my career as a controller, a CPA, and a consultant has been inventory or inventory related. There was either too much of the wrong product or not enough of the right product. The critical issues in operational assessments are always found close to inventory. The inventory syndrome can be defined as excessive levels of investment that prevent companies from reaching their goal of making a profit. *Drum-buffer-rope* (DBR) resolves many of the excess and unwanted inventory issues and is a simpler approach than one-piece continuous flow.

The discussion of TOC basics told the story of the scouts' march and their struggle to manage the variation of marching speeds of different scouts. Work centers in factories experience similar problems. Some work centers process work faster than others, which results in material sitting in queues waiting to be processed. Managing work flow has always been a problem, whether it is the factory floor or scheduling patients in a dentist's office. This also represents an issue in lean manufacturing and with Six Sigma. I will draw on these corollaries as I explain DBR.

In the scout example, we learned that the slowest scout had to set the pace and that he was the constraint. In a manufacturing situation, let us apply the constraint theory to the slowest work center. If we queue all work to start at the slowest work center, we run the risk of incurring unreasonable expense, especially if the slowest work center has a breakdown or stoppage for some reason. The scout troop also might not want to have the slowest scout out in front. We need to manage the pace of the scout march just as we want to manage the tempo of the work flow through the factory. Goldratt used the illustration of tying a rope between the scouts to set the pace to that of the slowest marcher and then allowed some slack in the rope to allow for variations that were likely to occur. Accordingly, the scout troop could be kept together and could maintain a regular cadence of marching. Thus, the concept is that the drum sets the cadence, the rope allows the scout troop to be linked, and the controlled distance between each scout creates the buffer.

This same principle is applied to factory work centers. The time relationships of DBR are shown in Figure 4.1. This approach is very similar to how Toyota (lean) employees use their kanban signal system. Toyota uses takt time to establish the rhythm for designing work cells and then determines the rate of consumption required to achieve workload balancing and one-piece flow. The significant point here is the constraint and how it can and should be managed. It should be noted further that Toyota does not have a cost accounting system inside its production area; the rhythm is coordinated throughout the plant

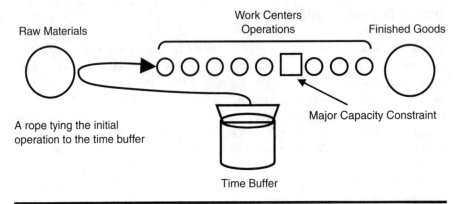

Figure 4.1. Drum-Buffer-Rope Synchronized Flow.

and for the plant as a whole based on customer orders. Toyota measures the cost of material, labor, and supplies going into the "black box," not the individual efficiencies of each operation. This eliminates all work-in-process inventory except for amounts contained in either the buffer or in the kanban.

It is important to realize that "a TOC shop may never get around to improving the operations of the nonconstraints" as stated in Noreen et al.'s *The Theory of Constraints and Its Implications for Management Accounting.* The point is: Do not spend money on additional salaries and invest more dollars to fix something that does not need fixing. It is much more important to concentrate organizational energy and dollars to improving a constraint as indicated by the simplicity of the five focusing steps. And now for the benefit of management accountants, why do we need to measure something that does not need to be measured, just for the sake of measurement? Goldratt, like Toyota, keeps it simple.

SIMPLIFYING A COMPLEX ENVIRONMENT

The TOC philosophy provides a framework of simplicity that can provide solutions to a wide range of problems. In developing the concept for this book, I wanted to provide an accounting approach and model that nonfinancial managers could understand and that financial managers could apply. There are many aspects of business that are complicated, but really good solutions tend to be pretty simple.

TOC directs us to ask the right questions and provides three good examples. Then we are given five focusing steps, of which the last one tells you that if a constraint is broken, go back to the first one and start all over again. We then have the goal, which is to make a profit, now and in the future. More importantly, it teaches that real-life systems have very few constraints, probably only one. Asking the right question is the key to the kingdom.

One of the reasons that TOC has to be simple to be effective is that it is focused on improvement, which requires change. The simpler we keep things, the easier it is to implement change. In lean, I described the principles of 5S, which is to keep things clean, neat, and everything in its place. We can relate to this with our own desks. When they are neat, clean, and uncluttered, we get more work done. So it is with TOC.

The just-in-time/total quality management movement was given credit for creating simplicity. It worked in spite of accounting. The motto of the movement stated:

- Do it
- Judge it
- Measure it
- Diagnose it
- Fix it
- Manage it

Do not wait to read about it in a report. DBR fits this criterion of simplicity. If we keep it simple enough, we will not need to worry about the accounting implications and the "cost world" mentality, therefore, will not be a factor.

If we eliminate inventory, we will not have to store it and or account for it. We need to make sure customers receive the product or service they want, when they want it, at the highest quality, and at an acceptable price that enables us to achieve our goal. In the absence of any inventory, one can be sure that any problems or constraints in the process will appear. The key is to improve the process continuously or subordinate it as indicated in the TOC five focusing steps. This initiates the actions that are necessary to create the needed cash flow for ongoing survival.

In any discussion of simplicity, I need to mention "Murphy." The reality is that something will always occur to upset even the most well-planned apple cart. Murphy is commonly mentioned throughout TOC writings and refers to "Murphy's Law," which means to count on the unexpected because the unexpected will always appear when and where it is least likely. The effective and well-planned use of buffers is a key component of TOC's simplistic approach. The most recent addition to TOC's arsenal of simple effective tools is the critical-chain path in project management applications.

THE CRITICAL CHAIN

The latest addition to the TOC toolbox is a constraint-based tool that impacts how projects are managed. Projects have long been a contentious management problem. They typically take longer than planned and incur huge cost overruns that soak up investment dollars and management resources. It has become a growing management trend to manage everything in terms of projects. Managing and measuring project effectiveness are a challenge for all organizations. Careful and effective management of projects has an impact on marketing, product development, and implementation of information technology systems, software development, and especially Six Sigma initiatives. Construction companies represent an excellent example of an industry that relies on projects to monitor and manage its activities.

Goldratt challenges the uncertainty of project management by applying the logic of TOC to resolve and demystify the issue of "project overload." TOC defines the three types of different and opposing commitments: (1) due date, (2) budget, and (3) content.

TOC focuses on the root causes of why projects are always delivered late and always over budget. The simplicity of the three questions representing the core of TOC is applied to the behavioral tendencies that are associated with project management. Goldratt identifies the following behavioral realities associated with project management:

- Additive Rule — Commitments of a project are based on adding up the duration and cost of the individual tasks.
- Parkinson's Law — Work expands to fill its time.
- 3-Minute Egg Rule — It is not quality if it is finished before the time is up.
- Student Syndrome — Waiting to start a task due to more important work at hand.

Goldratt's *The Critical Chain* exposes the behavioral realities that proliferate project mentality in organizations. The simple laws are spelled out in his Socratic style to explain the typical issues that haunt projects. We are reminded how projects labor under the paradigm of old rules and beliefs where change is required in order to achieve breakthrough results. Goldratt applies TOC to fix the problems instead of merely preventing them.

Project management relies on PERT charts and mapping the critical path to plan time lines, events, and the utilization of resources. Progress is measured based on the amount of work performed and also on the dollars invested in a project, compared to the remaining work and amount of investment required to complete a project. This measurement can result in overlooking individual problems because the project appears to be on target overall. This tendency allows a project to arrive at what appears to be completion, but because the critical path of the project events was overlooked, it now forces the project to take longer than expected.

DBR concepts are applied to overcome this problem by creating unique new ways to manage the project. In order to overcome the tendency of people to overestimate time, spend too much time completing tasks, and aggressively plan tasks, safety buffers are placed at the end of the project to protect its constraint, which is the critical path. This is called the project buffer so that no time is wasted in areas of the project that will not accelerate its completion.

A project will almost always utilize resources that will be required during different stages of its progress. Separate buffers that are termed "feeding buffers" protect these resources. Because of the critical nature of these feeding resources, the project then must be managed to place the feeding buffers in front of the noncritical resources to protect the critical path of the project. This is called critical-chain buffer management and is illustrated in Figure 4.2 to provide a sample diagram of the critical chain. The critical chain represents the longest sequence of project activities after resolving all of the resource contentions. Blocks of unscheduled time, called buffers, are provided to absorb cumulative delays and are placed at the end of the chain and also where the

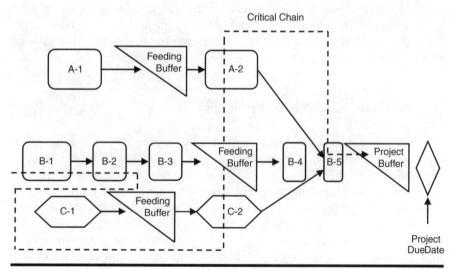

Figure 4.2. Critical-Chain Buffer Management.

noncritical chains connect to the critical chain. The chain equates to the weakest link example representing the constraint. Buffers are provided to cope with Murphy whenever he appears. Applying these actions results in overcoming any weak integration of project resources and will help to avoid dependency on in-project multiple resources.

Applying TOC in projects provides many opportunities for applying value-based management. It provides managers with tools that apply to controlling investment in equipment. It does not stop at just controlling the amount of investment; it shortens the time horizon in which companies can begin utilizing their asset investment. Time is money, which is something forgotten too frequently. Opportunities include introduction of new products to market, construction, and product design and development, including design for Six Sigma.

The constraints restrict the number of projects an organization can complete in addition to the time to complete given projects. Project environments are impacted by available capacity, so project overruns cascade to the organization's ability to process additional work. Effective buffering and constraint management generate increased capacity and reduce the tendency for multitasking of resources. The critical chain exposes the perils and problems that multitasking creates and explains how to allow the feeding buffers to consume high-priority tasks so that resources are used on tasks that are most critical for meeting project deadlines. This impacts the decision-making process in organizations by providing critical-chain buffer management by preventing delays and replanning projects that fall behind schedule. By providing visibility to the status of projects from the lens of critical-chain buffer management, the guesswork and the emotion of the unknown are removed from project management. Impacting how people think about the project translates into a dramatic improvement of the targeted results.

A STRATEGIC THINKING PROCESS

One of the key TOC tools is a process of thinking to create a road map that highlights directions for the strategic journey; a trip ticket, if you will, on application of all the TOC tools. Remember, the goal is to make a profit now and in the future. There are many businesses that can make a profit today but not sustain it in the future because they stopped performing at their highest level of capability. There is always room and need for continuous improvement. TOC asks key questions that are integral to strategy development and maintaining a focused strategy in achieving the goal. These same questions continue to drill at the core issues:

- What to change
- What to change to
- How to cause the change

TOC's approach is to ask these questions, then make the required changes. Without change, improvement fails to become a reality.

Goldratt uses the Socratic method whereby "Jonah" guides Alex Rogo (the plant manager in *The Goal*) through his dilemma by providing thought-provoking questions to stimulate problem identification and solution implementation. The strategic or focusing method is appropriately called the Jonah process. The current reality is that organizations are comprised of individuals with agendas and bias that make it difficult to identify problems and implement effective solutions. The Jonah process is effective because positive action becomes reality when people collectively buy in to an idea and solution they helped to conceive and implement.

All of the tools and techniques are worthless unless people utilize and apply them. The organizational silos, turf mentality, and executive egos represent ongoing obstacles and problems. The early years of the twenty-first century are providing even greater challenges because businesses, organizations, and people have become frozen in their own footsteps of inability to move forward toward the goal. The way to winning is learning how to use the tools we have at our disposal and move forward with their guidance and feedback.

I am going to enlighten and define the TOC Jonah techniques without providing detailed instructions. There are numerous sources of Jonah instruction and material, including the AGI-Goldratt Institute. This discussion is only intended to provide a basis for creating awareness.

The Jonah process begins with the awareness that organizations tend to solve problems and implement them in isolation. Major problems or needs represent a dilemma. The questioning technique to identify the constraint was clearly illustrated in one of my consulting projects, a dental practice of less than a dozen people, including the dentist.

We used TOC to achieve a breakthrough solution that transformed the practice. The practice had the dilemma of having only one dentist and more patients than the practice was capable of handling. After applying the questions relative to the goal of the dentist and the employees, we were able to quickly identify the constraint. The constraint was the dentist and how patients were scheduled. By applying DBR scheduling techniques and exploiting the constraint by adding an associate dentist, the practice was able to double its profit. By subordinating the constraint, elevating it, and starting from the beginning, the office stress and tension diminished.

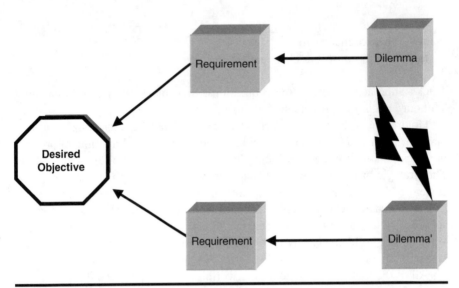

Figure 4.3.   Evaporating or Conflict Cloud Logic.

This example shows how a "breakthrough solution" was achieved using TOC. We utilized the Jonah process to:

1. Define the problem.
2. Create a breakthrough solution.
3. Implement the solution.
4. Achieve buy in from the key collaborators.

The first step was to identify and define the problem, which was achieved by gathering all the symptoms. The Jonah process terms this the *three-cloud technique* whereby at least three, or more, symptoms are identified. This is illustrated in Figure 4.3. It is the same technique used by a doctor, or dentist, to diagnose a patient. The technique uses an *evaporating or conflict cloud* to frame the dilemma.

This technique pinpoints core problems using effect-cause-effect to clarify the issues that create the dilemma. The use of the thinking tools helps to create understanding for facilitating change and selling buy in from presenting solutions in simple, practical ways. TOC developed the Jonah process and its tools to combat firefighting conflicts and disagreements. A conflict or firefighting cloud is developed for each symptom of the problem that is identified in the diagnostic process. This analysis is then used to develop what Jonah calls a current reality tree to map the existing situation. Current reality trees are useful lenses to examine the underlying issues and understand the magnitude of the problem and dilemma. TOC literature describes the prevalent tendency for the existence of conflicting policies within organizations that in turn represent a constraint that must be exploited. The strategic thinking component of the Jonah process uses reality trees to surface or raise assumptions underlying the conflict to clarify and guide understanding to achieve a potential breakthrough solution.

After achieving breakthrough ideas or solutions, organizational teams then can develop what TOC calls prerequisite and transition trees to identify the action steps and ensure buy in from the key collaborators. The mapping logic helps to clarify and identify options and potential solutions to facilitate conflicts and disagreements to achieve desired objectives and outcomes. TOC uses these techniques to achieve organizational buy in to overcome resistance to change. The process contains six steps, whereby the following checkpoints are resolved to achieve desired change:

1. Concurrence on the problem
2. Reaching agreement on the direction of the solution
3. Agreement that the solution will work
4. Agreeing on the associated risks
5. Agreeing on how the solution will be implemented
6. Agreement that the solution can be successfully implemented

This buy-in process provides clarity on the potential leverage that TOC can bring to problem solving when it is facilitated together with the mapping steps to convert undesired results into desired effects and objectives.

This tool is not, and should not be, restricted just to the application of TOC. Imagine the power of this concept when employed with lean manufacturing and Six Sigma. Balanced scorecards, discussed in Chapter 7, require buy in of strategy from top to bottom and from the bottom up. This represents another situation where TOC can help to enable other methodologies and vice versa.

A prevalent theme, and an objective of the mission, is to achieve breakthrough improvement of processes continuously. TOC is a tool that greatly simplifies understanding and, when used in combination with other methodologies, can leverage achievement of the goal dramatically. TOC helps to bring agreement on solutions that produce desired results and avoid disaster. The failure to commit and gain consensus represents continuing reasons why organizations fall short of the target. Top management down to employees in the trenches all need to understand the problem, realize the potential, and accept the challenge.

Although the problem is identified and defined, it still leaves us with unfinished work until the organization agrees on the solution and implements it.

TOC provides a basis for dialogue to help organizational teams understand the steps required for effective resolution and to realize why and how the problem evolved. By just understanding what the constraint is and the different ways it can occur, many of the barriers to progress are overcome. What ideas and policies are needed to pave the way for progress and improvement? TOC represents a tool that not only identifies problems, but also provides a vehicle for the team to achieve buy in on solutions. Buy in provides the foundation for commitment and action that results in a step toward resolution.

This discussion would not be complete without pointing out that constraints are often external to the organization. TOC has created strategic tools for understanding and coping with external constraints. The thinking process is directed toward developing win-win solutions in contrast to one-sided solutions where someone has to lose. The TOC material provides many examples where companies extracted concessions from vendors for faster delivery or improved quality that solved problems for both entities. This constraint is termed a "vendor constraint." TOC provides techniques for increasing the availability of the resource and creating a positive impact on the bottom line of both organizations at the same time.

Another external constraint is a market constraint. Assuming that price is not what is needed to overcome the market constraint, companies then need to increase the customer's perception of value through what TOC calls a "breakthrough offer" by providing alternative approaches for redirecting the focus away from price sensitivity. The bigger the problem that is solved for a customer, the greater will be the increase in actual and perceived value. Win-win victories are created by applying the TOC Jonah process to help the customer solve the problem, which in effect solves your problem. This process utilizes the three-cloud technique, firefighting clouds, and current reality trees to generate breakthrough ideas and breakthrough offers. In other words, all the TOC tools and techniques described can be applied to breaking external constraints in a similar fashion as they are applied internally.

TOC offers managers powerful tools with unlimited potential for identifying and solving a wide range of problems. Throughput accounting is one of the TOC tools and is described in Chapter 6. While the TOC management philosophy is powerful because it provides leverage and focus, it should not be applied in isolation. Its effectiveness is enhanced when applied together with other management philosophies. The tools *enable* each other.

This book has free materials available for download from the
Web Added Value™ Resource Center at www.jrosspub.com.

5

ACTIVITY-BASED MANAGEMENT AND MEASUREMENT

During the past half century, the productivity and global revolution turned the world of how we work and how we live upside down. Productivity has accelerated together with global outsourcing, which has applied increased pressure across the supply chain. New businesses have emerged with the technology bubble, bringing a proliferation of products and product lines. The decline of direct labor in our factories has been replaced with techno and administrative workers, dramatically shifting cost and expense incurred to produce products and services from variable costs to overhead. In an effort to compensate for the loss of relevance of management accounting, the accounting profession, academia, and controllers in industry have attempted to overcome the slide by assigning costs to activities in some effort to match costs with products and services. This activity analysis technique is called activity-based costing and management (ABC/M). This tool, and its many potential applications, is a critical component in improving the effectiveness of business processes through the use of activity-based analysis and continuous improvement. ABC/M is one of the enabling tools and techniques I feel is important. I will show you how it works, plus provide insight as to when and where to apply it.

The philosophies and techniques presented will not magically improve profit and build business value unless the underlying business processes are efficient and effective. The meaning of continuous improvement does not represent a magical solution to achieve breakthrough results. Continuous improvement is a necessary requirement just to stay in the game. It will not, by itself, provide a competitive advantage. ABC/M is a good tool for gaining strategic understanding, identifying the root causes of problems, and tracking the costs of overhead.

FIVE PRINCIPLES OF EXCELLENCE

The power of ABC/M is more than just the analytical process of identifying activities and their relationship to cost. It also is because of its ability to identify value and nonvalue activities. The capability to focus on differentiation of activities from resources and understand what an organization actually is helps to drive improvement and create excellence. Viewing the business from the window "what are we doing" in contrast to "what do we need to do" necessitates understanding and improving the business processes. Tom Pryor defines the "Five Principles of Excellence" as:

1. Continually manage activities, not resources.
2. Continually synchronize activities within business processes.
3. Continually eliminate wasteful activities.
4. Continually improve activity cost, time, and quantity.
5. Continually empower employees to improve activities.

These five principles provide a solid foundation for guiding ABC/M. These principles emphasize focused action that is applied properly to achieve improved results rather than generating analysis activity simply for the purpose of pinpointing costs. Understanding these five principles greatly facilitates knowing how and where to apply ABC/M to leverage the other tools and techniques contained in the tool kit.

Management of activities requires clear understanding of what currently is being done by the organization for the same reason that lean assessments are conducted. "Define" is a component of Six Sigma, as are the three questions asked when applying the Theory of Constraints. Activity-based analysis begins from a similar premise. What does it cost? What is the quantity of what is being done and the quality of the work or output generated? And last, how much time does it take to perform the activity?

The next principle focuses on synchronizing the activities as part of the ongoing improvement process. Improving an activity or process is of little or no value if it is not coordinated as part of the other processes within the organization. Continuous improvement should flow in rhythm with the beat of the organization. Establishing priorities and constraint identification needs to be clear. Spending the energy to improve a process, unless it fits the overall scheme, is paramount to waste because of the limitations on resources and capital.

Continuously eliminating wasteful activities will be an ongoing effort. It is important to direct the focus toward nonadded-value activities since overhead costs are not as visible. They represent the "hidden costs," and ongoing effort to flush them out in the open is an ongoing management challenge. The other component of this challenge is to concentrate on the customer and then flow back into the organization to improve the effectiveness of all related activities.

Customers demand low-cost, high-quality products and outstanding service in both timeliness of delivery and the quality of the service received. There should be little doubt as to why continually improving activity cost, time, and quality are included in the five principles. Again, when this principle is related to lean, Six Sigma, and the Theory of Constraints, it is easier to understand the interrelationship of these tools and concepts and how and why they can be mutually beneficial.

The fifth principle of employee empowerment is crucial. Toyota, Scandia, and others with successful empowerment programs secure support and buy in through communication to provide understanding at all levels of the organization. No one is more qualified to know what is going on than front-line employees that are operating processes. First-hand knowledge is the most accurate. Without employee involvement, there will be little or no continuous improvement effort for activities. Any effort to successfully initiate lean, Six Sigma, TOC, or activity-based management requires buy in and commitment. Posters, e-mail messages, and speeches will only represent nonvalue-added activities unless the proper commitment to training and communication is an integral component of the initiative.

Continuous improvement is one of the primary purposes and outcomes of activity-based management. It provides a valuable function by generating feedback and data that are critical in applying the profit-focused accounting tool kit. Let us learn more about how these tools work and gain understanding of the advantages that they provide.

ACTIVITY-BASED MEASUREMENT

Cost management evolved from double entry accounting systems used to create financial statements. Cost accounting data developed from cotton textile factories in the early 1800s and shaped the needs of business development until the 1950s and 1960s. Accounting systems use the general ledger and chart of accounts to capture categories of revenues and expenditures into financial state-

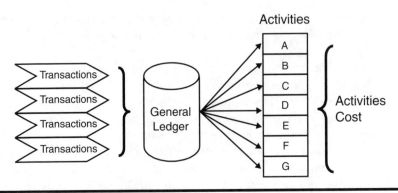

Figure 5.1.   ABC/M Reassigns Costs.

ments based on traditional approaches of grouping expenditures by departmental and functional categories. Activity-based costing emerged as a method to provide cost management with a way to reassign costs accumulated in the general ledger accounts. Figure 5.1 illustrates how data accumulated by accounting systems are then redirected so that decision makers can evaluate the impact on strategy and operations from different perspectives.

Based on the knowledge that ABC/M reassigns costs, it is then critical to understand what type of transactions drive overhead costs. In "The Hidden Factory," Miller and Volmann identified four types of transactions that drive overhead costs.

1. Logistical transactions — To order, execute, and confirm materials movement
2. Balancing transactions — To match the supply of material, labor, and machines with demand
3. Quality transactions — To validate that production is in conformance with specifications
4. Change transactions — To update manufacturing information

Logistical transactions include costs associated with indirect shop-floor workers in addition to activities associated with receiving, expediting, data entry, data processing, and accounting. Balancing relates to material planning, forecasting, and scheduling plus production activity control and procurement. Quality activity includes engineering and other quality-related activity. Change transactions relate to engineering change notices, routings, and other activity related to standards, specifications, and maintenance of the bills of material.

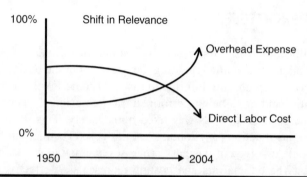

Figure 5.2. The Growing Relevance of Overhead Expense.

Beyond the "hidden factory," the costs of marketing, selling, distribution, and service are all significant contributors to overhead because successful businesses are driven by quality customer service and support. Global demands and cheap direct labor add to the overhead levels required to coordinate these contributors and drivers of overhead expenses.

The age of technology and requirements for information have made information technology overhead costs more prevalent entering the twenty-first century. Corporate overhead includes legal and human resources in addition to the typical functional responsibilities associated with headquarters expense. Direct material and direct labor are no longer the primary drivers of cost as they have been replaced by overhead expenses required to cope with the complexity and diversity of products and quality level demanded by the customer. Figure 5.2 depicts the stark contrast to changes that have been occurring in cost structures over the past fifty to sixty years.

During a recent operational assessment, an example of the "voice of the customer" occurred that is worth sharing. The interviews with the customer sales and service person were revealing. We learned that the customers regularly asked about product availability and when product could be shipped. The customer service person always had to reply with "let me call you right back to see what we have and when we can ship it to you." After these potential customers were unable to receive an instant answer, they responded immediately with "that's okay, we can get it from XYZ Company in 24 hours" and then did not place an order. These lost opportunities equated to approximately $2.5 million in sales for a company with under $10 million in sales. Management had no grasp of the activities occurring in sales and service, what they cost, and what the company lost by not having solid business processes in place to service and support customers effectively.

BUSINESS PROCESSES

The above illustration is a representative sample of the lack of management knowledge and understanding regarding the operation of the business processes. The only way to capture this information is to become involved in the details of the activities and tasks being performed. In the business process described, the gap in the business process was fixed immediately. This illustration is not meant to be a justification for adopting activity-based costing, but for management to become involved in business processes and activities. As involvement occurs, activity-based analysis and costing represents an effective tool to understand and improve processes.

The cost of complexity necessitates greater understanding of business processes and the activities and tasks occurring within them. What is a business process? A process is an activity that takes an input and adds value to it and then provides an output to either an internal or external customer. Industrial processes depend on machinery for their creation and come into physical contact with materials that will be delivered to a customer. These processes do not include shipping, distribution, or a billing process. A commercial process includes ordering materials, payroll, or processing customer orders and supports industrial processes.

These processes are comprised of activities that represent what gets done. Tasks are the individual steps or jobs within the activity required to perform the action. An example of an activity might be receiving material in the receiving department. A task would be counting how many boxes were received, and another task would be signing the receiver notice after completing the count. Activity-based costing looks at costs from both a product as well as a process point of view, as presented in Figure 5.3.

The top or vertical viewpoint represents the assignment of cost. People, machinery and equipment, and material are the resources generating costs that are assigned through the accounting system. The flow of the diagram shows the correlation of costs and how they are assigned to these activities and tasks. The horizontal flow of the diagram represents the process view. This shows the relationship to what drives the process to consume activities based on the tasks performed. Each activity has an input that causes or drives the activity to perform tasks within the process. Once the activity is initiated, it consumes resources in producing an output, a product, for either an internal or external customer. This output represents the workload from the activity and is quantified as the output measure. We begin to see how costs are assigned to resources shown by the vertical flow of what things cost. The horizontal flow shows why things have cost. Measuring the cost of the resource tells us what

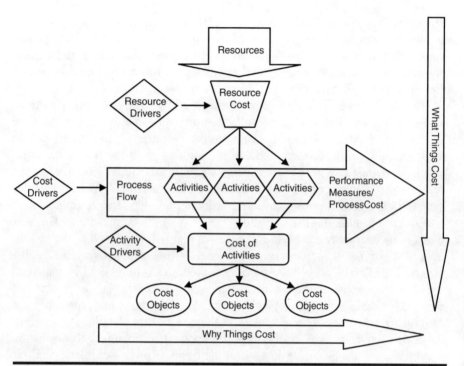

Figure 5.3.   Activity-Based Costing Flow.

we spent for the resource and helps us to understand why expenditures were incurred. The reasons for expending resources are called resource drivers.

Work activities represent what we do and consume resources in proportion to the activity level of tasks performed. The next step is to determine why we perform certain tasks, what they are, and how much they cost. These activities are called activity drivers and are used to quantify the consumption of resource costs. Outputs are then identified by a customer or a product, or both, and are called cost objects.

Activity-based costs that are measured quantitatively are shown as the vertical view in Figure 5.3 and create three types of drivers:

1. Resource drivers that trace costs to work activities (tasks)
2. Activity drivers that trace the cost of activities to cost objects (customers and products)
3. Cost object drivers that trace the cost object to other cost objects

Processes consist of at least two activities. They take time, consume resources, and produce outputs. Activity-based measurement prompts the following questions: What do processes do? What do processes cost? Answers to these questions are found by understanding the activities occurring within the process and the drivers that produce the cost objects or outputs.

This is a good time to go back and review a few basic concepts. Functions within an organization represent a collection of people in either one or multiple locations that share a common responsibility or purpose. Examples include sales, manufacturing, finance, and engineering and sit at the top of the organizational pyramid. Within these functions are organizational groupings called departments or cost centers that exist within the functional areas. Examples include field sales, accounts payable, receiving, test lab, and countless other categories depending on the size and complexity of the organization. The next levels in the hierarchy are business processes that will move across the boundaries of departments and cost centers to provide products and services to customers. The effectiveness of these business processes is monitored by matching activities to the cost of the resources generating the costs. The next step that needs to be addressed is identifying the critical detailed tasks that represent what the organization does. The answer is in the dirt and the details.

In developing activity analysis, it is important to obtain key information about the activities occurring in each of the business processes. Gathering this information is the first step in understanding how processes function and learning what people really do. This analysis needs to be developed from the bottom up and not from the top down. What activities are being performed and do they create value? Activities can be categorized as either primary or secondary. Primary activities contribute directly to the primary purpose of the organization, such as shipping product to customers where the activity output leaves the department or work center. This activity represents the way departments spend their time and consume resources of the organization. The primary mission of the organization is accomplished through primary activities. Secondary activities are then defined as activities that support the primary activities. Secondary activities, while necessary, tend to be administrative in nature, consume resources, take time, and cost money. Typically, 80 percent of an organization's effort is devoted to primary activities and the remaining 20 percent to secondary activities. Tom Pryor from ICMS, Inc. states that a desired ratio is 90 percent/ 10 percent or better. Higher ratios are indicative of unnecessary layers of bureaucracy. This is where ABC/M measurement helps to overcome smoke screens created by traditional accounting systems.

Identifying activities and relating them to the organization's business processes are similar to the goals of lean, Six Sigma, and TOC. This approach uses different tools with a different focus to reach the same destination. Regardless,

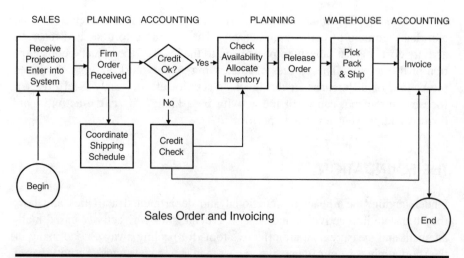

Figure 5.4. Process Map.

we are trying to provide the customer with unsurpassed service, high quality, and low cost/low price. Activities that provide the customer with these features are characterized as value-added activities. Analysis of the activities within the process will identify the activity drivers and allow classification as to being either value or nonvalue. Since activities consume resources we want to:

- Minimize cost drivers of nonvalue-adding activities
- Optimize cost drivers of value-adding activities

Activity cost drivers are used to measure the frequency and intensity of demands placed by cost objects (products or services). Activity analysis and measurement represents the foundation for continuous improvement as the root causes behind the activity drivers are identified. Figure 5.4 illustrates the flow of resources through the activities of the process to product cost objects.

This figure shows the dollars captured in the accounting system and the resources driving activity in the process to produce products for the customer. This will provide us with the performance measures and analysis indicating the cost and the value-added level of the activities.

DEFINING ACTIVITY DRIVERS

Activity cost drivers embody events that impact the consumption of resources, such as receiving material, moving material, expediting material, managing employees, or performing administrative tasks. These factors determine the workload required to perform an activity. They are used to trace and reassign activity costs to cost objects in proportion to the level of the objects' consumption of the activity. The process of identifying activity cost drivers determines the causes of differences in the level of activity effort. Analysis effort then focuses on the root causes of the activity by asking: Why is the activity performed and at what level it is performed?

THE FOUNDATION

Understanding the impact of functional and departmental activities and how they translate into activities and tasks is crucial as to why activity-based management and measurement are effective tools for peeling away a good many of the shortcomings of our financial and cost management systems. Activity-based costing has helped bring some relevance back to cost management because we now have tools to measure and optimize activities. This helps to provide a clearer picture of the real costs of serving customers and producing quality products. Being able to locate the sources of, and determine the reasons for, root causes is the essence of more effective continuous improvement of the processes. In the next chapter, I will begin unfolding how this tool, when used with a new accounting and reporting model, will provide more focused profit information. This use of activity-based management enables empowered employees to understand the impact of their tasks and allows them to focus on continuous improvement of their processes.

ACTIVITY-BASED COSTING AND ACCOUNTING

Using traditional accounting methods, direct costs capture raw material and direct labor using bills of material and routings as production flows through the work centers. Departments and work centers within departments are created to capture payroll and other costs directly attributed to the work centers. These are structured in the general and subsidiary ledgers to attempt to capture all the costs and expenses attributable to products. Departmental organization usually follows the flow of the manufacturing processes, with supporting functions (such as shipping and receiving, machine shop, warehouse, and quality) having their own departments. The expenses of all the related overhead expenses are then allocated relative to some attribute of a product unit such as direct labor hours or dollars, machine hours, or material dollars consumed in making a product. These conventional allocation methods are used to establish the burden rate for determining total product costs and the amount of overhead assigned to the inventory value of the product produced. This historical approach is fixed on the volume of production and the units or mix of products produced in an attempt to determine inventory costs and product cost for individual products. The failings of this approach are illustrated with an example that is presented in Chapter 6.

Activity-based costing focuses on activities. The difference in the two approaches is that activities consume resources, and products or services in turn consume activities. By assigning cost to activities and measuring the amount of activity required to produce the product or provide the service, it allows us to develop a more accurate picture of cost. Understanding the hierarchies of activities is necessary to achieve a grasp of how activity-based costing and accounting works. There are three primary categories of activities recognized in the application of activity-based costing:

1. Unit-level costs related to activities that vary based on units of service or product processed or serviced. The workload varies directly with the quantity of each activity driver.
2. Batch-level costs vary based on the work effort of the batch size or work produced. A machine setup cost of $1,000 will remain constant, but the batch-level cost per unit will vary depending on whether batch size is one or a thousand.
3. Cost object or product-level costs represent the identification of costs to sustain the organization, but the consumption of which cannot be specifically identified with a product, service, or customer. Facility costs can be included here where they cannot logically be traced to a cost object.

By employing the technique of more accurate identification of activity costs to products, companies have a tool capable of providing product cost information that is more reliable. This is especially true now that companies are offering a wider array of products. Association of activities as consuming resources to produce products tends to provide greater levels of accuracy of profitability by product and in the ability to identify and link costs throughout the supply chain.

Figure 5.5 presents Model Manufacturing Company, a typical example of a $10 million in sales company with product lines presented in a typical financial format. This is a glaring example that is all too similar to how most companies report their cost data under generally accepted accounting principles. A consistent and comparable set of data will be used to illustrate alternative applications of methodology. Figure 5.6 shows Model Manufacturing Company using ABC/M techniques that demonstrate the contrast compared to

	Widget 1	Widget 2	Widget 3	Widget 4	Widget 5	Total
Sales	$4,000,000	$2,000,000	$1,800,000	$600,000	$1,600,000	$10,000,000
Cost of Goods Sold:						
Direct Material	1,600,000	875,000	825,000	300,000	700,000	4,300,000
Direct Labor	500,000	225,000	225,000	78,000	220,000	1,248,000
Manufacturing Overhead	572,416	257,587	257,587	89,297	251,863	1,428,750
Total Cost of Goods Sold:	2,672,415	1,357,587	750,000	467,297	1,171,863	6,976,750
Gross Margin – $	1,327,584	642,413	492,413	132,703	428,137	3,023,250
Gross Margin – %	33.19%	32.12%	27.36%	22.12%	26.76%	30.23%
Selling Administration and Other	509,638	588,602	239,138	213,115	648,256	2,198,750
EBITDA	817,946	53,811	253,275	(80,412)	(220,119)	824,500
Interest Expense						187,500
Depreciation						201,282
Amortization						11,111
						399,893
Income Before Taxes						424,607
Income Taxes						148,612
Net Income						$275,995

Figure 5.5. Model Manufacturing Company — Traditional Cost View.

traditional accounting and illustrates the application of four categories of activity classification.

Figure 5.6 reflects four distinct levels of profit margin that, when aggregated, equal total operating profit before taxes. Activity-based management provides a three-dimensional view to capture process costs and the impact of the customer across the supply chain. The four levels of ABC/M used to determine profit margin as shown on the activity-based costing profit-and-loss statement are explained below:

1. Direct cost of material and supplies varies directly with sales and they are consumed as they are converted to product or cost objects.
2. Activity costs of product work flowing through processes connect to all the people activities associated with creating the product or cost objects. These activity costs are developed using bills of costs to accumulate activity costs relating to creating the product including direct labor, indirect labor, and all other support costs related to production. Figure 5.6 provides an illustration of the costs that impact product work activities.
3. Customer work activities gather the costs of the activity of processes with customer-specific work activities. These include order processing, invoicing, collection, accounts receivable, customer service, postsales services, and sales and marketing. Again, bills of costs are used to accumulate and reassign these activity costs.

	Widget 1	Widget 2	Widget 3	Widget 4	Widget 5	Total
Sales	$4,000,000	$2,000,000	$1,800,000	$600,000	$1,600,000	$10,000,000
Cost of Goods Sold:						
Direct Material	1,600,000	875,000	825,000	300,000	700,000	4,300,000
Direct Labor	500,000	225,000	225,000	78,000	220,000	1,248,000
Direct Costs	2,100,000	1,100,000	1,050,000	378,000	920,000	5,548,000
Gross Margin	1,900,000	900,000	750,000	222,000	680,000	4,452,000
Product Work Activities	362,300	325,316	189,549	122,575	429,009	1,428,750
Gross Margin	1,537,700	574,684	560,451	99,425	250,991	3,023,250
Customer Work Activities	317,302	491,537	146,308	134,575	486,528	1,576,250
Gross Margin	1,220,397	83,147	414,143	(35,151)	(235,536)	1,447,000
Business Sustaining Activities						622,500
EBITDA						824,500
Interest Expense						187,500
Depreciation						201,282
Amortization						11,111
						399,893
Income Before Taxes						424,607
Income Taxes						148,612
Net Income						$275,995

Figure 5.6. Model Manufacturing Company — ABC/M View.

4. Business-sustaining activity costs represent the costs not associated with products or cost objects. They include senior management, headquarters or corporate expenses, available but idle capacity costs, research and development, and other expenses where there is no direct cause and effect relationship with the final cost objects.

APPLICATIONS OF ACTIVITY-BASED COSTING

Activity-based costing provides managers with new and improved tools for understanding costs and profitability by product and customer. This translates to having better information to guide decisions and development of strategy. The bill of cost method for tracking activity costs of the layers of overhead for assignment by product and customer provides managers with the ability to better understand the "hidden costs." Translating costs into value- and nonvalue-added categories represents the addition of a valuable tool. Likewise, the ability to categorize activities as either primary or secondary allows organizations to attain new balance and levels of flexibility. The application of this capability will be a component of my discussion of profit-focused accounting, Theory of Constraints, and throughput accounting in the next chapter.

The enhanced understanding of process cost using activity-based management and analysis is a real plus. This chapter concludes with a discussion of the analytical tools that help to provide the ability to visualize business processes in correlation to process cost. This was a shortcoming of the earlier ABC/M versions. The enhancements, combined with increasing focus on continuous improvement emphasized by both lean and Six Sigma, make ABC/M a tool that businesses need to understand and utilize. In the chapter on balanced scorecards, more will be learned about how ABC/M fits with the scorecard techniques to produce enhanced focus for organizational strategy.

ABC/M provides an excellent model for use in predicting cost and profit margins when applying forecasts of future customer demand. The proliferation of product and service offerings has exploded, making it necessary to predict profitability based on the diversity of product mix by geographic region. The days of lengthy and unreliable budget drills are a thing of the past in today's competitive landscape. The just-in-time techniques applied to the supply chain require accuracy and speed in what I call the "customer-focused organization" of the twenty-first century. ABC/M allows explosion of process activity based on the demand for products that help organizations to adjust requirements for end products by the activities required to provide them. The predictive capability of ABC/M enables organizations to identify potential constraints accurately before they occur. This predictive ability can also be applied to business processes so they can be improved on a prospective basis. Another feature of predictive costing is the growing tendency of Internet B2B transactions and the need to have a truly accurate picture of product cost. The list goes on and new applications will emerge as more users start to push the capability of the tools.

ACTIVITY-BASED ANALYSIS

Activity improvement begins with analysis and the right tools. This section provides understanding of the time-tested tools for activity analysis and how to best apply them. GE was the first company to employ activity analysis and costing and developed the tools and techniques widely utilized today. Earlier, primary and secondary activities were identified together with value- and nonvalue-added activities. The first step is identification and definition, which requires finding out what people are doing and then categorizing the activities for analysis and then determining how to improve what is being done and enhancing it. Input is received into the activity and an output is generated from the activity.

Understanding the business and what it wants to do is a logical way to approach activity analysis. This is the very first step of the activity analysis regardless of who conducts the study. This brings up a good question. Who should conduct the analysis? My suggestion is that all process owners and their work teams should participate in the analysis in order to obtain lasting impact for continuous improvement. This will accomplish much more than having the financial function or an outside consultant provide a snapshot view of the process to identify activity cost for the purpose of tracking it to a product.

Questions should focus on the outputs of the activity and the customer for the output, whether they are internal or external to the organization. GE developed the activity dictionary, and this represents an excellent way to capture and define each activity. The definition should include all the activity inputs, outputs, and measurements of the outputs, together with the characteristics and cost drivers for each activity within a process. After capturing all the key elements of each activity, determine the amount of time each activity requires plus the amount of time spent waiting to perform additional steps. All of this information should be gathered for all activities within each department or work center plus the time required for each activity. You will then know how each department spends its time and the number of people required for each activity. Reviewing these activities within each department and tracing them through each process will help build understanding of the relationship between departments and functions consumed by each process. This information, when combined with departmental cost data, will yield insight into process and product costs.

Gathering activity information produces data on the amount of time devoted to nonrepetitive activities such as managing employees, administrative tasks, and training. Activities not required for meeting customer or external requirements are classified as nonvalue added. By identifying them and understanding how they fit into each process, companies will build a foundation for improving the efficiency of their processes. This is one of the key requirements for creating a value stream map.

Value stream mapping identifies all the process steps associated with converting a customer need into a product or service. The mapping technique provides a clear picture of all of the process steps that identify waste and opportunities for improvement. The classification of a nonvalue-added activity does not necessarily mean that it can be eliminated, but the mere illumination of it will provide an opportunity to improve on how it is performed. The mapping process can be nothing more than a pencil tracing of the flow of material, information, and steps required to create a product or service. Value stream mapping originates from the questions and answers that evolve from activity analysis. Value-added questions focus on competitive advantage through faster delivery and reduction of defects. Nonvalue-added questions center on tasks such as counting, inspecting, moving, delaying, storing, and expediting. The process team will identify and map all the value and nonvalue steps to improve the cycle time of the process. Continuous improvement usually focuses its initial effort on diminishing the impact of nonvalue-added activities, then looks at how value-added activities can be improved. Primary emphasis is then placed on improving customer-related value-added activities.

Value stream mapping is similar to, but different than, process mapping, especially in nonmanufacturing or overhead areas. Process mapping is a flow-chart of all the tasks, steps, and activities of each and every business process. It can be done using pencil and paper, sticky notes, or with one of the several computer software packages designed for this purpose. Many companies have never tackled this detailed, step-by-step documentation of how their business operates. This then becomes a very eye-opening analysis. Figure 5.4 shows a simple example of a process map.

The approach that I suggest is to identify the process owner (the key functional manager) and key employees that are the most familiar with the process and conduct interviews to define critical success factors and key performance measures. The next step is to analyze the process and define the process scope and activity drivers and map it "as is" at a high level. This analysis step should include defining the process attributes, the organizational roles and how they function, and who performs what tasks. After completing the high-level "as is" map, conduct workshop meetings with the process team to map the "as is" process steps and attributes in detail. This last detail-mapping step provides a basis for determining where and how the process can be improved. The detailed information becomes the foundation for conducting root cause analysis.

Employing some tried and tested tools enhances continuous process improvement meetings and the job of conducting root cause analysis. Let us discuss some of the common analysis tools. First is the 80 percent or 20 percent rule (Pareto's Law) that helps to determine where to focus the team's effort for maximum process improvement success. Improving 20 percent of the process will typically generate 80 percent of the savings. There will be many opportunities for improvement, but concentrating on the 20 percent that offer the greatest payback makes the most sense. Because continuous improvement represents change, it is important to post some early success.

Root cause analysis requires that causes and effects within processes be examined in close detail to provide clear understanding of the possibilities. The tool commonly used to conduct this analysis is called a "fishbone diagram." This tool identifies the relationship between a problem (or "effect") and all the possible "causes" of the problem. The diagram helps teams to identify the likely causes of problems, analyze them in greater depth, and then begin development of solutions. The diagram provides a foundation for brainstorming problems and finding solutions.

Brainstorming is a dynamic exchange of ideas surrounding analysis of a problem and the exploration of potential solutions. Continuous improvement teams should employ this tool to tap into the best ideas of the individual members of the process team and expand the entire thinking process in search of the best solution. Based on conducting many operational assessment-consulting projects, experience has shown that employees closest to the action always are aware of the problem and frequently have the best solution for the problem. Brainstorming meetings are more effective when they are facilitated. Storyboards are a tool that helps to achieve greater effectiveness.

The technique of storyboarding begins by first defining the problem. The process team members are then facilitated to generate and document all of their ideas. All of the ideas are then posted on the wall and grouped by major theme. The team members then list and arrange the ideas in the order that best solves the defined problem. Another approach to thinking outside of the box includes workouts. This is a technique used by GE where everything is laid out on the table, worked through, debated, and then the process team comes to closure. This is similar to the storyboard technique. Another tool that can be applied in conjunction with brainstorming is the "five whys," a technique of continually asking the same question to generate ideas. When a number of ideas have been posted, the process team votes on them and ranks them based on the vote received by each idea. Another approach often used to obtain consensus is the "fist to five" method. Each person on the team can hold up the number of fingers that indicate his or her level of support for an idea, ranging from a fist (equating to zero) to five (absolutely great). Rank all the storyboard ideas accordingly. This provides some sense of how teams can work to analyze and improve business processes.

This book has free materials available for download from the Web Added Value™ Resource Center at www.jrosspub.com.

6

BASICS OF THROUGHPUT ACCOUNTING

Simplified accounting and measurement for the complicated world of global business seems like a dream that could never come true. *Relevance Lost* (Johnson and Kaplan) and *Relevance Regained* (Johnson) provide a clear discussion on accounting's role in how business has suffered from the top-down management syndrome. This approach utilizes cost management data in an attempt to control and manage costs in contrast to allowing empowered employees to improve business processes. Eli Goldratt also picked up on the theme of misleading and useless cost accounting thinking and its disastrous impact on business operations and management thinking. The Theory of Constraints (TOC) answer to *Relevance Lost* is throughput accounting. Before launching into a detailed discussion and explanation, I will set some objectives and direction for profit-focused accounting to set the initial tone and then interject some of the suggested variations during the discussion of throughput accounting. Chapter 9 deals with the application of profit-focused accounting in more detail.

The profit-focused accounting approach will utilize some of the concepts offered by throughput accounting, especially its simplistic approach. All enterprise resource planning (ERP) systems employ bills of material or recipes to track raw material and routings to map operational processes and track direct labor though work centers. These data are included in the item master for each product manufactured. ERP systems also include information on setups and setup times and provide a foundation for planning and scheduling. Profit-focused accounting will track both raw material and direct labor as variable costs in contrast to just raw material as a variable cost under throughput accounting.

Profit-focused accounting will provide a bridge to generally accepted accounting principles (GAAP), and I will provide a simple way of applying overhead to determine inventory valuations. Activity-based costing and management will be a component of understanding the pool of overhead expense under throughput accounting, or standby expense as I call it. It will be necessary to utilize nonfinancial measures and balanced scorecards as enablers in this approach. Lastly, economic value added (EVA™) will be used to ensure long-term value building in contrast to a short-term view of profit. I thought it would be helpful to know the direction as I proceed with the basics of throughput accounting.

THROUGHPUT ACCOUNTING BASICS

Throughput accounting offers subtle simplicity in its approach to the complex tangle of misunderstanding and poor management decision-making tools developed by CPAs, cost accountants, MBAs, and academia over the past fifty or sixty years. The three key elements of throughput accounting include:

1. Throughput
2. Operating expenses
3. Assets

Throughput is defined as the rate that a system generates money (i.e., incremental cash flow through sales that correlates to sales less direct material using traditional accounting terminology). Operating expenses are defined as all the money the system spends in converting inventory into throughput. Direct labor is included under operating expenses and is assumed to be a fixed expense. Assets in throughput accounting are identical to assets in conventional accounting except for inventory. Inventory is defined as the money that the system spends on things it intends to convert into throughput. Goldratt termed "cost accounting as the number one enemy of productivity" and was adamant about avoiding the inclusion of labor and overhead in inventory due to the distortions associated with application of GAAP.

Throughput accounting is very similar to direct costing, sometimes referred to as contribution accounting. The table shown in Figure 6.1 compares the differences between direct costing and variable costing and helps illustrate the subtleties of the differences between the two methods. My concept of profit-focused accounting follows the contribution model, but with adaptation that will

Variable Costing	Throughput Accounting
Revenue	Revenue
(Direct Material)	(Direct Material)
(Direct Labor)	
(Variable Overhead)	
Contribution	Throughput
(Fixed Expenses)	(Operating Expenses)
PROFIT	PROFIT

Figure 6.1. Variable Costing Versus Throughput Accounting — Variable Overhead Includes Both Production and Nonproduction Expenses.

allow us to go beyond just keeping score. It will provide tools for value chain analysis, strategic positioning analysis, and cost driver analysis.

Variable costing assumes that contribution is sales less variable cost. Throughput is defined as revenue less totally variable cost. The difference lies in the categorization of direct labor as a variable cost. Direct labor is supposed to represent a cost that varies with the level of sales volume. In practice and reality, direct labor has more attributes of fixed expense because workers will not be terminated in direct ratio with volume for a number of reasons. Management does not respond to fluctuations in demand that quickly and has started to become sensitive to losing its trained workers. There are also many associated costs to the workforce such as healthcare, pensions, and in some instances costs related to organized labor unions. While there is some relationship to volume, reality is that direct labor is not truly variable. Linkage of direct labor hours to ERP and determining the capacity of work centers is why profit-focused accounting classifies it as a variable cost, not to associate it with the cost world. There are some industries, such as subcontractors, that classify direct labor as truly variable along with variable selling and shipping costs. TOC categorizes direct labor under operating expense because it is not truly 100 percent variable and to avoid the incentive to build inventories.

Revenue = Total Cost

(Price per unit)(number of units) = fixed cost + (variable cost per unit)(number of units)

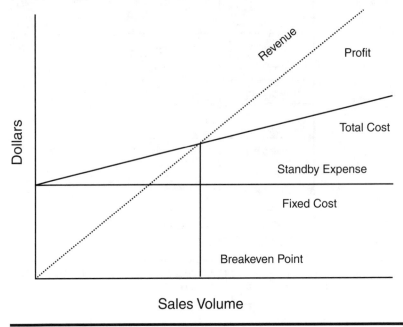

Figure 6.2. The Breakeven Model.

The original purpose of direct costing was to use it as a pricing tool to utilize all the potential unused capacity of a production facility. The traditional breakeven model shown in Figure 6.2 provides an illustration of how any sale that generates a contribution or variable margin will add to the goal of making more profit. Early in my career in the 1960s and 1970s, I was taught about the principles of contribution accounting and to use this contribution tool to establish selling prices. Our competitors, who used traditional cost accounting methods, tended to make huge errors in their pricing submissions and my use of contribution accounting gave our company a competitive edge. I would always price products using the two methods with some knowledge of what our automotive manufacturing customers were willing to pay, thereby applying target-costing techniques to earn sales volume at a profit. This represented a similar approach as described in *The Goal*, but with a twist. Today's reality of the global competitive situation entering the twenty-first century is that it negates the effectiveness of the breakeven model, as the customer takes control of the market relative to quality, service, and price. In actuality, all expenses are variable in effect. Productivity has increased and companies now have an abundance of unused capacity with weak demand. The model is useful as a tool for understanding, but falls short of reality.

I found contribution accounting to be effective because all levels of the organization understood the simplicity of its presentation. Contribution accounting was developed originally when companies in the United States did not have to face any difficulty in selling excess capacity. It was an effective pricing tool that fully exploited the resources of the organization. Understanding the need to exploit unused capacity occurred with one of my clients. The client manufactured high-quality printed folding cartons and decided to lease an additional printing press that significantly increased his monthly operating expenses. The company was losing money by applying traditional product costing and calculations to set selling prices. Once the need to soak up the increased capacity of his plant was understood using contribution accounting, he started to price products competitively in a way that increased sales and contribution so that the business became profitable. The breakeven model does work in some instances, even though for most instances it is obsolete in today's global environment. The primary point is that operating expenses (or fixed cost in the breakeven model) graphically illustrate the relationship of variable contribution to fixed expense in the determination of profitability.

The TOC reasoning for utilizing contribution accounting is to avoid building visual profits by continued production for the purpose of applying overhead. Traditional cost management systems are required to include some overhead in valuing inventory. Accordingly, overhead is applied to product cost using some method of allocation based on direct labor, machine hours, raw material, or some combination of these methods. The most common method was and still is calculating burden rates based on direct labor. Overhead can be either over- or underabsorbed based on plant efficiencies or production levels. In Chapter 5, the declining impact of direct labor was seen, as shown in Figure 5.2.

The best way to illustrate the distortion of burden absorption is to use a simplified example. We will assume a burden rate of 100 percent of direct labor. Our model assumes no sales during the month. We used $1,000 of raw material and $500 of direct labor to produce widgets, which were placed in finished goods inventory. Overhead expenses for the month totaled $500. According to GAAP, we are required to apply $500 of overhead at a rate of 100 percent, which will value the widgets produced at $2,000 and allow us to report no profit or loss on our simplified profit-and-loss statement. Figure 6.3 summarizes these simple transactions.

Applying variable costing (profit-focused accounting), a loss of $500 will result as opposed to breaking even using GAAP. Throughput accounting would have reported a loss of $1,000, since direct labor is included in operating

Burden Absorption

Assume no sales and all production for the month was complete and the burden rate is 100 percent of direct labor.

Sales	0
Raw Material	1,000
Direct Labor	500
Burden	500
Inventory	2,000
Overhead	500
Absorbed Overhead	(500)
Profit	0

All overhead is included in inventory.

Figure 6.3.   The Overhead Distortion.

expense and not in the valuation of inventory. While this represents a simple and unlikely scenario, one can understand how the different methods produce different answers using the same cash outflow. We see that profit is increased based on the flow of production to inventory and not based on sales.

THROUGHPUT ACCOUNTING METRICS

Throughput accounting offers some different views of measurement relative to throughput and inventory. Its approach creates a focus on bottom-line results using global operational measurements. These bottom-line measurements identify net profit as the absolute measure and look at its relationship with the amount of investment made by the owners or shareholders of the enterprise. Throughput accounting measures the cash flow generated by throughput less operating expenses and the investment in inventory. Goldratt recognized the need to make a profit, but also the ramifications of profit to the amount of investment needed to generate throughput and create the amount of cash required for survival. *The Race,* written by Goldratt and Robert E. Fox, discusses the bridge between actions necessary to achieve the goal. They feared, and correctly so, that the "cost concept" plus intuition was not the correct bridge to direct actions needed to maintain and accelerate our competitive position. It was more like walking off a gangplank than bridging the proper actions for managing constraints to achieve targeted performance results.

Throughput accounting identified the keys to achieving and maintaining a competitive edge as:

- Superior quality
- Better engineering
- Higher profit margins
- Lower investment
- On-time delivery
- Shorter lead times

Throughput accounting is focused on the goal of optimizing profitability and linking the relationship to the three components necessary for its achievement. *The Goal* was written at a time when maximum utilization of productive capacity was a key issue. Throughput is defined as sales less direct materials, so the emphasis was to maximize it in contrast to the "cost world" approach that focused on cost reduction. Throughput accounting is predicated on managing constraints to optimize inventory levels and control operating expenses, resulting in higher net profit and achievement of higher returns on investment.

The proponents of throughput accounting place the weight of their message on applying TOC as a management philosophy and a tool for decision making. *Throughput Accounting* by Thomas Corbett defines the basic elements of throughput accounting and describes potential fallacies of applying product costs associated with product mix and making bad decisions. *The Measurement Nightmare* by Debra Smith provides an excellent description that explains the mess associated with applying GAAP to throughput accounting and how to bridge the gap. Each effort provides understanding of a little-understood concept that offers great possibilities.

One of the driving forces of throughput accounting is its predication on maximizing throughput and how it accomplishes its objective. Primary obstacles to maximizing throughput are scheduling and identifying constraints. Goldratt has provided us with some tools that are truly potent once we gain understanding and know where to apply focus and how to gain leverage.

Goldratt has truly tried to help us not only to recognize problems associated with the "cost" world, but he also has provided a new decision process that was missing between the available data and the information that was needed. By asking the right question, we access the information we need because we can apply different decision procedures. Throughput accounting recognizes that throughput is the highest priority. It is no different than Jack Welch of GE saying, "the only real security we have is satisfied and loyal customers." There have been extensive efforts to reduce costs, but increasing sales of the right products will produce greater profit than all the effort in the world to control and cut costs.

Throughput accounting places its priority on maximizing throughput and minimizing any delay of throughput. It is not a sale until the product is delivered and ultimately not until it is paid for. We need to remember the Boy Scout march of Chapter 4 and the description of drum-buffer-rope (DBR). Goldratt provides in-depth discussion of throughput maximization in *The Haystack Syndrome*. This may not be his most well-known effort, but it represents one of his best efforts. He tackles the difficult issue of production scheduling with a detailed explanation of effective application of local performance measures to optimize throughput.

Focus is placed on avoiding late orders and developing measurements that correlate to lateness called throughput dollar days. This measure represents the throughput value of a late order times the number of days late. This measures the effect of not doing what was supposed to be done. Avoiding delays will require using inventory to buffer for the inevitable disruptions that always have an impact on the perfect plan, the inevitable "Murphy." This can be in the form of unexpected changes such as a machine breakdown, weather problems, or an out-of-control process that produces excess waste. Buffers utilize time and inventory to protect capacity-constrained resources. Inventory dollar days represent another unique throughput accounting measurement.

Conceptually, DBR is predicated on providing a process of synchronizing the flow of product utilizing a production plan starting with the customer order. Then it creates a dynamic schedule utilizing TOC principles of protecting the constrained resource (slowest Boy Scout). This represents the application of the basic concept of profit maximization. This scheduling approach includes providing a buffer at the constrained resource with both time and material. Another buffer is created at the shipping point, to ensure against late deliveries. Success in this application lies in identifying the constraint utilizing the five focusing steps.

1. *Identify* the system's constraint.
2. Decide how to *exploit* the system's constraint.
3. Subordinate everything else to the above decisions.
4. *Elevate* the system's constraint.
5. Do not allow *inertia* to become the system's constraint. When a constraint is broken, go back to step one.

The circular flow following the concept of DBR is illustrated in Figure 6.4. Flow begins with customer demand and circulates from an order issued to an

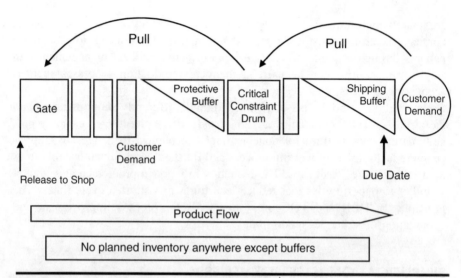

Figure 6.4. Drum-Buffer-Rope Scheduling.

order shipped. The buffering concepts are shown for both the capacity-constrained resource and the nonconstrained resources to help you visualize the application. The cadence of the production rate of the capacity-constrained resources sets the pace for the flow of the process. DBR was designed for use in conjunction with the five focusing steps. It does not need to be strictly a TOC tool, as it can be applied together with material requirements planning modules contained in all ERP systems.

A throughput prospective — realizing that the market is frequently, if not always, the constraint — provides direction for companies to look beyond themselves and have the customer provide insight versus a strict cost-cutting strategy. Taking the best of TOC concepts provides a blueprint for improving your own process before you start improving those of your vendors or customers. Clean up your own house first before tackling the entire neighborhood. The DBR and TOC approaches provide tools and logic that will generate a progression of constraint identification. After exploiting it, subordinating it, and elevating it, you go on to identifying the next constraint. This allows companies to fix what needs to be fixed in a more cost-effective and time-efficient fashion. This leads to a journey of continuous process improvement that lends itself to application of lean Six Sigma approaches.

DBR applications represent solutions originally designed for production. They are also applicable to marketing since the flow starts with the customer demand and the cadence is then maintained by the constrained resource. There are many opportunities to apply DBR in nonproduction processes and in nonmanufacturing industries. I successfully applied the concept to scheduling patients through a dental practice. It is an effective process management tool and its applications can be used in many nonproduction processes such as accounting and customer service.

In addition to motivating companies to think differently about planning and the results of TOC, companies are able to identify underutilized capacity plus new market opportunities for nonconstrained resources. Effective DBR application reduces levels of work in process and finished goods inventory that frees up and accelerates cash flow. The reduction in work in process creates greater visibility to opportunities that reduce lead times and shorten cycle times. The principles of DBR and TOC offer new tools for process improvement and exploitation of strategic opportunities.

SIMPLIFICATION IS EFFECTIVENESS

Effectiveness begins with understanding and then taking appropriate action. Throughput accounting brings simplicity and offers us a model we can utilize to gain relevance on how accounting can help to improve the effectiveness of business operations and strategy. Accountants have been trained to provide details and perhaps have struggled to understand the simplicity of throughput. The concept of sales less direct material, when grouped with all other cash outflows, which includes operating expenses with the exception of investment, does not fit with the training we received. The problem is that not much has changed, so the public and private sectors of the accounting profession lag behind the productivity advancements that have occurred since the mid-1980s. Furthermore, management has not been any help because it has also been trained and motivated by an outdated model. This creates issues for the accountants to change in more dynamic ways, since they have had to answer to MBA-trained management or to management that has its foundation in the "cost world" tradition.

I learned my management and cost accounting the hard way and through application of tools on the job. It was survive or sink. The manufacturing company I worked for after my initial stint in public accounting was one of the first companies to employ direct costing or contribution accounting. This was way before *The Goal* and throughput accounting. We utilized a standard cost system and tracked all the variances utilizing contribution accounting. No adjustment was made to inventories except at the end of the year so our traditional financial statements were in conformance with GAAP. We made the adjustment using straightforward calculations to allocate overhead in inventory based on the relationship of direct labor to manufacturing overhead. The biggest problem with this simple contribution model was in the allocation of variances from standard to product lines. Since most ERP systems allow the capture of actual costs, this is no longer a problem. Also, the process flow of the manu-facturing processes can be identified by the ERP system using the bills of material and routings. Even the cost of setups and changeovers can be captured. The devil is in the detail, and one of the greatest opportunities that companies have is cleaning up the detail within ERP systems. Flattening the bills of material and cleaning up the accuracy of the routings will take companies a long way down the road to process improvement.

The system that I used and enhanced for over twenty years was very close to throughput accounting in concept and how it was applied and presents a good model. My profit-focused accounting model captures sales less direct material, direct labor, and other identifiable variable costs for each product line and business unit. Other operating expenses excluding interest, depreciation, amor-tization, and taxes are standby expense. We then measure the profit that is the responsibility of operating managers as earnings before interest, depreciation, amortization, and taxes. This model is in the spirit of throughput accounting and I believe enhances it. Taking our approach a bit further, we then apply activity-based costing and management to track the nonproduction-related standby ex-penses to identify the business processes and their costs. By applying DBR, TOC, lean thinking, and Six Sigma, organizations can then fine-tune their operations in a more simplistic way, focusing on business processes.

The overview of the profit-focused accounting approach is presented in Figure 6.5. This model has a significant advantage in presentation and appli-cation by being simple and understandable. The format helps to build a basis for achieving employee empowerment. Once the empowered employees have an accounting scorecard they can understand, they have a foundation for making contributions toward continuous improvement.

While the breakeven model is no longer valid, its simplistic approach helps to increase understanding. Direct labor is more semi-variable than fixed, but it is easier for most employees and managers to visualize where the category fits when it is shown as variable. Standby expense under contribution accounting theoretically represents all expenses that do not vary with volume, or fixed cost in the breakeven model. This can be equated to operating expenses under throughput accounting. Today's business model has shifted to contain more operating expense as a percentage of total costs than any other category. The profit-focused accounting model groups expenditures by department in standby expenses as transactions are collected and recorded in the general ledger. A

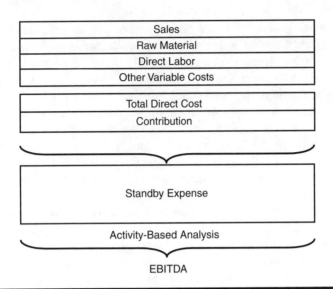

Figure 6.5. Profit-Focused Accounting Approach.

departmental report is then provided to measure and budget these "fixed" expenses. It is a traditional and simple way for managers to relate to these expenses in a profit-and-loss report. How standby expenses relate to the processes within functions of the organization requires activity and process analysis. This analysis can be helpful in further understanding costs attributable to products and customers.

This approach to simplicity realizes that managers do not make finance decisions and cannot make investment decisions in a vacuum. This P&L monitoring has therefore stopped short of how those factors influence the bottom line. Those expense categories enter the calculation of return on investment and EVA™, but can create smoke and fog when it relates to a grass-roots understanding of process cost. A structure has been developed for enabling understanding of what needs to be understood in a way that facilitates addressing identification of root causes and constraint identification.

STRATEGIC THINKING PROCESS

What should be the role for accounting in an empowered continuous improvement–focused organization? This question covers a vast area of possibilities. Throughput accounting offers some clues. By creating clarity and providing simplicity, accounting should be a key player on the team. The similarities between TOC and Toyota offer support for the approach taken by profit-focused accounting. TOC provides much more than offering three metrics with which to keep score; it has developed a strategic planning approach beginning at the desires of the customer. This is Toyota's focus, but in applying similar but different tools and approaches.

Toyota calls its plants the "black box." *Profit Beyond Measure* by H. Thomas Johnson and Anders Bröms indicates "Toyota has a comprehensive array of information systems, accounting and otherwise, with which to *plan*, in advance of operations, and to *report* results of operations after the fact. But information from such systems is *not allowed to influence operational decisions.*" The accounting system calculates the cost of what is made in the "black box" by reporting material, labor, and the investment activities that occur, but does not have a cost system that tracks operating costs. The point is that accounting reports keep the score. Scorekeeping will impact and help to guide strategic thinking, not make operational decisions. Accountants should keep score and they should be part of the planning process.

The scorekeeping process will report the expenses assigned to departments under functional classifications. The problems started when these standby or operating expenses were allocated to products and the cost system was used to measure efficiencies based on volume and utilization. The issue is process cost, especially those processes not related to converting material into products. Processes flow vertically across departmental structures within the organization to accomplish their objectives. This is illustrated in Figure 6.6, where we see that departments and functions flow vertically, but the processes that the activities and tasks perform flow horizontally.

As you remember from Chapter 4, processes were defined as any activity or group of activities that takes an input and adds value to it and provides the output to an internal or external customer. Toyota's "black box" is filled with production processes. What is depicted in Figure 6.6 are business processes that support the "black box." These processes include processing orders, payroll, receiving, shipping, inventory control, accounts payable, accounts receivable, purchasing, sales, and all the many processes performed within the functional silos. Accounting has a unique opportunity to simplify reporting. Through application of activity-based analysis, it maps and determines costs associated with all of the horizontally flowing processes located within operating expense. My approach is to avoid integrating activity-based costing into the scorekeeping process. The objective is to provide an enabling analytical tool for improving the processes and understanding the components of operating expense. Activity-based analysis should only be applied to the processes contained within oper-

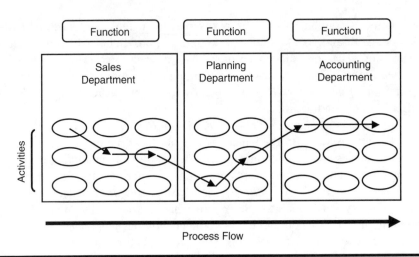

Figure 6.6. Horizontal Flow of Process Through Organizational Structure.

ating expense and not to the variable throughput components of revenue and variable costs. Allocations of costs within these categories are flawed and can lead to distorted information and bad decisions.

Accounting now becomes the bridge over which data can flow into a format to provide useful information for making strategic decisions. Many businesses have never identified their processes and documented them in a fashion that builds a foundation for improving them. This discussion is appropriate here because TOC requires identifying the constraint and solving conflict surrounding it. Simplifying the scorekeeping roles will help eliminate reports that add little or no value and release valuable time that can be devoted to documenting processes and identifying constraints. Accounting now becomes an effective member of the empowered continuous improvement team as opposed to a useless attempt to manage by "cost world" mentality.

The planning process using profit-focused accounting concepts offers exciting new possibilities. The simplistic approach provides greater speed together with an accurate score. Improving the business processes will help to enhance this by speeding up the accounting-related processes. The activity-based analysis data provide a foundation for eliminating the budgeting process and moving to a predictive forecasting model that incorporates trend formats that provide for identifying future possibilities, in contrast to twenty-twenty hindsight of cost management.

In this section on strategic thinking, it is important not to limit the analysis to the strict boundaries of the organization. TOC and the principles of DBR stretch back to the voice of the customer and creating win-win situations. All

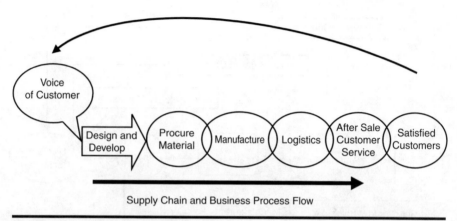

Figure 6.7. Flows of Value Activities.

too frequently, managers limit their thinking and fail to consider the value activities with the organization. Figure 6.7 illustrates the flow of value activities that occur in a company.

The value chain starts at raw material and flows through the functional activities that drive value to the customer. Following DBR, the value chain really begins with the customer and flows through the chain and back to the customer. Unlike management accounting, the value chain offers strategic opportunities for win-win solutions. Much has been made of the global economy, but managers frequently fail to see the following opportunities for helpful linkages:

1. Suppliers
2. Customers
3. Internal process linkages
4. Business unit value chains within the company

Figure 6.8 illustrates the complexity of the supply chain and the necessity to incorporate a broader scope from a strategic planning and forecasting viewpoint.

Identification of constraints and process mapping become even more critical. They offer an even more compelling reason for extending analysis backwards in the chain to the suppliers' supplier and forward to the customers' customer.

Chapter 9 discusses the application of new possibilities for the profit-focused accounting model. However, it should start to become clear that no single tool represents the Holy Grail. The more we can simplify a complex environment, the better are our chances for success. We have to avoid adhering to old

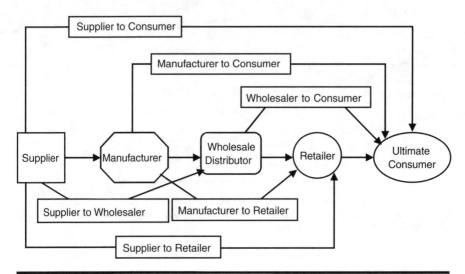

Figure 6.8. Supply Chain Complexities.

tools that are no longer capable of getting the job done. The organization needs to have its team understand its unique strategic focus and be capable of seeing the scoreboard during the game. The best attributes of throughput accounting and activity-based analysis have been developed into tools that will enhance constraint identification and process improvement in consideration with the concepts proscribed by DBR and to provide a view of the entire value chain in ways that represent win-win solutions. The impact of strategic focus and creating balanced scorecards will be added to the tool kit as we move forward.

This book has free materials available for download from the Web Added Value™ Resource Center at www.jrosspub.com.

7

BALANCING
THE SCORECARD

A new method of scorekeeping has evolved out of the need for businesses to manage in the "information age." Traditional cost management and the generally accepted accounting principles model of accounting and financial reporting have had their impact diminished as relevant tools to guide managers. Employee empowerment drives the need for nonfinancial metrics to help monitor the effectiveness of business strategy and its execution. Balancing the multiple perspectives of business focuses on utilizing alternative views of the organization by looking through a multipurpose lens. This effectively executes a vision that represents the core capability of the scorecard and the reason for its emergence as a meaningful management tool.

Today's pace of innovation and productivity has literally exploded, creating new demands and requirements for organizations. The customer is a new force in the marketplace driving the way business must compete to survive. Traditional accounting tools are not effective in measuring the impact of the customers and their requirements. Companies are forced to develop relationships to retain existing customers and engage new customers in new markets at the same time. This drives the necessity to introduce innovative products and services at an accelerated rate of speed. The new customer requires customized, high-quality products produced at the lowest cost and delivered on time.

These new competitive pressures require companies to access the maximum benefit from their employees in order to achieve the required improvement in processes, quality, and customer response time. Never before have companies and their employees had to deploy and effectively utilize information systems and technology to remain competitive with companies that have this culture and capability.

Robert S. Kaplan and David P. Norton published *The Balanced Scorecard* in 1996 based on the premise that the relevance lost because of reliance on financial measurements had not been regained and businesses were taking incorrect action all too frequently. Managers were making decisions based on their flawed reliance on past performance instead of using drivers of future performance for creating strategic direction. The failure of the traditional financial accounting model has created the search for understanding and a new pathway to the future that includes activity-based costing, throughput accounting, and the utilization of nonfinancial metrics. The balanced scorecard has evolved as yet another management system to address the needs of information age companies to provide focus across all levels of the organization. Kaplan and Norton followed *The Balanced Scorecard* with *The Strategy Focused Organization* in 2001. Balanced scorecards are another effective tool for the profit-focused accounting tool kit that can provide impact when properly used in the right situations.

UNDERSTANDING BALANCED SCORECARDS

The foundation for creating and employing balanced scorecards starts with the organization and its vision and strategy. There is no shortage of strategies, but frequently the vision ends up being a consultant-facilitated series of retreats and meetings that are bound into a notebook that collects dust on executive bookshelves. This results in very little action and less understanding. The success of Toyota and many other companies that nurtured just in time and total quality management rested on the complete empowerment of their employees. There is no effective execution of strategy without a process of understanding throughout the organization, from top to bottom. Balanced scorecards are intended to provide a two-way channel for communication, where all levels of the organization understand the vision and are responsible for executing the strategy. Success lies in aligning empowered employees with the strategic vision and maintaining focus utilizing financial and nonfinancial measurements in the scorecards.

Before an organization can utilize the balanced scorecard framework, it must first identify and articulate the strategic vision. I have stated that typically there is no shortage of strategies, but there is continual failure to convert the strategy into reality. Balanced scorecards provide a framework for translating strategy into operational terms so that the scorecards do not become a hodgepodge of financial and nonfinancial metrics that lack direction. Figure 7.1 shows the

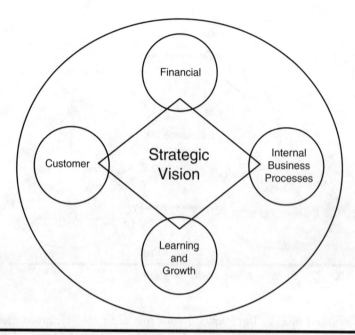

Figure 7.1. The Balanced Scorecard Is a Strategic Management System.

framework for a meaningful translation of strategic vision into operational components from four different perspectives.

Balanced scorecards look at a business from four perspectives. Focus on measurements and strategic action steps are categorized to aid effective execution of the strategic vision. The four perspectives recognize the significance of the following key focus areas:

1. Financial
2. Customer
3. Internal business process
4. Learning and growth

What balanced scorecards provide is retention of financial metrics by providing measurements that allow focus on customer-related issues, effectiveness of internal business processes, and the value of empowered employees. The identification of customer needs and measurement of customer satisfaction are factors that financial measures do not capture. Likewise, the level of quality and effectiveness of internal business processes have relied on statistical process control and other continuous improvement metrics such as cycle time. This will never be clearly identified in accounting financial reports. Learning and growth rep-

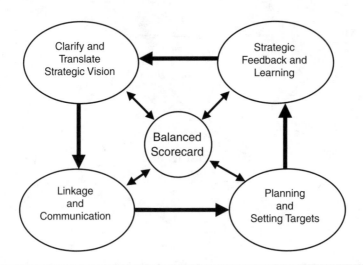

Figure 7.2. The Balanced Scorecard Concept.

resent organizational and employee issues that are not determined effectively from historical financial information. I do not believe any financial system will ever provide effective ways of measurement and monitoring all of the activities and perceptions needed to evaluate and communicate strategic action required for organizational success. Figure 7.2 portrays the concept of the balanced scorecard, showing vision and strategy as the center of focus and connecting to the four perspectives described above.

Balanced scorecards represent a way to create understanding at all levels of the organization because they penetrate beyond just tabulating dashboards of critical success factors. Financial targets are driven by what occurs within the organization to create products and services for internal and external customers. By linking financial targets to specific strategies, the balanced scorecard approach creates a platform for communication and consensus. From this platform, the organization establishes feedback mechanisms based on goals and targets that are established based on the strategy. Effectiveness is driven by placing focus on what needs to be done by the employees who perform the activities and tasks within the internal business process and linking to the voice of the customer. Rewards for goal attainment are then linked to measurements that monitor progress from top to bottom and vice versa. By aligning all of the critical strategic initiatives, organizations are then able to enhance strategic feedback and provide for continuous learning and employee involvement needed to achieve and sustain long-term value.

A key element of understanding the balanced scorecard is the importance of visualizing how the management system translates the mission of an orga-

Figure 7.3. Translating a Mission into Desired Outcomes.

nization into desired outcomes. Figure 7.3 illustrates how we take the mission of why we exist, utilizing the core values, to a vision of what we want to be. Strategy represents the game plan and utilizes balanced scorecards to focus and implement the strategic vision. By using balanced scorecards, strategic initiatives are developed so that employees are focused to do what they need to do at all levels of the organization. These initiatives are translated into personal objectives so that employees are empowered and have understanding of what they need to do and why they need to do it. This careful communication creates organization-wide consensus that translates into strategic outcomes. As Figure 7.3 illustrates, the focusing and alignment process creates satisfied shareholders, delighted customers, effective processes, and a motivated, prepared workforce.

Understanding the concept of strategy is essential in applying the balanced scorecard management system because it brings clarity to why the traditional cost and financial model has become outmoded. Kaplan and Norton identify the following three missions that a business unit can adopt:

1. Growth or build — This implies a goal of increased market share that is usually associated with high-growth industries. This is characteristic of the demands occurring in today's information age.
2. Sustain or hold — This mission is focused on protecting market share and the competitive position of the business unit.

3. Harvest — This reflects a goal of maximizing short-term earnings and cash flow.

While some businesses can still be categorized as hold or harvest, there are many more that are being forced by global competition to grow or go out of business. Measuring the impact of strategy associated with action plans is easier since the risks are minimized, the time horizons are shorter, and the importance of strategic planning is lower than for businesses falling into the growth category.

Growth industry business will be more driven by the need for continuous strategic planning and attention to implementing it successfully. The pace of activity is faster for growth-oriented businesses, requiring more knowledge about cause and effect relationships than a sustaining or harvest business. By nature, managers of growth businesses will need more information to guide them and process outcomes will necessitate using nonfinancial metrics. Reliance on strictly accounting and financial measures will not help managers in environments with higher levels of uncertainty as dictated by the age of information. The balanced scorecard is a good tool for understanding and providing guidance in an environment of continuous process improvement.

The information age is driven by knowledge-based strategies that require deployment of intangible assets. The issues become customer relationships combined with innovative products and services. Increasingly, greater emphasis will be placed on high-quality and responsive processes. This requires businesses to improve processes through initiatives such as lean thinking for greater speed and Six Sigma control. Employees will need the feedback mechanisms to improve their skills and maintain high levels of motivation. I think the balanced scorecard is a necessity to help overcome the culture shifts that will occur from the rapid pace of change.

A simplified balanced scorecard example will help bring clarity and understanding to the concepts as shown in Figure 7.4. The financial measure shown is ROCE or return on capital employed. For the customer perspective, customer loyalty and on-time delivery are shown. Process quality and process cycle time are the scorecard metrics from an internal business process perspective. The scorecard presents a measure of employee skills, which might be training days or a similar measure for the learning and growth perspective.

THE VALUE CHAIN PERSPECTIVE

The need for the balanced scorecard stems from the accelerated pace of business in a global economy that has a foundation built on knowledge-based strategies

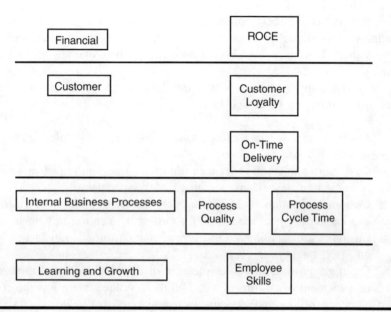

Figure 7.4. A Simplified Balanced Scorecard Example.

that employ intangible assets. The changing dynamics of the impact of the customer perspective and how it influences the "value chain" drives the growing need for knowledge-based strategies. Earlier I mentioned a growth or build strategic theme that necessitates a strategy of differentiation in contrast to a cost leadership strategy. This set of circumstances takes companies into the Twilight Zone, where the same old historical financial models again fail to provide the necessary guidance.

The first step in building value chain understanding begins with the customer. The scorecard is predicated on strategic linkage to identify the customers and their needs. You cannot satisfy customer needs until they are identified. These are then translated into specific missions and strategy objectives. This starts by identifying your customers, their characteristics, habits, and preferences. What products or services do they want and how do we create a relationship with them that translates into effective strategic action?

Winning strategies for capturing and retaining customers begins first by identifying them and then by differentiating them. How do we interact with them and what represents the most strategic way to interact with them in the most cost-efficient and effective manner? It is important to determine who is the true ultimate customer in the increasingly complex supply chain. Are we serving a customer where we are a vendor supplying a link within the supply chain, such as a computer or appliance company that then sells to the customer? The analysis should define the market, our strategic fit within it, and our share of the market. In other words: Where do we fit in the dynamics of the market chain?

The customer perspective is broken into five categories or core areas where scorecard metrics can be established:

1. Market share — This represents your share of all the sales to the given market that you are serving.
2. Customer acquisition — A measure of the rate you attract or win new customers or new business with existing customers.
3. Customer retention — Measuring your ability to retain your customers and comparing it to the norms for customer retention in your industry.
4. Customer satisfaction — A measure of your customer's satisfaction based on price, quality, and service.
5. Customer profitability — A measure of the profitability of a customer or a segment of customers based on the revenue stream less the cost of attracting, selling, and servicing, including the cost of products and services provided to those customers.

The customer perspective consists of the customer value chain based on identification of needs that are comprised of product/service attributes, relationship, and the image or reputation of your organization. From identification of need, the chain then links to how the organization satisfies the demands and wants of its customer through the effective interaction of its internal business processes and employees.

The internal value chain is shown in Figure 7.5 and graphically presents the customer value proposition as it flows from identifying the need to satisfying the need. This model shows the flows from innovation design and development to customer management and operational excellence. Measuring the speed of response from need identification to delivery in the market typically represents a critical competitive advantage factor that will influence scorecard metrics.

The supply chain time line represents the time required to make, market, and provide postsales service to satisfy the customer's need. The supply chain time line will vary depending on where the company fits into the "dynamics of the market chain." The chain is shown in Figure 7.6 and presents an array of possibilities. Another view of the value chain is presented in Figure 7.7 and reflects some clue of the level of business processes that will impact the activities.

The "flow of the generic chain processes" helps us understand how variations and fluctuations in process costs can impact the competitive playing field.

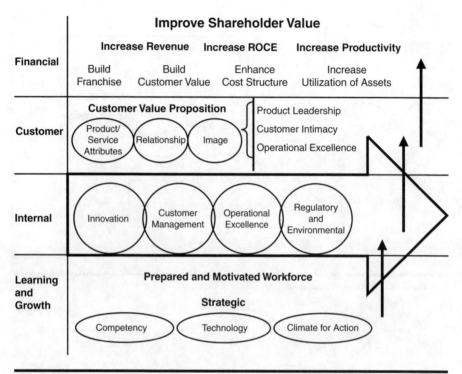

Figure 7.5. The Internal Business Process Value Chain Perspective.

The scorecards will help create a strategic focus and linkage through the use of nonfinancial metrics, but do not represent the "silver bullet" solution since the other management philosophies and systems will have to be components and pieces of the puzzle. Gaining understanding of the value chain is critical to realizing that competitive advantage based on differentiation will require the application of new tools and measurements, including nonfinancial metrics, in order for organizations to execute their strategies successfully.

WHAT DOES THE SCORECARD MEASURE?

The answer to the question of what the scorecard will measure will vary from company to company depending on the industry and strategic vision. It starts with a clean sheet of paper and evolves based on input from the top to the bottom, gaining two-way consensus. Kaplan and Norton, the authors of *The Balanced Scorecard,* liken it to a digital dashboard in the cockpit of an airplane that provides key data that the pilot and crew can monitor throughout the flight.

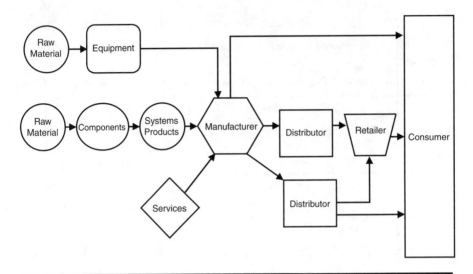

Figure 7.6.   The Dynamics of the Value Chain.

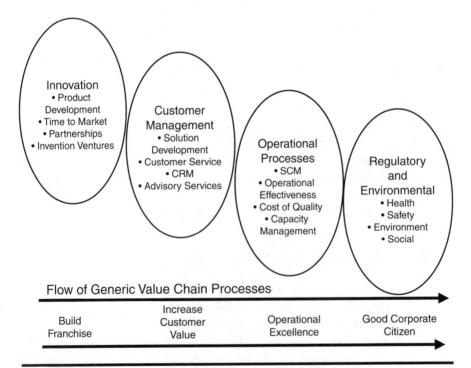

Figure 7.7.   Value Chain Impact on Processes and Activities.

I will explore this concept to help provide visualization of how it functions and how it links to profit-focused accounting.

The scorecard is called balanced because of the emphasis placed on the four perspectives that an organization must consider to evaluate how it is performing in the past, present, and future. Each of the four perspectives will be explored before we move forward to strategic linkages and alignment. Measuring in a balanced way provides *perspective* on how organizations are doing on what they are trying to do. I will offer some additional perspectives that will build on the four original key views from which to measure and evaluate:

1. Customer perspective — How do customers perceive us?
2. Internal business perspective — Internally where and at what must we excel?
3. Innovation and learning perspective — How can we continuously improve and build value?
4. Financial perspective — From a shareholder view, how are we doing?

Customer

Customers are interested in factors such as time, quality, performance, service, and cost. The weight of these factors will vary between customers, industries, and organizations. Developing the right measures for each organization's scorecard will be different, but most companies will want to measure:

- Market share
- Customer retention
- Customer acquisition
- Customer satisfaction
- Customer profitability

Some of this information will be available within the organization. For other measures, such as customer satisfaction, it will be necessary to employ an independent resource to survey and capture information. An organization will want to measure the causes or factors that directly impact the increase or affect revenue. Chapter 11 provides insight on developing simplified approaches to developing scorecards and Chapter 13 offers a thorough review of performance metrics.

Internal Business Processes

The customer factors and associated revenue will be directly impacted by how well the internal process drives the internal value function relative to the organization's vision and strategy. These measures will be focused on core competencies, processes, and managerial decisions that have a direct impact on factors influencing the customer perspective. We have already looked at the tools that companies have been utilizing to achieve world-class business process performance. The focus normally will encompass manufacturing, engineering of productivity processes, and development of new products that fulfill the needs of the customer. Achieving process excellence includes productive, developmental, and commercial process activities. Scorecard measurements will monitor performance of operational excellence of the internal organization that relates to the effectiveness of employee actions. Measurements within the internal perspective normally are broken down to impact various levels of the organization such as departments and work centers. Examples include cycle time, quality, product and cost measures, and order fulfillment that is fast and timely. I will provide some examples of how measurements are cascaded down through the levels of the organization later in Chapter 11 when I discuss application of the scorecard concept.

Innovation and Learning

The knowledge-based "information age" is characterized by high-speed change and a continual shifting of blurred market boundaries. Success in such a competitive environment hinges on the worker's ability to innovate and learn new skills in order to keep pace. The scorecard measurements of this prospective include employee retention, employee productivity, and employee satisfaction, which generate results in executing differentiated strategies and building value. The measurement framework should include consideration of how staff competencies, technology infrastructure, and a climate for action enable and drive employee satisfaction. Employee satisfaction is shown as the driver of employee retention and employee productivity. A strategy of taking care of employees and their needs has proven to be one of the best ways of creating delighted customers. Employee surveys are usually one of the ways information on employee satisfaction is developed. Training and developing new employee skill sets are being implemented in many organizations. These are measured both in time devoted to the effort and number of employees trained. Other measures include the number of employee suggestions. The team approach to continuous improvement and culture change has also been applied in some industries. Employee stock ownership, gain sharing, phantom stock, and other compensation motivators have been tried with varying degrees of success. Innovation and learning are areas where significant opportunities for development and improvement exist. However, true success will require paradigm shifts and in some instances overcoming cultural barriers.

Financial

Scorecards must be balanced, which means the financial measurements indicate how the company is progressing in its achievement of strategic goals and objectives. Survival requires success on the bottom line. I would argue that the financial measures combine a blend of both short- and longer-term metrics that are aligned with the strategy of the organization. Profit-focused accounting is predicated on employing the essentials of throughput accounting that captures the elements of speed, simplicity, and a goal of profit and return on investment. In later chapters, I explore the tools for measuring and emphasizing value creation over the long haul in contrast to quarter-to-quarter earnings per share. The key word here is balance. The focus needs to ensure that progress toward the top to bottom strategy is being achieved and to provide signals regarding the need for any course corrections.

Simplicity and speed are critical to create scorecards that are predictive and forward in applying and measuring strategy. Placing a throughput emphasis on the financial scorecard directs attention toward sales and cash generation in addition to monitoring the level of investment to execute the strategy. One of the criticisms of scorecards is the delay in providing the needed information to managers responsible for monitoring performance. The reality is that if all the efforts to improve customer satisfaction, quality, and enhanced employee learning and retention do not translate to better earnings and return on shareholders' investment through creation of value, then the organization will need to re-evaluate its vision and implementation of action plans.

The throughput approach focuses on sales less variable cost that translates into cash flow. All of the improvements from streamlining processes and the elimination of waste will not flow to the bottom line if there is a deceleration of throughput. If excess capacity is not utilized or sold, and idle employees are given additional work resulting in increased throughput, profit will drop and return on investment will suffer. This creates a "catch-22" when the creators of the savings become victims of layoffs and downsizing. This represents one of the major challenges of strategies of differentiation and innovation.

The financial metrics need to be tailored to the organization and its strategy. The dashboards can be innovative with such concepts as daily profit-and-loss and flash reports that provide "in-flight" monitoring of financial progress. The dashboard might include metrics such as orders placed or backlog of orders. Profit-focused accounting includes a trend format approach that allows long-term metrics to be measured based on the latest current forecasts of expected results. For example, return on sales, return on assets, and return on investment can be presented based on projected annual results. In essence, financial measures need to be linked with the other perspectives and be indicative of progress.

ACHIEVING STRATEGIC ALIGNMENT

Strategic alignment cannot begin until we know and understand the strategy. Understanding strategy starts with making sure we are on common ground. Strategy should represent a vision of who the organization is, where it is going, and how it is going to get there. These questions need to be answered before aligning strategy. Success evolves from development of good strategy and good execution. This ongoing process involves setting objectives and implementing action plans that will result in achieving the desired success.

Action plans will almost certainly require building an organization that is capable of successfully carrying out the strategy. This may require building an organization that fits the direction of the conceived strategy. Can the organization go where it needs to within the time frame of the plan? Answering this question then leads to creating the cause and effect relationships required to create the process that will be needed to communicate and build scorecards. It is first necessary to raise the hypothetical question regarding an action and determining what its effect will be. Alignment of the organization with the strategy deals with building the chain of communication required for actions to be translated into the desired results.

The scorecard should be constructed to reflect the strategy of the organization. The process of building the scorecard becomes the context for shared communication and creating the level of understanding needed to successfully execute the strategic vision. The outcome measurements tend to be lag indicators reflecting the results of a strategy. These typically will be profitability, return on investment, market share, or similar metrics associated with results. On the other hand, lead indicators are utilized with the scorecard to predict or indicate future results of the strategy. These predictive indicators are called performance drivers and are indicators of an organization's strategy. Effective scorecards will include a balanced mix of lag and lead indicators that are developed by generating understanding throughout the organization regarding the balanced scorecard initiative and its intended objective. The understanding will be top down and bottom up. When properly executed, this will produce an empowered and engaged effort to identify the right blend of measurements and performance drivers for building scorecards and creating alignment with strategy at all levels and from all perspectives.

Alignment with strategy is an essential element of developing appropriate cause and effect relationships. This step might include the development of budgets to provide resources necessary for funding activities critical for strategic success. Another step might include linking reward systems that motivate all levels of the organization to pursue the target objectives that are reinforced by the scorecards. The scorecards will help to monitor the changes necessary for successful execution of the strategy. The monitoring process must ensure that all of the lead indicators link to the financial targets that are critical for strategic success.

Through correct alignment and by mobilizing employees, the organization will be able to check to see that the proper information, communication, and operating systems are in place and functioning properly. Additional change initiatives will require implementing best practices and programs for continuous improvement. This new strategy and communication tool will provide timely and appropriate feedback to both leadership and employees who are responsible for converting the strategy into reality. The scorecards provide the organizational team with the necessary tools to identify where and when to make "in-flight" course corrections.

One of the reasons balanced scorecards become such a useful tool is that change will never happen in exactly the perceived manner and within the pre-scribed time as it was planned. Having scorecards that are responsive to lead indicators using predictive trend formats is critical to success. The Theory of Constraints and activity-based analysis offer tools that go hand in hand with creating meaningful scorecards. Activity identification linked with process costs is essential in creating and building scorecards that are aligned and linked to strategy. Another scorecard tool is constraint management and identification. This can help organizations to identify and make changes where they are needed. These examples show how application of multiple tools as *enablers* can produce greater impact than when they are applied by themselves.

Balanced scorecards tell the story of strategy and their effectiveness depends on making strategy the focal point of the entire organization. Alignment occurs when the entire organization becomes completely absorbed in the details of the strategy and converts it into actionable steps that result in effective execution. The scorecards provide a communication tool and link to the strategy partici-pants that lets them know how they are doing and if they need to do something different so they can adjust accordingly. The alignment process is developed when the communication of the organization's vision is mapped out and all the employees see and understand what they need to do and then relate it to what is needed from other activities to accomplish the objective. The predictive drivers of required action are measured and monitored. If the lead indicators chosen provide positive results, then the lag financial metrics selected will provide proof on the bottom line.

This book has free materials available for download from the
Web Added Value™ Resource Center at www.jrosspub.com.

8

LEAN CONSTRAINTS: SIX SIGMA CONTROL

We have traveled through a learning discussion of how productivity emerged from the mid-twentieth-century era of mass production and a "cost world" mentality to the competitive survival environment of today. The torch for just in time and total quality management has developed into separate philosophical camps, each with its staunch supporters, to the following management systems or methodologies:

- Lean manufacturing or lean thinking
- Theory of Constraints/throughput accounting
- Six Sigma
- Activity-based costing and management
- Balanced scorecard

All of these tools have distinguishing attributes. When leveraged and combined for the "best fit" for appropriate situations, they could generate a significantly greater impact on bottom-line profitability. They each offer similar areas of focus:

- The customer is the number-one priority
- Low cost
- Highest quality (products and service)
- Delivery when and where the customer wants it

These tools can work together or at least *enable* better results when used appropriately to solve problems and eliminate waste while giving customers what they want and when they want it. After providing insight on combining the productivity tools, I will offer guidance on executing the strategy and monitoring the results using the accounting and scorecard tools. Application of all these tools implies and requires change. These ideas then become more than just other good ideas that did not get implemented.

IMPLICATIONS OF CHANGE

Lean manufacturing and Six Sigma projects create changes that will produce a significant impact on organizations and how they operate. These programs change the way processes function and flow, how product quality is monitored, and how new products are designed. This affects people and the way they work, and frequently the security of their jobs. Many companies attempt "lean" projects led by manufacturing people on the shop floor, with little or no understanding of the initiative by finance, marketing, and other functional areas of the organization. It becomes another "flavor of the month" fast fix to improve productivity and profitability without achieving and balancing buy in from the entire organization. This represents "bad change" that often results in failure and can produce resistance for further change and new initiatives.

Six Sigma projects also fall into the "not well understood" category and quickly build barriers to change. Because of the successes at GE, Motorola, Allied Signal, and other companies, executives frequently think these programs are the answer to never-ending profitability and growth in share value. These executives fail to make the effort to understand all the components and steps necessary to make it work. They do not make a commitment other than a casual embrace. It gets delegated to someone down the line. Concern does not develop until the desired results fail to materialize within the expected time frame.

Failure to comprehend the implications of change touches the heart of what lean manufacturing and Six Sigma are intended to accomplish. If these programs do not make extensive changes and revisions in how products are made and services are delivered, then they miss the mark. For these reasons, training and understanding are crucial. Because of the existence of functional silos, differences in understanding frequently block the flow of effective communication and achieving the buy in needed for successful change. I have grouped three management philosophies together for this very reason. TOC is an effective tool that can help to accelerate the application of "lean Six Sigma."

The Theory of Constraints (TOC) is a broader approach than "lean Six Sigma" because of its application of leverage throughout the organization and across the value or supply chain. It offers a strategic thinking process together with tactical problem-solving tools that can facilitate understanding and buy in. The very essence of the thinking process drives to the heart of change:

- What to change
- What to change to
- How to cause the change

These questions go to the nature of the problem and highlight the dilemmas that can throw initiatives off track. After creating the right level of focus, TOC then provides effective tools and methodologies to implement change. It helps take care of the functional fences and silos that develop. Changes are much more than fixing a process or applying quality measurements. They involve policies, strategies, work practices, and human relations.

The proliferation of many ideas, systems, and methodologies has created "change management fatigue" to the point that organizations are unable to improve the processes and systems to provide the quality of performance measurement and management desired by most forward-thinking companies. Organizations have been burned by ineffective efforts to change to new management concepts that were touted to be the answer to instant profitability. This has been compounded by efforts to integrate new enterprise resource planning (ERP) systems that, in some cases, have fallen short of expectations. The shortfall was due primarily to poor implementations resulting from inadequate training and weak senior management support. I have had several consulting engagements where all that the employees needed was to learn how to use their technology tools properly. There were also other situations where employees did not receive the level of support from senior management, which resulted in doing business the same old way.

The implications of change reach down to the individuals of an organization and the success they achieve ultimately extends up to senior management. If senior management does not understand the need and fails to provide the right tools and training, then very little positive change will occur. Success is dependent on leadership and the need for individuals within the organization to achieve consensus and buy in. Another critical factor is the need for initiatives to achieve some early visible success. Gaining traction for lean manufacturing and Six Sigma projects in the early going improves the chances for making and sustaining necessary long-term change.

Change strategies should be kept simple to improve the odds for gaining traction and achieving success that is visible throughout the organization. People understand success. Successes will be more clearly and quickly understood by keeping things simple. This builds an environment that will be embraced with greater enthusiasm. The roots of change hinge on success, and any tendency toward change fatigue needs to be overcome by the clarity of vision and communicative support from senior management.

What are the few things you need to focus on to achieve the greatest impact? By narrowing the focus to the 20 percent of the factors to change, you will likely achieve 80 percent of the targeted objective. By simplifying, you will gain traction by achieving lean Six Sigma targets by hitting 80 percent of the savings in a shorter time frame versus never attaining 100 percent of the opportunity.

I added TOC to lean manufacturing and Six Sigma because it provides focus and leverage. It is a simple approach that emphasizes maximizing throughput by exploiting constraints. The measurements are few and easy to understand, and this accelerates the speed of understanding and measurement. More importantly, the approach to gaining understanding and buy in makes this a critical ingredient for achieving greater success with the changes required by lean Six Sigma.

Let's face it, lean Six Sigma is all about making radical changes in how we make products, how we serve the customer, and how the organization functions. Organizations need to address these radical changes in anticipation of aligning with a clear vision and feeling the flow of how they will provide a positive impact on future results. Another option is to wait until it becomes necessary to make changes in reaction to events. The less desirable option is when the organization is in a chaotic crisis. Effective leaders need to define reality to avoid reactive crisis by providing a communicative buy-in process.

The buy-in process needs to include addressing the need for change and why it is necessary. Senior leadership needs to communicate the vision so the team understands clearly who wants the change and has a sense of understanding for the need and the pressure the changes will create. The expected results of the changes brought about by lean Six Sigma and how the efforts will benefit customers and impact the business should be communicated. Then the organization needs to understand lean manufacturing and Six Sigma and how the organization's capabilities will be improved as a result of applying them. Organizations also need to understand and prepare for the challenges of applying "lean Six Sigma." The last step should include communication of who will be involved, how this will affect individuals, and what they will gain as a result of the change initiatives.

THROUGHPUT MEASURES

The ultimate purpose for applying the principles of lean manufacturing and Six Sigma is the same as TOC, which is to make more money. The simplified approach offered by TOC is called throughput, which is defined as the rate at which the organization generates money through sales. Throughput will be impacted by other metrics used to monitor the speed of the process and the preciseness of control over the process relative to quality. However, it will ultimately boil down to cash flow generated from sales, which relates to the value added from what the customer paid the manufacturer, over and above what the manufacturer paid for material and services to satisfy the customer. Throughput is affected by customer demand, quality, and the differentiated value of the proposition of the offer provided by the manufacturer to the customer. Lean manufacturing and Six Sigma initiatives must ultimately relate to an increase in throughput and utilization of capacity created as a result of streamlining efforts.

Inventory represents all the money the system spends on purchasing things it plans to convert into throughput. TOC defines inventory as the investment in property, plant, and equipment plus money spent for raw material, work in process, and finished goods accumulated in the manufacturing process and warehouses. TOC defines property, plant, and equipment as "passive" inventory as contrasted to "active" inventory. Most lean manufacturing effort, as is TOC, is focused on minimizing or eliminating "active" inventory. Frequently, lean and Six Sigma initiatives create excess capacity that must either be used to generate additional throughput or sold to reduce the level of investment.

One of the main issues facing companies is measuring the success of lean and Six Sigma. Many of the measurement issues correlate to understanding, the need to demonstrate success, and the "cost world" thinking used to determine progress and measure improvement. Throughput measures defined above can be used to monitor the rate of overall improvement. Productivity can be measured or determined by dividing throughput by operating expense. The speed at which inventory is converted into throughput is determined by dividing throughput by inventory, commonly known as turns. The faster the rate at which we convert inventory into throughput, the higher the turns. The inventory turns ratio and return on investment are common measures and reach far beyond indicating quality levels and cycle time. TOC uses leverage and focuses on creating profit through growth and helps companies avoid the trap of reducing waste and increasing speed without generating profit. The elimination of waste or increasing cycle time without increasing profitability and generating increased cash flow will generate more change fatigue and fail to produce the desired gain from improvement.

LEAN SIX SIGMA: CONTROLLED OPTIMIZATION

This segment is intended to explain the advantages of blending lean with Six Sigma. Lean manufacturing manages processes through application of continuous improvement toward elimination of operational and organizational waste to create value. This typically results in achieving significant increases in process speed. Six Sigma enhances this concept by providing continued control of the improved processes. Reduction of variation and the elimination of process defects are enabled by using Six Sigma tools and process speed and the acceleration of throughput created by applying lean manufacturing. Going a step further, enabling TOC to set priorities and measure the potential benefits allows companies to generate even greater bottom-line impact. I will provide an overview of using lean to achieve process optimization and follow it with a discussion on the application of Six Sigma tools to maximize the bottom-line impact of combining the use of these two methodologies.

LEAN: PROCESS OPTIMIZATION

Lean focuses on the removal of waste that includes material, people, and time. Time wasted is time that you will never get back and this represents the largest opportunity for lean. In most factories, material spends approximately 95 percent of its time waiting in queues for the next operation to be performed. If the waiting time can be reduced by applying the 80/20 rule, this then increases the potential for reducing the investment in all categories of inventory. This acceleration in speed translates into increased profitability with reduced levels of investment achieving the desired gains in the rate of throughput versus investment.

While I cautioned about measuring using local factors, it is appropriate to explain cycle time and the impact it has on achieving lean objectives. Cycle time represents the total lead time required from when raw material enters a production facility or process until it leaves the facility or process. The process time actually devoted to working on a product for a customer can be termed as value-added time versus nonvalue-added time spent waiting. Process cycle efficiency can be determined by dividing value-added time by total process lead time. This metric can be used as an indicator for evaluating and monitoring lean process improvements. In *Lean Six Sigma,* Michael L. George states, "while process efficiency will vary by application, an average of 25 percent is world-class." Analysis of process cycle efficiency is an excellent tool to evaluate the potential for reducing costs.

The sheer slowness of most processes offers huge potential for improving profitability through acceleration through reduction of time waiting versus value-added activity time. The first place to look is inventory because if you can see it, it is waiting. If it is waiting, it is also taking up space. The opportunities for improvement are dramatic because excess inventory hides opportunities for improving profitability. One example that I can share emerged from a client where we conducted an assessment. They had so much inventory that they completely lost two forklift trucks in that vast sea of excess stock. This is a somewhat extreme example, but imagine the potential of what shorter cycle times and reduced inventory can provide:

- Opportunities for increased revenue growth (capacity)
- Reduced material handling people and equipment
- Reduced storage costs
- The need for customer service activity lessens

There is a dramatic reduction in the amount of overhead related to inventory that supports the argument for throughput (profit-focused) accounting, which will be explored in the next chapter. In addition to looking for opportunities for accelerating process speed, do not be limited strictly to manufacturing, as frequently there has been little attention devoted to commercial processes. This lack of focus opens the door for ways to add lean speed to the entire organization. Activity-based management analysis, discussed in Chapter 10, examines acceleration of nonmanufacturing processes.

VALUE STREAM MAPPING: APPLYING 80/20 FOCUS

We have talked about focus and leverage, so it should be no surprise that locating the right 20 percent of the processes to improve will provide us with an 80 percent improvement in cycle time. Locating the high-priority 20 percent requires starting with activities that directly impact the customer. The objective is to identify and remove the waste in the products that customers want to purchase from you. Process activities that create, produce, and deliver the desired products the customer wants to buy are called value added, and the activities that do not meet these criteria are termed nonvalue added. Nonvalue added does not mean nonessential; we want to minimize their impact by reducing the time they consume or eliminate them where possible.

Value stream mapping involves identifying all the activities and tasks starting at the customer and working back through all processes and mapping them. This may be with pencil and paper or using computerized mapping software. After the identification and mapping have been completed, it is then necessary to group them as follows:

1. Customer value added (definitely create value)
2. Business value added (create no value, but are necessary)
3. Nonvalue added (eliminate or minimize the activity)

The value stream relates to products or families of products that can be directly correlated to creating value or throughput. Customer value-added activities should be those adding a form or feature to a product or service. Analysis should then be conducted to assess if the activity produces a differentiated advantage such as price, service, or quality. The activity then is evaluated from the eyes of the customer relative to the perceived value it provides.

Business activities relate to necessary, but not value added (such as legal and financial), requirements. An analysis of business activities is then evaluated to identify potential improvement opportunities. Nonvalue-added activities frequently include handling, inspecting, expediting, and other similar tasks that are targets for elimination or reduction. Acceleration that can reduce or eliminate the time required to satisfy the customer, with the greatest profit impact, should include application of the 80/20 rule to achieve the maximum impact from the available resources.

The mapping of the process flow should document the "as is" state that will typically show more nonvalue-added activities in the processes than value-added activities. Setups for tooling or machine configuration will be identified together with the amount of time and personnel required. Some of the value stream information will be contained in the item master of the organization's ERP system. The other activities associated with meeting the customer requirement will have to be developed from analysis and mapping the process steps. This will require a significant effort, but the rewards are worth it. The next step is to create a process flow map that reflects a "to be" vision that incorporates improvements to meet the 80/20 optimization criteria. A Six Sigma black belt or an internal or external operational consultant usually conducts this step.

LEAN TOOLS

Lean tools were described in Chapter 2 in some detail. In order to provide a foundation for more complete understanding, it is appropriate to touch on the key tools employed in lean initiatives and compare them to the TOC waste-reduction approach. Let us first look at the "lean tools" that are employed:

- Pull system versus push
- The 5S
- Kanban
- Product family focus
- Reduction of waste and cycle times
- Use of production cells

- Value stream mapping
- Kaizen events

TOC applies the following tools:

- Pull system versus push
- Strategic leverage points
- Logistical applications
- Buffer management (drum-buffer-rope [DBR])
- Market offers (market constraint)
- Throughput accounting
- Policies and procedure constraints
- Buy-in process

Lean and TOC both pull product through the manufacturing process based on real customer demand that is radically different than traditional manufacturing, where products are pushed through the systems and customers are supplied from finished goods inventory. This is a much faster process that avoids any incentive to overproduce. Through the elimination of wasteful steps in the process, the time required to meet customer demand can be accelerated.

TOC uses DBR to manage the critically constrained resource logistically through the use of material buffers in addition to creating a shipping buffer to avoid unforeseen events (a.k.a. Murphy) to ensure timely delivery to the customer. In contrast, lean utilizes takt time to set the pace of production to provide a single-piece continuous flow through the process, one step at a time, with no utilization of buffers. Lean utilizes kanban signals to signal workers when to start and stop working. The ideal is no work-in-process inventory and no idle time. The concept of DBR works very similarly to the kanban system although they are different logistically.

The 5S methodology was described in Chapter 2 as a regimen of cleanliness and order. This ties into the concept of lean flow, whereby the entire plant is organized in cells that allow for a reduction in the distance parts must travel through the production process. The cellular approach also provides for greater flexibility in the process and the teams are skilled at performing fast setups.

TOC does not employ kaizen or value stream mapping, but it does place emphasis on the heart of change that focuses on improvement through reduction of effort, time, space, cost, and mistakes focused on maximizing throughput. Kaizen utilized in lean initiatives is focused on continuous improvement. TOC implies that continuous improvement means growth. When the constraint is the market, TOC provides greater focus on those factors that overcome it such as

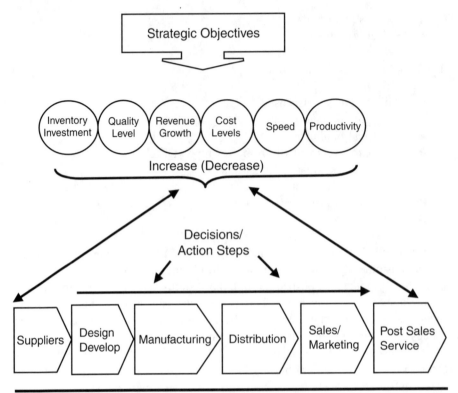

Figure 8.1. Linking the Critical Points of Leverage.

delivery performance, increased cycle times, designing in new product features, and achieving superior quality.

A focus on throughput versus local optimization ensures cash flow and profitability. TOC can provide better insight to understanding nonphysical constraints. Nonphysical constraints include policies, strategies, measures, work practices, and human relations. These situations frequently provide larger obstacles to creating a lean Six Sigma environment than the critically constrained resource within the production process. These issues are real and the application of the thinking process of TOC provides the ability to both identify and remove these nonphysical barriers to progress.

Linking leverage points in the value chain starts with the voice of the customer and includes all of the components and related decisions that are required to delight the customer. The source of flow starts with the customer and then evolves through a variety of linked activities that are portrayed in

Figure 8.1. TOC can speed up the interactions required for the organization to successfully cope with these linkages that might not occur in traditional lean Six Sigma initiatives. It can provide the necessary octane in the fuel tank to make the bus go a little faster. If we remember that speed is cash, then it can start to make more sense with greater impact. This component is really part of the buy-in process offered through the strategic problem-solving ability of TOC to connect the logistical connections required to enhance lean Six Sigma.

SIX SIGMA TOOLS

Six Sigma offers many effective tools that provide the controls and assurance needed to achieve the desired levels of quality and control over process variation. One of the elements of the tool kit is personnel trained in applying Six Sigma tools. The team structure needed for successful application of Six Sigma was discussed in Chapter 3. The tools used to achieve the desired results are explained in more detail, especially as they relate to lean Six Sigma.

The improvement process and implementation are achieved using the DMAIC (define, measure, analyze, improve, control) process and its tools. The flow of the DMAIC model and relationships to steps of the process are presented in Figure 8.2.

This model has been created and is applied in utilizing Six Sigma. The diagram shows the order in which the process steps occur and then loop back. Since the tools are an essential component to the success of the lean Six Sigma approach, the most commonly used tools (see Figure 3.3 in Chapter 3) and objectives of the DMAIC approach are highlighted.

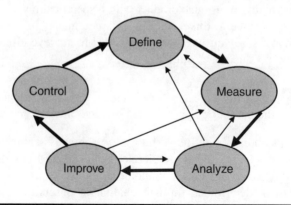

Figure 8.2.   The DMAIC Model.

Some of the specific DMAIC tools and applications require further comment. Michael George uses the term "time traps" in *Lean Six Sigma* to categorize the areas of time waste that occur in slow processes representing processes that are the most expense. By identifying these "time traps," the 80/20 rule can be applied to achieve dramatic savings very quickly. The key to locating the time wastes is through the use of supply chain accelerator software contained in advanced planning and scheduling software offered by major software companies. The George Group effectively used this at Caterpillar to identify opportunities for speeding up and improving the control over processes. The software calculates minimum batch sizes and helps identify possibilities for setup reduction, application of design of experiments (DOE), mistake proofing, and implementation of DBR synchronization or kanban single-piece flow.

Setup reduction always represents an opportunity for gaining acceleration. Time lost due to setups is time lost forever, translating to lost revenue. Setups are either internal or external and should be separated in their application. Internal setup requires that the machine be stopped for work to be completed. However, external setup steps can be performed while the machine is still in operation. The objective should always be to convert as much of the internal setup to external setup, thereby reducing the amount of time that the machine needs to shut down.

My consulting work involves a relationship with a lean manufacturing consulting firm. We always take video of the current state of the setup. This enables us to analyze details of the changeover that were not immediately obvious. It also provides a visual tool for the operators to examine during the process of brainstorming ways to remove or accelerate steps. This enables us to make every effort to streamline the internal setup procedures and movements. The final component to speeding up setups is to ensure that the changeover was completed and ready to produce product within specification without having to shut down the machine to tinker with it. This is a matter of applying the right mind-set to make sure you have what is needed to achieve elimination of any variation when production is started.

DESIGN OF EXPERIMENTS

DOE represents an extremely powerful tool to achieve breakthrough improvements in product quality and to accelerate the speed of production processes. This tool is applied to accurately pinpoint solutions to problems that are not easily detected or determined through qualitative observation. Essentially, it takes the guesswork out of problem solving and provides more accurate answers in the shortest amount of time.

DOE is used typically in situations when multiple factors (two or more) are involved in a process to correct a quality situation or improve the process. The usual approach is either trial and error or to test each variable factor one at a time in an effort to identify the best combination. DOE starts by establishing the objectives and criteria for the experiment. This step helps to avoid trying to study either too many or too few factors and ensures that the proper responses in the experiment are being measured. It also helps avoid arriving at a conclusion that has already been determined.

Experiments are structured and organized to determine the relationships between factors affecting a process and the output of that process. By conducting and analyzing the results for controlled tests, it is possible to quantify the factors within the experiment and the effect that they have on the output through the observance of changes that are introduced methodically throughout the experiment. The experiments normally utilize analytical software developed for DOE applications that produces graphical images of the factors and the outputs. The results of the experiment are used then to direct the process improvement or determine the need for additional experimentation. DOE is a very powerful tool that removes the guesswork and dramatically speeds up the improvement process. This DMAIC tool is one of the most effective methods for eliminating product defects and speeding up processes, which translates directly into increased throughput.

ROBUST DESIGN

DOE utilized in Six Sigma efforts placed growing and increased demands on "design for Six Sigma" (DFSS) to develop new products of the highest quality at the lowest cost. This led to use of "robust design," developed by Dr. Genichi Taguchi of Toyota. Robust design concentrates on improving the fundamental function of a product or process through the utilization of flexible designs and concurrent engineering. The key to its effectiveness is the ability to accelerate and reduce the amount of design and engineering time to accomplish this objective, thereby producing improved quality and reliability at the lowest cost all in the same effort.

Robust design offers faster, high-quality results with minimum costs by focusing on the few requirements that are really significant and then optimizing the others to achieve lower costs. This is achieved through the ability to classify the variables with products and processes into "noise" (random and expected variation), control, input factors, and output factors. The ideal parameters of the product or process are then determined mathematically as to the requirements and specification required for perfection. The data are then arrayed so that a minimum number of systematic experiments can be run to determine the added cost of tighter tolerances against the benefits to the customer. This approach has helped to reduce the cost and time of development by 50 percent or greater in many instances. TRIZ (Theory of Inventive Problem Solving) has further enhanced the robust design approach through the use of model-based technology for stimulating and generating innovative ideas and solutions to problems.

TOTAL PREVENTIVE MAINTENANCE

One of the biggest problems faced in manufacturing is the unexpected breakdown of equipment. This represents another example of time lost is lost throughput. I used the example of the failure of a $25 bearing that shut down a critically constrained resource for three days, which caused shipments to a customer to be a week late and resulted in a serious loss of cash flow. Excessive machine breakdowns are indications of a process that is probably not producing acceptable quality and is likely accounting for scrap and waste due to the unplanned stoppages and start-ups. A good total preventive maintenance program can extend the life of machinery that helps minimize investment. The details for establishing and operating a good total preventive maintenance program is beyond the scope of this book, but the example is a clear reminder of its importance.

MISTAKE PROOFING

Mistake proofing is to build processes or engineer operations so that they prevents mistakes or defects from occurring. This is called "poka-yoke" and was developed by Shigeo Shingo as part of his Zero Quality Control system. The concept either uses devices to detect or prevent defects or process methods to avoid them. The result is savings in time and resources by doing things right the first time.

EFFECTIVE PROJECT SELECTION AND EXECUTION

The success of lean Six Sigma should be measured based on the greatest bottom-line profitability improvement and the most effective use of assets and time to achieve results. The time to achieve results must be effective or the initiative will fall under the category of another well-intended but unsuccessful effort. Success means to select the most lucrative opportunities to streamline business processes and introduce new high-quality innovative products in the most efficient time possible.

Selecting only the best projects and managing them effectively will produce the highest return for our effort. We need to eliminate waste, speed up the slowest processes, or employ DFSS that produces the maximum throughput. All opportunities should be evaluated utilizing the DMAIC process and assigned a priority based on the throughput increase and determination of the economic value added (EVA™) or profitability return the project generates on invested capital less the weighted average cost of capital. Throughput was explained in Chapter 6 and earlier in this chapter.

EVA™ is the rate of return less the weighted cost of capital times capital. This is calculated by taking the spread between the rate of return on the project and multiplying by the economic book value of the capital committed to the project. This concept will be discussed and described in greater detail in Chapter 12. There are only three ways to increase EVA™:

1. Enhance operating profitability
2. Make investments that add value over the cost of capital
3. Eliminate investment from unused or uneconomic activities

This prioritization method will force selection of projects that generate the greatest bottom-line impact. The evaluation methods such as the 80/20 rule, value stream mapping, measuring cycle efficiency, and other identification tools should be used to create a pool of opportunities, but they should be ranked using the impact they have on EVA™.

MULTIPROJECT MANAGEMENT EFFECTIVENESS

A key element to success is effective management and execution of projects. TOC has developed a variation of DBR scheduling called critical-chain buffer management. This concept has been expanded to include multiproject management that encompasses project planning, execution, and management.

The first rule of multiproject management is to apply global measurements to set the ranking priority for lean Six Sigma projects. All projects must be prioritized and sequenced. This is absolutely necessary because there inevitably will be far more opportunities than the resources of the organization are capable of addressing. The key is to sequence the projects in order of the greatest payback. There is a tendency to try to accomplish projects that appear first and then continue adding projects into the queue without regard to the overall impact of bottom-line payback. This is called multitasking multiple projects.

Project multitasking is a growing problem in complex organizations. A solution to multitasking is explained in *The Critical Chain* by Eliyahu Goldratt and is termed critical-chain buffer management. This has been further expanded to the "TOC multiproject method." Proper application of this tool will speed up the cash savings generated through more effective implementation of lean Six Sigma projects.

Briefly, here is how the tool functions. The first step is to define and prioritize the projects. Critical chain evaluates all of the time estimated to complete each project and identifies all of the resources needed to complete the necessary tasks. The timing of each project is structured and synchronized as to time of project initiation and expected completion. The key to this approach lies in staggering the projects and the flow of work in order to achieve the maximum utilization of resources. This is accomplished through identification of the most critical and heavily loaded resource and then buffering and controlling the pace of all the projects to the drumbeat of the critically constrained resource. All projects within the organization are subordinated to the critical chain through the staggering concept. Capacity buffers are placed to protect the drum resource and subsequent projects to allow for unanticipated disruptions that inevitably will occur.

Frequently, nonconstrained resources will be required to work on multiple projects in ways that create variation or "noise," and time buffers are provided to cover these situations that are called feeding buffers. The buffers within the project pipeline then provide signals of where potential delays might occur and highlight areas to adjust the schedule to provide opportunities for correcting the multiproject schedule. Effective management of the multiproject process can be achieved through application of TOC and critical chain by properly monitoring and utilizing both types of buffers. The purpose here is to show the opportunities for achieving greater acceleration and bottom-line impact by applying the right tools for the job.

ALIGNMENT OF LEAN CONSTRAINTS

Lean manufacturing and TOC are aligned in some areas and divergent in others. The beauty of these philosophies and methodologies is they are really trying to get to the same objective, but in instances with different focus. The primary areas of agreement include value, the value stream, flow, pull versus push, and achieving continuous improvement. They differ in where and how they focus in generating profitability.

Lean attacks waste and TOC places its emphasis on increasing throughput. TOC feels that if the constraint is the market, it is likely that you are providing the customer with what he or she wants. The emphasis of lean initiatives very frequently is localized or internally directed in the effort to streamline and eliminate waste. My purpose is to focus on profit and accounting for it in more optimal ways to provide continuing value to the customer and the shareholder. I think you should try to achieve "having your cake and eating it too" by prioritizing lean initiatives that increase sales in conjunction with the most efficient and effective way to produce and deliver quality products to the customer.

Throughput is not just sales; it is the net cash flow generated by the sale. Eliminating waste is part of the process of maximizing throughput. The elimination of waste increases capacity that can generate additional throughput. However, if the creation of increased capacity by the elimination of waste is not measured relative to EVA™, then the lean initiative has failed. Continually making a return on investment in excess of the cost of capital is crucial.

Lean initiatives focus on product families, and improving specific product processes may fail to produce increased throughput. TOC focuses on the system and improving the flow through and around the critically constrained resources in an effort to maximize throughput. The ability to create balance is important. The TOC approach needs to be cognizant of the value stream approach and, vice versa, lean enterprises must be aware of the constraint. Spending excessive energy and effort improving nonconstrained resources results in wasted opportunities for maximum profit improvement. Understanding the complete value chain, and how your organization fits within it, is imperative.

TOC utilizes DBR and buffers the critically constrained resource until variability in the system is reduced or eliminated. Lean enterprises remove the inventory buffers that cover up variability and attempt to employ single-piece continuous flow using kanban replenishment. The TOC approach uses DBR scheduling to achieve the same results. DBR is easier to understand and implement, which makes it a good choice for many organizations. Since the goal of the two scheduling techniques is to reduce inventory, it makes sense to give consideration to both approaches. In situations where a great deal of effort is required to bring processes to the level of capability to utilize single-piece continuous flow, then DBR scheduling might be a better choice.

I regularly monitor lean and operational management discussion groups to maintain a sense of issues being faced by companies conducting lean initiatives. One of the issues is measurement and how to do it. The measurement issue continually indicates the struggle with the creation of lean savings and what to do with the underutilized capacity that it produced. Lean initiatives require the effort of people who might become redundant due to the failure to create additional throughput. This problem argues that lean and TOC need to be linked to avoid the loss of trained workers and wasting excess productive capacity. The key to success is to understand the two philosophies, the tools, and knowing where and how to best apply them.

THE BEST OF THREE WORLDS

Three powerful philosophical approaches and methodologies have been provided in this chapter. My purpose was to provide the basic understanding of their functionality and best application. While each of the worlds has its followers and fans, it is my belief that many organizations would be well served by using all three disciplines balanced to accommodate each specific circumstance.

Maximum success is dependent on understanding each of the approaches and how to apply it for maximum benefit. Lean offers the advantage of accelerating the removal of waste from the organization. Six Sigma provides control tools and techniques that help to sustain lean applications. Both have had successes. The allure of lean thinking is that it can create huge increases in productivity and has been a popular competitive focus for many companies. Six Sigma proponents tend to drive a total strategic approach that can be expensive for smaller businesses to adopt. This is an issue not only because of the financial investment required to implement Six Sigma successfully, but many smaller organizational structures are not capable of making the necessary culture shift.

TOC has achieved success. This approach to measurement is simple while providing an incredible amount of focus and leverage. Again, lack of understanding at senior levels in particular has slowed its potential capability to provide an impact. While the approach may be too simplistic to some, it is probably because the unique complexity of how to apply and use the many strategic and tactical tools that it offers has not been fully absorbed and understood. When the depth of the philosophy and its potential are understood and blended together with lean Six Sigma, I believe the possibilities are unlimited.

My recommendation to businesses and organizations of all sizes is to grasp the basics without looking for the ultimate answer and understand how the three approaches can best apply and fit your situation. I will conclude this analysis of the three methodologies with tips and suggestions for how to maximize all three tools.

First, start applying lean concepts to drive out waste using the approaches described. In making this suggestion, please remember that lean initiatives should include a lean assessment. Establishing a baseline of where you are is critical before you decide where you are going and how to get there. Second, learn the basics of TOC measurements and the thinking process. Blend them together as a lean/TOC program. These steps will provide initial momentum and start to eliminate waste, reduce inventory, and increase profitability from the generation of additional throughput. I would suggest this progression prior to jumping into a Six Sigma program. My logic is that you can generate more profit impact and return on investment in the shortest period of time.

Third, I would suggest that while the lean/TOC effort is beginning to take hold, the Six Sigma process should be evaluated and understood. By developing this learning foundation, you will begin to realize how Six Sigma provides process control to the changes being adopted and implemented. Even if a formal Six Sigma program is not launched, you should use and apply the tools. The key elements of the tool kit and applications have been mentioned and described.

In conclusion, I think that it is critical to maintain perspective. Use the measurements to establish bottom-line priorities for launching projects and TOC multiproject tools for managing them. The key to getting the most out of all three worlds effectively is the knowledge you and your people develop to pursue improvement continuously.

This book has free materials available for download from the
Web Added Value™ Resource Center at www.jrosspub.com.

APPLICATION OF PROFIT-FOCUSED ACCOUNTING

Having your cake and eating it too is a tough mountain to climb. Over my career, I have seen relevance lost and to some extent seen it partially regained. Based on this experience, I believe there is a way to enhance the accounting impact significantly that will improve the way organizations measure and manage. My hypothesis centers on offering the best of three worlds by applying throughput accounting, activity-based management, and a balanced scorecard approach. This creates a value-based approach to measuring, monitoring, and executing strategy. Profit-focused accounting provides a new model for applying these concepts and utilizing these tools.

WHY WE NEED TO CHANGE

In Chapter 1, the rise in productivity was correlated with the decline of the relevancy of a centuries-old accounting model. Changes have occurred at a blurred rate of speed, yet the same old accounting traditions still permeate the thinking of many accountants and senior management of companies. We have seen some earlier documented initiatives, but the breakthrough still has not been made allowing organizations to feel they have the answer.

Accounting records history and generally accepted accounting principles (GAAP) drive the rules for recording transactions. They set the rules for matching revenue and expenses and categorizing what is an asset and what is a liability. Even with new technology, the books must be closed in order for financial statements to be issued monthly, quarterly, and annually. The process is too slow, and investors and managers alike too frequently look at revenue and earnings on a monthly and quarterly basis with no comprehension or understanding of what really drives and supports the reported results. The failure to understand the numbers correlated with the real drivers of profitability, when combined with the lack of speed and flexibility of the system, has left managers to devise their own basis for managing and executing strategy.

Activity-based costing and management (ABC/M) has provided some needed guidance when used properly. The balanced scorecard approach has also proven to be an effective enabler of strategy execution that has helped to improve communication and understanding. Throughput accounting also has provided some progress toward breakthrough and effectiveness. Each of these methodologies has proponents who extol the virtues of their tools and ideology. However, each takes us only part of the way to where we need to be.

The problem still comes back to the old broken model and grappling with the integration of the continuous improvement and process measurement of ABC/M and the application of nonfinancial and financial metrics of balanced scorecards. We need tools that are simple, fast, and flexible that not only report the bottom line, but also aid the process of making pricing decisions, planning, performance measurement, and enhancing investment analysis. How do we integrate accounting reports aligned with strategy and reflect measurements that are meaningful tools for controlling and planning production?

Taking it a step further, we need tools that help manage knowledge assets and the development of new products. We also need a model that can cope effectively with valuing assets, particularly inventories, in accordance with GAAP in ways that are effective but do not create improper incentives to overproduce. Measurement of lean Six Sigma and understanding the cost of quality and its strategic implications are reasons why we need to change.

The global supply chain and the customer value chain have driven businesses to search for new answers and new solutions. The rapid pace of change required to create and maintain market leadership and innovation has changed the ball game. The cost structure is dramatically different today. Overhead or standby expense has grown to keep pace with the complexity of business and the increase in product lines offered to the market. Conversely, direct labor as a percentage of total cost has dropped dramatically. This shift changes the focus of cost management.

Why has overhead taken the lead in consuming expenditure dollars? There are many reasons for this trend. One of the primary drivers is increased complexity of product lines that companies have introduced in an effort to meet competitive customer demand. Correspondingly, it is a technological world driven by information and knowledge, and this trend has shifted cost relationships. Companies are driven to innovate new products faster and management has become project driven. Multiproject management is now a new management challenge. Accounting scandals have further exposed the shortcomings of the traditional accounting model. It is clear beyond a doubt that we need to overhaul the existing model. Businesses need reliable processes and systems that focus on the needs of today, not yesterday.

HOW IT WORKS

The first step in creating a profit-focused accounting model is to make sure that it is simple but with adequate flexibility to provide effective solutions that are capable of overcoming limitations inherent in the old model. As we observed in lean Six Sigma programs, fewer moving parts improves quality and functionality with less chance of breakdown. Today's financial statements consist of components that are understood only by accountants and even then are embedded with explanatory footnotes.

Throughput accounting is about as simple as it gets. Throughput, less operating expenses, equals profit. Most accountants get a little too squeamish with such simplicity, so I expanded it to have more of the look and feel of a traditional financial statement presentation without sacrificing simplicity and flexibility. The basic framework includes three building blocks:

1. Throughput (sales less variable expenses or incremental cash flow)
2. Operating expenses (standby expense)
3. Assets (same as traditional accounting after we build the GAAP bridge)

Figure 9.1 illustrates a simple three-product-line company and the components of the income statement. I am allowing flexibility by including direct labor and other variable expenses in addition to raw material in the determination of contribution. There is no overhead or burden contained in the income statement except for an annual or quarterly adjustment to allow for conformity to GAAP. I discuss ways to establish this adjustment and where to record it on the financial statements in a later segment of the chapter.

Standby expenses contain all other operating expenses except for depreciation, amortization, and interest. Operating expenses (or standby) are grouped by department in the general ledger. The departmental segmentation is a common approach for most companies. The approach may vary from company to company. I explain how to report departmental expense using a trend format standby

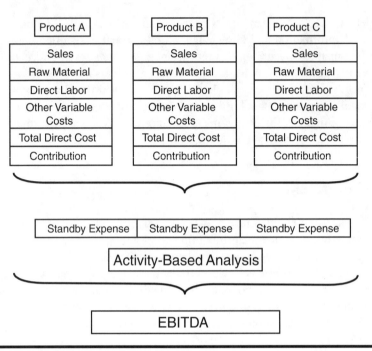

Figure 9.1. Profit-Focused Accounting Model.

expense report in a following section on trend formats. Figure 9.1 indicates that activity-based analysis is conducted to provide a drill down to earnings before interest, depreciation, amortization, and taxes (EBITDA).

Most managers do not have control over financing decisions, so I excluded the impact of financing from the earnings statement. Depreciation, amortization, and taxes are also excluded since these are factors beyond the control of operating managers. Return on investment calculations and economic value added (EVA™), both crucial measurements, do contain the impact of these excluded items. The objective was to create a simplified format that would be comprehended easily by operating managers. A platform was created that embraces the elements of throughput accounting and process cost and continuous improvement were applied by injecting activity-based management. While activity-based costing can be integrated into the accounting system, simpler and more effective results will be accomplished from analytic off-line activity-based costing studies without incurring the cost and time required to revise and implement a new cost accounting system. Before I incur the wrath of all the Theory of Constraints devotees, they need to understand that it is only applied to standby or operating expenses to achieve visibility of commercial business processes.

It is not applied to variable production processes where allocations could lead to bad decisions. It is an *enabler* to provide insight and not a structural component of the integrated accounting system.

SPEED AND FLEXIBILITY

One of the ways speed is achieved is by simplifying the reporting format. The approach recommended utilizes daily scorecard reports that contain financial and nonfinancial metrics. The daily scorecards contain sales information and updated information on new orders. These scorecards also contain nonfinancial measures that can be reported almost in real time so that corrective action can be initiated. These daily scorecards are then accumulated into a weekly scorecard. The creation of such a responsive proactive environment allows the entire organization to become more in tune with the day-to-day and week-to-week pulse beat of operations. Information is exchanged more freely and quickly, which helps everyone to be on top of the action. The activity-based management approach nurtures an atmosphere of process focus. By building confidence in the processes, reliability is then shifted to input and knowing the output, which translates into speed.

The clarity and simplicity of the profit-focused accounting approach are based on measuring and reporting real results by *avoiding* the tangle associated with the complexity of *burden rates and allocations.* The terminology is simple and easy to understand. This simplicity is enhanced because there are less data to gather, which reduces the time needed to collect and report them. Focus is then directed to throughput, cash flow, and asset turnover.

Tightening the commercial business processes used in managing data provides system reliability, accelerating the time line for closing the general ledger each month and producing financial reports. The daily and weekly scorecards help to make the monthly closing process more routine. By reducing the amount of pressure on financial departments, they are better positioned to complete monthly closings faster and do it right the first time. Monthly closings are a series of projects that require management. Application of critical-chain project management concepts can be used to insert buffers in the time line of action steps required to produce and distribute financial reports. By buffering the due date for reporting and working back, financial departments can improve the time needed to meet the deadline. Performing project steps prior to the end of the month creates buffers. For example, the weekly scorecards can be used to identify problem areas that require corrective action or to make adjusting entries where necessary. After the end of the month, all the necessary standard journal entries can be processed in line with the critical-chain project schedule, resulting in simpler and faster financial closings. This acceleration provides management access to more meaningful data before they become stale. These accelerated monthly statements can be correlated to the daily and weekly scorecards.

Accounting departments can extend and enhance the process focus combined with technology to produce lean paperless transactions. This can be applied to accounts payable and accounts receivable so that transactions occur in real time. Vendors, when qualified, are paid automatically without the necessity of matching receiving reports with invoices. This is possible through vendor-managed inventory and external kanban systems. A similar arrangement can be established with customers. All the communication is conducted electronically utilizing electronic data interchange, the Internet, and computerized faxes. By taking lean thinking into the accounting function, the speed of month-end closings is almost real time. Even Internet auction payments are made from bank account to bank account. Bank statements are reconciled on-line without the need to receive statements and checks from the banks.

THE TREND FORMAT APPROACH

The trend format approach to scorecard and financial reporting provides a multipurpose view of data. The profit-focused accounting model enables readers of financial statements to look at the best estimate of projected full-year results while presenting monthly and year-to-date results compared to plan and last year. This format worked effectively for many years in a complex multinational environment where I was the corporate controller. *Complex* can be defined as multiple profit centers in multiple countries with extensive and diverse product lines. Understanding is a critical attribute when communicating financial data to different levels of managers in any organization. It becomes even more challenging when the primary language of these managers is not always English. I am recommending the simplicity of this format because it worked extremely well over a number of years with many different managers.

The reason it works well is because it is simple and it is visual. The reader is capable of quickly grasping the key messages provided by the scorecard. Figure 9.2 presents an example of the top-level income statement. Let us discuss and explain this format and how it functions to establish an initial foundation. Once the concept has been established and understood, I will present and describe some of the enhancements that can be applied.

The statement shows revenue, contribution, contribution percentage, standby, and EBITDA. The statement shows each month of the year and has columns for the current year, original plan, and last year. Actual results are reported for each month and compared to plan and last year for the critical categories

Month	Sales $			Contribution $			Contribution %			Standby $			EBITDA $		
	Current	Plan	Last Year	Current	Plan	Last Year	Current	Plan	Last Year	Current	Plan	Last Year	Current	Plan	Last Year
JAN	835,000	833,333	708,333	363,225	371,000	315,250	43.5%	44.5%	44.5%	305,000	302,250	267,608	58,225	68,750	47,642
FEB	830,000	833,333	708,333	373,500	371,000	315,250	45.0%	44.5%	44.5%	301,250	302,250	267,608	72,250	68,750	47,642
MAR	835,000	833,333	708,333	369,905	371,000	315,250	44.3%	44.5%	44.5%	303,000	302,250	267,608	66,905	68,750	47,642
APR	835,000	833,333	708,333	369,905	371,000	315,250	44.3%	44.5%	44.5%	303,000	302,250	267,608	66,905	68,750	47,642
MAY	835,000	833,333	708,333	369,905	371,000	315,250	44.3%	44.5%	44.5%	303,000	302,250	267,608	66,905	68,750	47,642
JUN	835,000	833,333	708,333	369,905	371,000	315,250	44.3%	44.5%	44.5%	303,000	302,250	267,608	66,905	68,750	47,642
JUL	835,000	833,333	708,333	369,905	371,000	315,250	44.3%	44.5%	44.5%	303,000	302,250	267,608	66,905	68,750	47,642
AUG	835,000	833,333	708,333	369,905	371,000	315,250	44.3%	44.5%	44.5%	303,000	302,250	267,608	66,905	68,750	47,642
SEP	835,000	833,334	708,334	375,750	371,000	315,250	45.0%	44.5%	44.5%	305,000	302,250	267,608	70,750	68,750	47,642
OCT	835,000	833,334	708,334	375,750	371,000	315,250	45.0%	44.5%	44.5%	305,000	302,250	267,608	70,750	68,750	47,642
NOV	840,000	833,334	708,334	378,000	371,000	315,250	45.0%	44.5%	44.5%	305,000	302,250	267,608	73,000	68,750	47,642
DEC	840,000	833,334	708,334	378,000	371,000	315,250	45.0%	44.5%	44.5%	305,000	302,250	267,608	73,000	68,750	47,642
YTD*	1,665,000	1,666,666	1,416,666	736,725	742,000	630,500	44.2%	44.5%	44.5%	606,250	604,500	535,216	130,475	137,500	95,284
YEAR	10,025,000	10,000,000	8,500,000	4,463,655	4,452,000	3,783,000	44.5%	44.5%	44.5%	3,644,250	3,627,000	3,211,296	819,405	825,000	571,704

*FEB

Head Count

	Current Month	Last Year Month
Direct	65	
Standby	23	

Measurements

	Current	Plan	Last Year
EBITDA % Sales	8.2%	8.3%	6.7%
ROI %	10.5%	10.5%	4.7%
ROI Turnover	3.83	3.82	3.4
EVA	64,728	66,511	(56,500)
Inventory Turns	6.5	6.5	6.0

Figure 9.2.   The Trend Format Income Statement.

Month	Sales $			Contribution $			Contribution %		
	Current	Plan	Last Year	Current	Plan	Last Year	Current	Plan	Last Year
JAN	835,000	833,333	708,333	363,225	371,000	315,250	43.5%	44.5%	44.5%
FEB	830,000	833,333	708,333	373,500	371,000	315,250	45.0%	44.5%	44.5%
MAR	835,000	833,333	708,333	369,905	371,000	315,250	44.3%	44.5%	44.5%
APR	835,000	833,333	708,333	369,905	371,000	315,250	44.3%	44.5%	44.5%
MAY	835,000	833,333	708,333	369,905	371,000	315,250	44.3%	44.5%	44.5%
JUN	835,000	833,333	708,333	369,905	371,000	315,250	44.3%	44.5%	44.5%
JUL	835,000	833,333	708,333	369,905	371,000	315,250	44.3%	44.5%	44.5%
AUG	835,000	833,333	708,333	369,905	371,000	315,250	44.3%	44.5%	44.5%
SEP	835,000	833,334	708,334	375,750	371,000	315,250	45.0%	44.5%	44.5%
OCT	835,000	833,334	708,334	375,750	371,000	315,250	45.0%	44.5%	44.5%
NOV	840,000	833,334	708,334	378,000	371,000	315,250	45.0%	44.5%	44.5%
DEC	840,000	833,334	708,334	378,000	371,000	315,250	45.0%	44.5%	44.5%
YTD*	1,665,000	1,666,666	1,416,666	736,725	742,000	630,500	44.2%	44.5%	44.5%
YEAR	10,025,000	10,000,000	8,500,000	4,463,655	4,452,000	3,783,000	44.5%	44.5%	44.5%

*FEB

Figure 9.3. Trend Format Sales and Contribution Report.

providing the throughput emphasis. Month-to-month comparisons to original plan and last year are made, as well as year-to-date comparisons and the best estimate for the full year. This is a multifaceted presentation of data comparison and trends for the key operational measures presented all on one statement. This top statement is supported by sublevel trend format sales and contribution reports by major product lines/customers in addition to standby expense by department. Examples of these reports are presented in Figures 9.3 and 9.4.

The trend formats provide a flow for easier understanding. Product line profitability is easier to understand because the reports show sales and contribution without being fogged by overhead allocations. Operational management is not allowed to become confused with distortion resulting from over- or underabsorption of overhead due to inventory fluctuation and valuation. The impact of their decisions becomes easier for them to understand. The breakeven model is not truly reliable today because all expenses become variable to some extent. However, managers are able to visualize and understand how much they need to sell and the throughput margin rate that must be achieved to cover standby expense. It gets them into the game and helps them understand what it means.

The statement format allows for ongoing sales and operational planning that helps to remove the functional silos and unite the organization. Ratios are provided for return on sales, inventory turnover, and EVA™ through the application of the most current forecast of full-year results. This capability is not

	People			Salaries $	Fringe $	Supplies $	Other $	Total $
Month	TY	OP	LY	TYOPLY	TYOPLY	TYOPLY	TYOPLY	TYOPLY
JAN	6	6	5	25,000	3,750	3,000	4,000	35,750
FEB	6	6	5	25,000	3,750	3,000	4,000	35,750
MAR	6	6	5	25,000	3,750	3,000	4,000	35,750
APR	6	6	5	25,000	3,750	3,000	4,000	35,750
MAY	6	6	5	25,000	3,750	3,000	4,000	35,750
JUN	6	6	5	25,000	3,750	3,000	4,000	35,750
JUL	6	6	5	25,000	3,750	3,000	4,000	35,750
AUG	6	6	5	25,000	3,750	3,000	4,000	35,750
SEP	6	6	5	25,000	3,750	3,000	4,000	35,750
OCT	6	6	5	25,000	3,750	3,000	4,000	35,750
NOV	6	6	5	25,000	3,750	3,000	4,000	35,750
DEC	6	6	5	25,000	3,750	3,000	4,000	35,750
YTD*	6	6	6	50,000	7,500	6,000	8,000	71,500
YEAR				300,000	45,000	36,000	48,000	429,000

Year

*FEB

Figure 9.4.   Trend Format Standby Expense Report.

effectively provided by traditional financial statement formats. The statement format can show financial and nonfinancial metrics to include:

- Inventory dollars and turnover
- Percent of on-time delivery
- Total assets and investment
- Head count
- EBITDA per employee
- EVA™

I will explore the attributes of the throughput trend format of profit-focused accounting in subsequent sections of the chapter. The key advantage can be summarized as simplistic future focus on the goal.

ENTERPRISE RESOURCE PLANNING

Enterprise resource planning (ERP) is the tool used by most companies to plan their operations. It contains the accounting modules that produce financial reports. ERP and all of its applications are beyond the scope of this book, but I do want to utilize some of its attributes. A typical ERP system relies on data generated from steps presented in Figure 9.5, which shows the key planning activities that

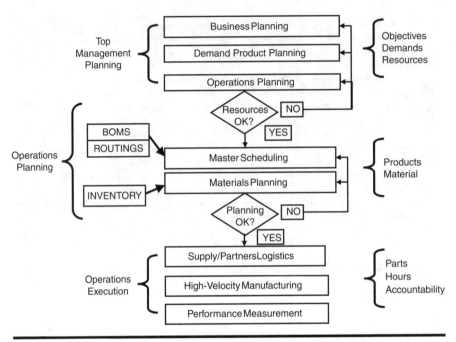

Figure 9.5. The ERP Model.

significantly impact accounting data. The bills of material and routing process steps are contained in the item master that feeds material planning and logistics. Vendor masters and customer masters contain critical information that flows to the accounting module that is a component of an ERP system. Figure 9.6 portrays the complexity of interactions using these data. I structured an accounting and reporting model that would minimize any changes to the existing accounting system to accelerate the pace at which organizations could access the advantages of a new reporting approach.

Details of routings and bills of material are contained in the item master for each product within the ERP system and drive the planning system and supply chain logistics of the organization. By including direct labor in the determination of contribution, a version of throughput accounting can be provided that is not materially different from the Theory of Constraints (TOC) model. Routing steps map the direct production process so the material requirements planning system can be used to identify the lean time traps as described in Chapter 8. The accounting system is also an integrated module of the ERP system, representing a further reason to avoid making structural changes. My goal is to offer a new thinking and reporting model that changes the impact on the bottom line.

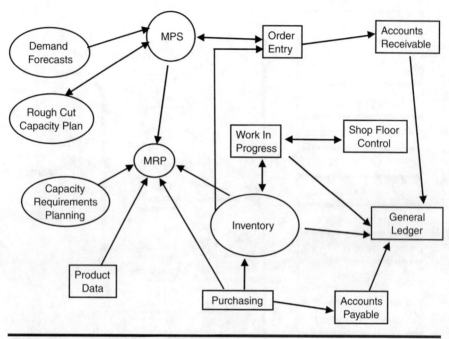

Figure 9.6. ERP Interactions and Flows.

ERP systems help to manage the flow of inventory in the system. How the system values inventory will change so that only actual material and direct labor are used to accumulate costs as product flows through the system before it is shipped to the customer. Some inventory will be required to buffer critically constrained resources and establish shipping buffers. A key to controlling waste is precise accuracy of the bills of material, routing steps, and the accuracy of perpetual inventories. Everyone wants to focus on streamlining and acceleration, but effective lean Six Sigma and TOC programs must have a foundation of accurate data. Effective use of the ERP/APS (advanced planning system) allows focus and leverage to occur at the proper locations in the value chain.

THE BRIDGE TO GAAP

Profit-focused accounting, like throughput accounting, calculates contribution or throughput without including or using any overhead factors in its determination. Accounting purists will quickly want to rebuff this technique until they understand how I provide for achieving compliance with GAAP. While some

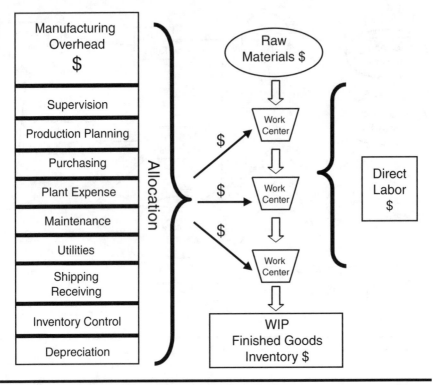

Figure 9.7. Traditional Cost Flows of Product Costs.

inventory will be necessary for buffers, the objective is to eliminate it to the extent possible.

In its basic form, inventory valuation represents the amount of raw material, direct labor, and manufacturing overhead. Traditional cost accounting systems accumulate these costs as work flows through the factory. Walk out on any factory shop floor and observe the process flow. Figure 9.7 provides a graphic illustration of how costs flow through the system and how they are accumulated in the various inventory buckets depending on their state of completion. The perpetual inventory modules capture the quantities and cost of product.

There are various options for how the ERP system values products and how costs are accumulated as material flows through the process. Among the options are actual average costs for raw material and actual labor using LIFO (last in/first out), FIFO (first in/first out), and actual average using actual or standard costs. Every company has its own system and policy for handling these costs. The system will also indicate how overhead is allocated to inventory from manufacturing overhead. Typical manufacturing overhead is presented in Figure

9.7 and in Figure 9.10 for Model Manufacturing Company. The allocation methods are entered on the item masters of the ERP system for each product produced. You can choose to not check this flag and that will disable the overhead allocation feature. You will then view only material and labor costs in the system. Journal entries are used to record changes in the overhead in inventory accounts in the general ledger. You do not need the system to drive these entries. This will allow use of the ERP system to use direct costs as defined and permit adjustment of overhead in inventory for financial statement purposes to be entered via a journal entry using the GAAP-bridging calculation.

The following example shows the factors that affect the value of overhead in inventory:

Inventory in units (beginning)	100,000
Overhead rate	$10
Overhead in inventory (beginning)	$1,000,000
Inventory in units (ending)	105,000
Overhead rate	$10
Overhead in inventory (ending)	$1,050,000
Increase in the value of overhead in inventory	$50,000

There are only two factors that will influence the value of overhead in inventory:

1. The quantity of units in inventory
2. The overhead rate applied to the quantity

Any combination of changes in these two factors will create a change in the value of overhead in inventory. GAAP requires that overhead be included in the valuation of the inventory asset account for financial statement purposes. This requirement is not likely to change, so for the purposes of our accounting model, it just needs to be addressed. There are many different thoughts and opinions on determining overhead value in inventory and they will vary depending on the company and the industry. The typical methods include direct labor, direct material, machine hours, and other indicators of volume. I am advocating that any variance from fluctuations in overhead valuations be excluded from management operating financial reports. They should be treated much like financing and capital spending costs, consistent with the EBITDA measurement philosophy. Activity-based analysis is used to create a bottom-line focus that will be discussed in a later section of this chapter. Strategic cost implications are also discussed later in the section dealing with throughput value streams.

Application of lean/TOC strategies will reduce inventory levels and help keep them at lower levels with little fluctuation. When the inventory is reduced initially, a material reduction in overhead contained in inventory will impact the bottom line adversely. After this initial correction, there should not be material fluctuations of inventory volume. Assuming overhead rates remain relatively constant, the overhead valuation account should not have a material impact on the value of assets and earnings.

Both lean and TOC will provide for a steady level of inventory through the application of synchronous flow concepts using kanban or drum-buffer-rope. Unless the company is publicly traded, only one adjustment for overhead variance will be necessary at the end of the year to comply with GAAP financial statement requirements. Publicly traded companies will require quarterly adjustments. During my years as a corporate controller, I successfully applied this approach with the full approval of our auditors. One caution however: it is suggested that the overhead variance be carefully monitored throughout the year to avoid any surprises.

ACCOUNTING FLOW AND IMPLICATIONS

It will be helpful to understand the accounting flow and to illustrate how the model will record key transactions. Changing accounting systems is a major barrier, so new reporting models are offered, not necessarily a major overhaul of the accounting system. Companies can use their existing systems, and by rethinking the flow of accounting transactions and journal entries, they will be in a position to utilize the benefits of throughput accounting and activity-based costing without the need to make structural changes. There are many analytic tools on the market to enable companies to evaluate and analyze existing data in different formats. Understanding the flow of information through the business processes and then knowing how to use and interpret the financial data make up the key premise of the model.

Figure 9.8 shows the flow of journal entries to record cost of goods sold and contribution. The key transactions, assuming the use of a standard cost system, are shown in the T accounts for each account. If an actual average cost is used, the transactions through the variance accounts will be eliminated. Purchases are recorded at actual, and then the account is credited with a corresponding debit or credit to purchase price variance and a debit to raw material to show acquisition of inventory. Refer back to Figure 9.7 to understand the flow. Raw material is credited and work in process (WIP) is debited to reflect the start of production. Direct labor is recorded as incurred and is moved into WIP at standard cost, with any variance from standard being debited or credited to labor variance. Scrap is recorded as a variance from standard, as goods are moved from one work center to another. The material and labor are accumulated

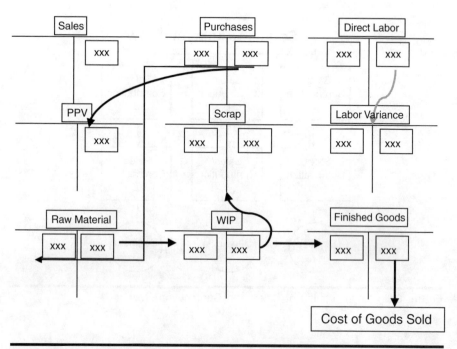

Figure 9.8. Transaction Entries to Record Cost of Goods Sold.

as incurred in WIP until the product is completed. When all work is completed, the product value is moved from WIP into finished goods. When the goods are invoiced to the customer and a sale recorded, finished goods are credited for the cost of the product and a debit is recorded in cost of goods sold. All variances are recorded as costs in the period incurred, and contribution or throughput is determined by subtracting material, direct labor, and variances from sales.

Raw material is recorded either at standard or using the actual average method. Labor and expense are recorded to each work center or cell at actual or standard. The movement of work can be based on actual transactions using work orders or through the utilization of backflushing. Backflushing is a procedure that allows deduction from inventory records of assembly or subassembly components produced by exploding the bill of materials using the actual count of product produced and either moved to the next work center/work cell or to finished goods inventory. Any difference remaining in a WIP center after the backflush is treated as a scrap or labor variance and expensed. This process is focused on production required to meet customer demand with no emphasis on efficiencies. The true emphasis is placed on the amount of throughput or

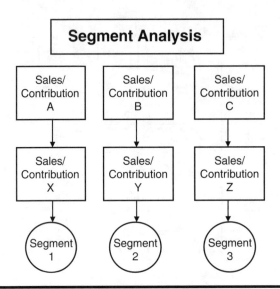

Figure 9.9.   Segmentation of Sales and Contribution Flow.

contribution generated with only the limited inventory needed to provide constraint buffers.

The transactions and accounting journal entries explained above are how most companies flow production transactions through their ERP system. These steps were described to show that it is possible for companies to utilize profit-focused accounting/throughput accounting with literally no change to their accounting system except for the removal of over- and underabsorbed overhead (burden).

I suggest presenting product segments or families in a sales and contribution format that will tie into the top-level combining statement. A sample flow is shown in Figure 9.9 and the report for Model Manufacturing Company is presented in Figure 9.10. The trend format sales and contribution report utilizes column headings for the current year, original plan, and last year. These statements can be organized to reflect product lines, market segments, geography, customer, or other configurations depending on the need of the organization. The statements offer the same attributes of actual results for the month and year to date together with the latest estimate of full-year results compared to the original plan and last year. These statements can contain nonfinancial metrics, production units, or other information such as scrap or backorder data. The contribution or throughput is presented representing sales less raw material and direct labor and expense and contribution as percentage of sales.

Month	Sales $			Contribution $			Contribution %		
	Current	Plan	Last Year	Current	Plan	Last Year	Current	Plan	Last Year
JAN	835,000	833,333	708,333	363,225	371,000	315,250	43.5%	44.5%	44.5%
FEB	830,000	833,333	708,333	373,500	371,000	315,250	45.0%	44.5%	44.5%
MAR	835,000	833,333	708,333	369,905	371,000	315,250	44.3%	44.5%	44.5%
APR	835,000	833,333	708,333	369,905	371,000	315,250	44.3%	44.5%	44.5%
MAY	835,000	833,333	708,333	369,905	371,000	315,250	44.3%	44.5%	44.5%
JUN	835,000	833,333	708,333	369,905	371,000	315,250	44.3%	44.5%	44.5%
JUL	835,000	833,333	708,333	369,905	371,000	315,250	44.3%	44.5%	44.5%
AUG	835,000	833,333	708,333	369,905	371,000	315,250	44.3%	44.5%	44.5%
SEP	835,000	833,334	708,334	375,750	371,000	315,250	45.0%	44.5%	44.5%
OCT	835,000	833,334	708,334	375,750	371,000	315,250	45.0%	44.5%	44.5%
NOV	840,000	833,334	708,334	378,000	371,000	315,250	45.0%	44.5%	44.5%
DEC	840,000	833,334	708,334	378,000	371,000	315,250	45.0%	44.5%	44.5%
YTD*	1,665,000	1,666,666	1,416,666	736,725	742,000	630,500	44.2%	44.5%	44.5%
YEAR	10,025,000	10,000,000	8,500,000	4,463,655	4,452,000	3,783,000	44.5%	44.5%	44.5%

*FEB

Figure 9.10.   Model Manufacturing Company: Profit-Focused Accounting Model.

The reporting model breaks out standby expense by department on a trend format basis. Figure 9.11 shows an example from a functional perspective. Trend format standby expense reports similar to the example presented in Figure 9.4 are presented for each department within the functional groupings. The same approach is followed for standby expense regarding column headings and the

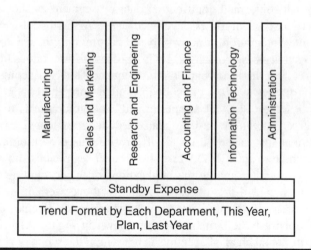

Figure 9.11.   Model Manufacturing Company: Standby Expense Report.

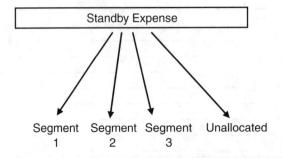

Figure 9.12. Activity-Based Analysis of Standby Expense Performed Based on Activity to Provide Deeper Understanding of the Composition of Operating Expense.

ability to report the current month, year to date, and estimated full year. This format offers a completely different way of looking at departmental and functional expense. The section on budgeting as a dynamic process will provide insight on linking trend format standby reporting to continuous planning. Standby expense or operating expense offers unique challenges. It contains the personnel and related costs of innovation activities that represent the key to building future value and profitability.

The profit-focused accounting model goes beyond throughput accounting and balanced scorecards by applying activity-based costing as a component of the new reporting model. The model segments sales and contribution by product segment and customer groups, even to a specific customer, if needed. The next step is to conduct activity-based analysis that enables segmenting standby expense to match up with sales and contribution data by segment as shown in Figure 9.12. Activity-based analysis is developed using ABC/M tools and does not require the total integration of activity-based costing into the existing accounting system. Activity-based management is a process of continuous improvement that is discussed in the next chapter. The frequency for conducting analysis is dependent on factors such as the shift in product mix and changes occurring in the activities and tasks that are performed. My preference is to develop an analysis matrix that can be easily updated as changes occur. I have designed a sample format that can be used to sift profit-focused accounting sales and contribution down to an EBITDA level by product segment as shown in Figure 9.10. The key to understanding the implications of the accounting flow is that all the format changes I describe are possible without overhauling an existing accounting system. If you do want to make changes to the chart of accounts, I have developed a basic structure that is shown in Figure 9.13. Providing a detailed departmental chart of accounts is not within the scope of this book, but the broad structure will provide a starting guideline. While an overhaul might

- Assets 1000
- Liabilities 2000
- Shareholders' Equity 3000
- Sales 4000
- Direct Cost of Sales 4400 to 4999
  - **Material 4500**
  - **Labor 4600**
  - **Purchase Price Variances 4700**
  - **Scrap, Waste, and Inventory Variances 4800**
  - **Freight and Variances 4900**
- Direct Labor Control and Variances 5000
- Standby Expense 6000
- Interest 7000
- Depreciation 8000
- Taxes 9000

Figure 9.13.   Profit-Focused Accounting Chart of Accounts Structure.

not be needed, it may be necessary to tighten the bolts and tune it up if the system is not producing the level of reliable data needed by management and for reporting compliance. Also, there are several good analytic software packages capable of bolting on to your existing software that can produce the formats I have described in addition to providing real-time digital dashboards to monitor results.

A BOTTOM-LINE FOCUS

The standby trend format of our reporting model combined with activity-based analysis is essential given the shift in importance of overhead or operating expense. Reliance on just throughput is not enough, nor does the "cost world" approach provide the needed tools. Activity-based analysis of standby expense used in conjunction with segment reporting of sales and contribution allows organizations to look at the strategic implications of where their company's activities fit from the perspective of the value chain. This represents an enhancement over the "cost world" approach.

I have mentioned application of value-based management using EVA™. While this approach could be adopted on a top-level basis, it will not provide the view from a product or business segment standpoint. In today's world, where speed and innovation are critical, companies need the ability to drill to the bottom line for many reasons. The expanded capability of throughput accounting to understand the linkages within the value chain gives companies new advantages. They can now fully utilize and adopt throughput accounting and the advantages it offers without losing the ability to analyze the competitive elements needed in a world driven by technological change. Pursuing strategies of differentiation is facilitated and enhanced by the profit-focused accounting version of throughput accounting.

BUDGETING: A DYNAMIC PROCESS

Budgeting is a laborious job that consumes an organization often without creating impact. Budgets are almost always out of date before they are completed and require large chunks of time, which prevents focus on real-time priorities. Budgeting becomes everyone's wish list with hidden cushions and an inaccurate assessment of reality. The trend format model developed uses the original plan similar to a budget in the sense that once it is set for the year, it does not change, therefore providing a reference point.

I have developed an approach to create an original plan continuously and quickly on a moving two-year basis. The approach is based on maintaining a two-year projection so there is always a basis for developing the current forecast each year and a new original plan at the end of the year. The monthly trend format is applied to sales and contribution by product line, rolling up to total sales and contribution. The same concept is also applied to standby expense by department, with a roll up to total standby for each month. The suggested column headings for use with the rolling plan concept are presented below:

- This Year — Current Forecast/Actual
- Plan Year 1
- Plan Year 2

The concept uses Plan Year 1 as the original plan at the start of the beginning of the new accounting period. The format provides for the latest monthly data for two full years in addition to the current year.

This working framework is aided by using the capability of the ERP system, activity-based analysis, and balanced scorecards to monitor execution of the organization's strategy. I discuss application of activity-based management in Chapter 10 and application of balanced scorecards in Chapter 11.

The advantage of trend formats as a predictive management tool has been shown. Current forecasts will be developed differently depending on the company and industry. However, the forecast data can be converted into operational terms using the finite scheduling capability of the ERP system or an advanced planning and scheduling system. All of the bills of material and routing steps are documented in the system and can be used to convert sales demand by product into contribution by product using this data. The system can also be used to apply the process foundation to two years of data except for any new product innovations anticipated. Two-year data and current forecast data can be gathered using Web-based tools or e-mail if information needs to be collected from multiple locations.

The real key to the two-year rolling plans approach and maintaining current forecasts is application of activity-based analysis to standby expense by department. Activity-based analysis is used to identify the key activity drivers for all of the processes flowing through the standby departments. These activity drivers will need to be updated periodically to maintain an accurate picture of process flow. Once these data are gathered, they will be updated and maintained through a process of continuous improvement. Transactional flows that influence the volume of activity can be obtained from the current forecast analysis of sales and contribution by product and market segment. Departmental and functional data are maintained in trend formats. Process activity flow is monitored using the capability of ABC/M. The trend formats are also used to maintain and monitor nonfinancial measures using balanced scorecard concepts.

The trend formats enable organizations to view results in predictive ways that enhance the execution and measurement of strategic themes. The profit-focused accounting approach using trend formats provides a wide range of options for integrating a more effective approach to planning using throughput accounting and activity-based analysis. Budgeting, as we know it, can become a thing of the past. I have just scratched the surface of possibilities and potential for applying the new concepts introduced to you.

PROFIT-FOCUSED MANAGEMENT OF PRODUCT DEVELOPMENT

The continuing success of organizations in today's competitive environment is more dependent on innovation and development. The innovation may be in new products, new technologies, or new services. Greater use of knowledge assets and directing activity through projects will be required for achieving and maintaining a competitive edge. Traditional accounting and cost management systems do not offer much guidance for organizations as they move into the "information age."

Throughput accounting, or profit-focused accounting, offers significant advantages because it can provide greater visibility and flexibility for monitoring and measuring the effectiveness of product and segment profitability as shown using the trend format throughput approach. Another possible approach is to capture product development standby expense using work orders. This collects costs from a variety of standby departments and then organizes and groups them using project management. This allows organizations to look at the current forecast of future results with greater predictability. In addition, we can look at the departments performing the development work using the same future predictive view. Since project management is the vehicle used to keep this activity on target, this approach can be used in conjunction with critical-chain project management and TOC multiproject management.

In most instances, organizations will utilize input from multiple departments to contribute to product development. These departments will charge their effort and other expenses to a variety of projects, each with its own critical chain. The cost of each project will be monitored using the same trend format. This provides a matrix view for a total product development as a department that is broken down for each individual project on a month-by-month basis. Microsoft Project or a similar software tool can be used to develop the project schedule that corresponds to the trend format matrix view for each project.

Critical-chain buffers are included in the individual project plans for the critical-chain and feeding buffers to protect overloading noncritical resources. Project work orders are used to accumulate the cost of each work order by project, and contributing resource departments charge to these work orders using a departmental rate. Product development includes the cost of each work order that is expensed with the cumulative cost maintained in the work order and is also reflected in the matrix control for each work order. The trend format provides control of cost by each work order, by department, and for total product development expense.

My approach to providing work order and project control is not limited to just product development. Application of the matrix organization and multiproject management approach can be adapted to construction or other complex situations, lending itself to visual control and management from a matrix perspective. In my career as a controller, we used the matrix management approach to evaluate operations from the perspective of both manufacturing management and marketing management including product development.

THROUGHPUT VALUE STREAMS

Lean initiatives place a great deal of emphasis on value stream mapping, which tracks all the activities required to convert customer needs into delivered products and services. The trouble with lean programs is that they can fail to capture the throughput concept driven by bottom-line profitability. Throughput also helps to identify availability of excess capacity that is the result of lean programs. Both lean and TOC recognize the value from the customer's perception; true value is not created in an organization until the sale is made and the cash is in the bank. The profit-focused accounting approach takes care of any misconception that may arise from following one or the other approaches. I combine them so a trend format of sales and contribution emphasis enables lean programs using a TOC approach to better capture maximum benefit from value stream mapping and analysis.

Another reason to identify throughput value streams is to provide a foundation for performing strategic analysis of value chain positioning and cost drivers. A value chain represents the link of activities that create value from providing raw materials through the many steps and processes required to deliver a product to the end customer. It is important to consider both up- and downstream linkages when conducting value stream mapping and analysis. The creation of a throughput connection to the value chain combined with activity driver analysis as proscribed by the model will ensure more effective measurement and understanding of lean Six Sigma programs.

I advocate using the combination of all three accounting and measurement tools to consider options that are encountered in developing strategic themes and evaluating strategic options. Frequently, the cost drivers will involve technology, and my model will offer greater assurance of consideration from the perspective of empowered management and continuous improvement. The activity-based analysis approach also helps to avoid the evaluation of a value stream analysis based on just throughput or volume output.

A BASELINE SCORECARD

There are many approaches to keeping score and there are many measurements, both financial and nonfinancial. In concluding this chapter on applying the concepts that have been discussed, I felt it would be useful to share a scorecard that can be used by organizations to create a baseline of their "current state" before launching forward on new programs. This scorecard answers many frequently asked questions about metrics. It is not all-inclusive, but it provides a simplistic summary of a critical few measures an organization should consider. Besides, everyone wants a list, so Figure 9.14 presents my suggested list of measures (also available for download at www.jrosspub.com).

This scorecard is not a balanced scorecard; I will discuss those in depth in Chapter 11. What this scorecard provides is a view from seven perspectives:

Measurement	This Year	Last Year	Assessment Team Comments
Financial Performance			
Net Sales			
Operating Income as Percent of Sales			
EBITDA			
R&D Cost as Percent of Sales			
Percent of Sales from New Products			
Capital Investment as Percent of Sales			
• % For New Products			
• % For Capacity			
• % For Safety and Environment			
Working Capital as Percent of Sales			
EVA-Economic Value Added			
Operational Performance			
Manufacturing Cycle Time			
Performance to Takt time			
Raw Material Inventory $			
Raw Material Inventory Turns			
WIP Inventory $			
WIP Inventory Turns			
Finished Goods Inventory $			
Finished Goods Inventory Turns			
Total Inventory-Days on Hand			
Product Service Quality			
Defects per 1000 Units			
Average First-Pass Yield Percentage			

Measurement	This Year	Last Year	Assessment Team Comments
Customer Satisfaction			
Customer Satisfaction Index			
Customer Return Percentage			
Delivery Performance			
Average Quoted Lead Time			
Late Shipments			
• Measured in $			
• Measured by # of parts affected			
• Measured by # of customers affected			
Abandoned Customer Phone Calls %			
Employee Satisfaction			
Employee Turnover			
Absenteeism			
Number of Suggestion per Employee			
Number of Suggestions Implemented			
Hours of Training/Education per Employee			
Safety & Ergonomics			
Injuries			
Medical Costs per 100 Associates			
Lost-time Accidents			
Supplier Performance			
Supplier's Delivery Performance			
Supplier Defects per 1000 Units			

Figure 9.14.   Baseline Scorecard.

1. Financial performance
2. Operational performance
3. Product service and quality
4. Customer satisfaction
5. Employee satisfaction
6. Safety and ergonomics
7. Supplier performance

This scorecard can be used to conduct an internal benchmarking assessment. It will help to provide a basis for understanding where the organization stands now and areas where it has opportunities to make improvements. Calculation and determination of these metrics plus other measures are fully described in Chapter 13. This scorecard is not designed to replace the trend format; its purpose is to create a baseline for better understanding the historical performance. The metrics can be used in developing a balanced scorecard, if they fit and apply to the strategic themes of the organization.

Another reason for including the list of metrics is that they can be included with the trend format as key measures to be monitored on an ongoing basis. Some of them have already been included in our templates. While I provided a list of performance measures, I think it is important to understand that the mere creation of a digital dashboard and tracking a list of suggested measures will not guarantee continuous profit and performance improvement. However, understanding what these measures mean and what they impact in an organization is critical. My feeling is that effective application of throughput accounting, activity-based analysis, and executing strategies using balanced scorecards as suggested is the way to compete successfully in the twenty-first century.

WAV Web Added Value™

This book has free materials available for download from the Web Added Value™ Resource Center at www.jrosspub.com.

10

APPLYING ACTIVITY-BASED ANALYSIS

Chapter 5 provided the foundation for activity-based costing and management. It describes the basics and how they fit into our new accounting and measurement model. Like all methodologies and tools, it does not represent a panacea for every situation and it does not solve every business problem. There is not one right answer and there is not one right tool. Activity-based costing helps to bring clarity to cost management in areas where traditional cost management failed. Analyzing activities and processes in conjunction with the other profit-focused accounting tools is a necessity for organizations to meet today's business challenges. We will now gain greater understanding of where and how to effectively use activity-based analysis. Unless you know where to apply the tools and how they can be most effectively utilized, they will not be of any benefit.

IMPROVEMENT AND OPTIMIZATION

The real key to activity-based costing and management is process and activity analysis. Once organizations go beyond their traditional functions and departments, real improvement becomes a possibility. When the business processes are identified, together with the activities and tasks that make them flow, it is then possible to know what changes to make and where and how to make them. This section is intended to direct attention toward continued improvement and ongoing optimization of operational effectiveness.

The real meat of activity-based analysis lies in using it to achieve continuous improvement in conjunction with lean and Six Sigma programs, balanced scorecards, and throughput accounting. While activity analysis can be conducted in manufacturing and production to better understand the processes, application of lean strategies and the Theory of Constraints to achieve operational excellence is better suited to this task. Standby expense, as it is defined under profit-focused accounting, represents a gold mine of opportunity and represents a more appropriate application for using activity-based analysis to help make proactive strategic and operating decisions to improve the effectiveness of business and commercial processes.

The objectives of activity-based analysis are to:

1. Eliminate or minimize low value-adding costs
2. Streamline value-added activities by enhancing and improving efficiency and effectiveness
3. Identify the root causes of problems and fix them
4. Provide a basis for improving the understanding of product costs caused by poor assumptions and incorrect allocation of costs

In order to accomplish these objectives, it is necessary to conduct the necessary analysis of all processes flowing through the standby departments. The first step is to identify all the processes and the activities that consume time in each standby department. You will recall that each activity requires inputs, which causes an activity to occur, and that one or more outputs will result. The workload of the activity can be measured and called "output measures." The simple diagram in Figure 10.1 will help us to understand this concept and the link to business processes.

Value analysis tools will be needed to capture and gather all the key information regarding each activity for each process. Since activities consume resources, it is necessary to document the resources consumed by each activity and determine the cost of the output. This information makes it possible for organizations to determine the cost of each activity and process contained in the functional standby departments. Figure 10.2 provides a perspective of how transactional costs captured within the general ledger are redirected by activity-based analysis to create a more strategic and operational view of cost and its impact.

The general ledger captures every transaction and records them by account and department. This becomes the basis for creating financial statements. After re-evaluating this information based on analysis of process activities, it is then possible to create a clearer picture of the operation from the perspective of process flow and costs.

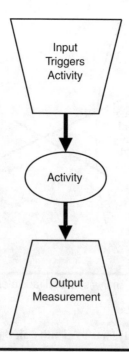

Figure 10.1.   Concept of Activity Input and Output.

VALUE ANALYSIS

Value analysis begins with defining what the organization is doing in relation to every aspect of meeting customer needs from securing the order to fulfilling and servicing the order. Each step of the value chain must be expanded to consider each activity and task required to maintain the flow of value through the chain. The organization utilizes processes to enable this flow. Processes can range from extremely complex to very simple and usually consist of a series of activities that are further decomposed into series of tasks. The drawing in Figure 10.3 provides visualization of this flow.

Every process flowing through the functional standby departments needs to be identified and then documented. A useful identification analysis tool is the creation of an activity dictionary to define each activity and gather key descriptive data. The dictionary would list the inputs, outputs, performance measures, cost drivers, and activity characteristics. This tool is a good check to make sure that all activities have been accounted for and to ensure that all of the activities will be linked to detailed flowchart maps of each process.

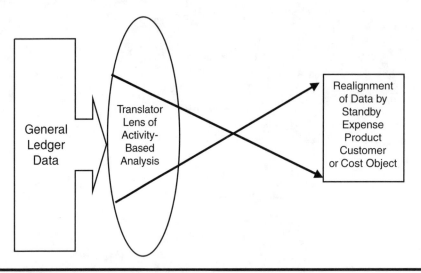

Figure 10.2. Activity-Based Analysis Cost Translator View.

The purpose of value analysis is to identify all the activities and then classify them as either primary or secondary. Identification should begin by categorizing and analyzing the time spent by each person within each department and matching it to activities. By creating data on how much time is spent on each activity, these activities can then be grouped as primary or secondary. Primary activities are those that take up at least 5 percent of a department's time, and any activity consuming less than 5 percent of the department's time would be classified as

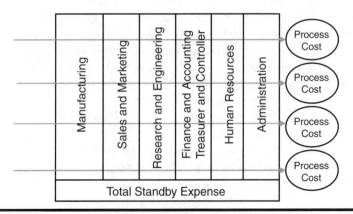

Figure 10.3. Process Hierarchy, Cost Drivers, and Activity Flow.

secondary. Primary activities are those that contribute directly to the purpose of the department. For example, the primary activity of the accounting department is to record and account for transactions. Secondary activities support the primary activities and required time such as training or attending meetings. These activities are necessary, but not primary.

The next required step is to identify activity input, such as an accounting clerk processing the receipt of vendor invoices and entering them in the accounts payable voucher register. The output would be invoices posted. The next step might be to process these invoices for payment and prepare checks. The checks then need to be signed and then placed into envelopes for mailing. The envelopes need to be run through the postage meter and mailed. Identification of all these primary and secondary activities must be acknowledged as to the input and the output. The output measure for mailing envelopes would be the number of envelopes mailed. If the clerk had to re-enter invoices because the incorrect account distribution was made, this would be classified as a nonvalue-added activity. These activities would be included and linked with the accounts payable process. The activity is producing financial reports, the output is the report, and the output measure is the number of financial reports produced.

Performance measures are indicators of the work performed and the results from an activity. These indicators can be both financial and nonfinancial. The value analysis effort should consider how long the activity took, how well it was performed, and then link the activity to the cost. Value added is generally considered an activity necessary to meet customer or external requirements. Any activity representing waste or efforts to eliminate or minimize it might be classified as nonvalue added. The objective is to focus effort toward improving the efficiency and effectiveness of activities that enable a company to become more competitive or exceed customer expectations.

Activities consume resources in order to accomplish their objective. Resources can be purchased externally or provided from internal sources. The cost of the activity represents the sum of the external and internal resources consumed. Examples of the resources include people and their respective cost, machinery, equipment, facilities, and all related costs required to support the business structure. This includes capital, credit, and the use of technology. Events or occurrences that initiate activities trigger the consumption of resources, resulting in the creation of activity cost. The frequency and intensity of demands placed on the activities determine the amount of cost incurred. Process improvement results from the minimization of demand from cost drivers of low value-added activities and the optimization of demand from cost drivers of high value-added activities.

We link all the activities to functional processes by standby department utilizing value analysis to identify the cost driver relationship by the type and

	Widget 1	Widget 2	Widget 3	Widget 4	Widget 5	Total
Sales	$4,000,000	$2,000,000	$1,800,000	$600,000	$1,600,000	$10,000,000
Cost of Goods Sold:						
Direct Material	1,600,000	875,000	825,000	300,000	700,000	4,300,000
Direct Labor	500,000	225,000	225,000	78,000	220,000	1,248,000
Direct Costs	2,100,000	1,100,000	1,050,000	378,000	920,000	5,548,000
Gross Margin	1,900,000	900,000	750,000	222,000	680,000	4,452,000
Product Work Activities	362,300	325,316	189,549	122,575	429,009	1,428,750
Gross Margin	1,537,700	574,684	560,451	99,425	250,991	3,023,250
Customer Work Activities	317,302	491,537	146,308	134,575	486,528	1,576,250
Gross Margin	1,220,397	83,147	414,143	(35,151)	(235,536)	1,447,000
Business Sustaining Activities						622,500
EBITDA						824,500
Interest Expense						187,500
Depreciation						201,282
Amortization						11,111
						399,893
Income Before Taxes						424,607
Income Taxes						148,612
Net Income						$275,995

Figure 10.4.   The Activity-Based Financial Statement.

level of activity. Costs are matched to products and segmented using value analysis to identify cost at the unit level, by batch level, and by business-sustaining level costs. Unit-level costs can be identified by activity and with cost drivers that can be tracked and will vary depending on workload demand. Batch-level costs will vary based on the volume of work, such as receiving and processing accounts payable invoices. Unit-level costs typically will be direct costs as shown in our model, and batch-level costs will be from processes occurring with standby departments and will relate to the volume of work flowing through the organization. There is a third category that relates to sustaining the business which includes corporate-related expenses that place demands on work activity but are not attributable to specific products or customers. An example of Model Manufacturing Company presenting an activity-based costing financial statement illustrating these components is provided in Figure 10.4.

Before leaving this section to describe the activity cost matrix, it is important to summarize and review activities and how they connect with business processes. Activities represent a verb plus noun description of what a company does. Some examples of activities are as follows:

- Receive raw material
- Move raw material
- Inspect incoming components
- Test components
- Process accounts payable invoices
- Ship customer orders
- Administrate tasks
- Process financial reports
- Perform setups
- Expedite material
- Train employees

There will be multiple processes within each function. Examples of processes within the financial function include:

- General ledger control
- Payroll
- Accounts receivable
- Accounts payable
- Cost accounting
- Cash management
- Financial reporting

The list could be expanded considerably and extended to other organizational functions. We should now begin to see how processes are a web of activities crossing departmental boundaries and functional borders. Envision processes as being a connected series of activities that consume a certain amount of resources, and the amount of resource consumed then represents the cost of each activity as presented in the example shown in Figure 10.5. The next section will provide examples from Model Manufacturing Company to illustrate the flow of costs from functional departments and functions to activities. By taking this concept a step further, it evolves into a demonstration of how activity costs flow to products and customers.

ACTIVITY COST MATRIX

Model Manufacturing Company was created to illustrate how data would look from different perspectives. The activity cost matrix summarizes the activities

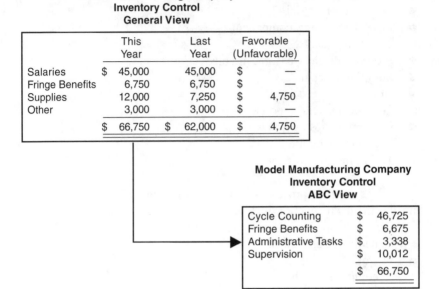

Model Manufacturing Company
Inventory Control
General View

	This Year	Last Year	Favorable (Unfavorable)
Salaries	$ 45,000	45,000	$ —
Fringe Benefits	6,750	6,750	$ —
Supplies	12,000	7,250	$ 4,750
Other	3,000	3,000	$ —
	$ 66,750	$ 62,000	$ 4,750

Model Manufacturing Company
Inventory Control
ABC View

Cycle Counting	$ 46,725
Fringe Benefits	$ 6,675
Administrative Tasks	$ 3,338
Supervision	$ 10,012
	$ 66,750

Figure 10.5. Value Analysis Template.

for each standby department of our model company to provide a clear comparison of the data. Each department and its activities are summarized together with the cost of each activity by department. The activity cost ties out to total standby expense. The percentage of time devoted to each activity within the department is determined in order to identify opportunities for reduction of nonvalue-added activities. This analysis should be done only for the operating expenses that we call standby and not for the production processes.

Direct production activities are documented in the enterprise resource planning (ERP) system, making it easier to access activity and process costs for analysis and improvement. The same concepts are pertinent in efforts to minimize nonvalue-added activities. A matrix was created to identify activity and process cost so that any changes in activity levels can be correlated to the level of expense. The matrix analysis facilitates trend format forecasting and establishes a basis for monitoring continuous improvement initiatives.

In many instances, business processes may require activities and tasks from more than one department. Once the cost of an activity has been established, the cost of processes can be developed. If the output quantities change or variation in department expense occurs, the activity costs will be different. These shifts will impact process costs, as will changes in the amount of nonvalue-added activities. Analysis and identification of activity and process costs form the foundation for continuous improvement efforts and identification of product and customer costs that provide for segmentation of profitability required for strategic and competitive analysis.

PRODUCT AND CUSTOMER PROFITABILITY MATRIX

Activity-based analysis allows organizations to view profitability by product, product segment, and by customer in greater depth than afforded by traditional cost analysis and throughput accounting. Operating expense or overhead, as previously mentioned, represents a growing percentage of the expenditure pie and greater significance in its strategic impact on profitability. Activity analysis was applied to Model Manufacturing Company to decompose standby expense by the five product lines. The matrix allows us to determine standby expense by product line.

Simply identifying standby expense with a product segment does not mean that eliminating the product segment will cause the associated standby expense to disappear. Reviewing the profit-focused accounting income statement for Model Manufacturing in Figure 10.4 provides useful insight for applying this application. My recommendation is to create a model of activity analysis that fits each company's business and industry situation. Development of such a model should become a key component of the continuous improvement effort. The model will first serve as a baseline for business processes, reflecting the "as is" current state, and then evolve to a "to be" future state model, indicating where and how to improve the effectiveness of the organization's businesses processes.

Continuous improvement should be the goal for activity analysis, whether the initiative is lean or Six Sigma, and the ultimate measurement should be bottom-line impact. The model that is offered is a fictional example and does not include all of the activity and task analysis refinements that should or could be employed to segments or that present profitability by product or by customer. Only by taking a consistent set of data and viewing it from multiple perspectives is it possible to gain a sound understanding of the possibilities. When this type of approach is followed, the shortcomings of traditional cost management become evident. The throughput accounting model is simple and creates the needed speed, but fails to provide the insight required to conduct strategic and competitive analysis *without understanding the impact of business processes buried in operating expense.* The activity-based analysis model should not be integrated into the accounting system as there are too many changes and variations that can and will occur that can send erroneous signals, creating inaccurate

Basis	Widget 1	Widget 2	Widget 3	Widget 4	Widget 5	Total
Units	5,000	5,000	2,000	2,000	5,000	
Selling Price	$ 10.00	$ 8.00	$ 6.00	$ 5.00	$ 4.00	
Sales	$ 50,000	$ 40,000	$ 12,000	$ 10,000	$ 20,000	$ 132,000
Direct Material	20,000	17,500	5,500	5,000	8,750	$ 56,750
Direct Labor	6,250	4,500	1,500	1,300	2,750	$ 16,300
Contribution — $	26,250	22,000	7,000	6,300	11,500	73,050
Contribution — %	53%	55%	58%	63%	58%	55%
Product Work Activities	4,529	6,506	1,264	2,043	5,363	19,704
Gross Margin	21,721	15,494	5,736	4,257	6,137	53,346
Customer Work Activities	3,966	9,831	975	2,243	6,082	23,097
Gross Margin	17,755	5,663	4,761	2,014	56	30,249
Business Sustaining Activities						8,217
EBITDA						$ 22,032

Figure 10.6.   Customer Profitability Analysis.

results. Monitoring the following components of the analysis model will help to determine if any revisions are necessary:

1. The mix of the number of employees or work activities changes
2. The distribution profile or mix of cost activities consuming resources changes
3. New activities developed or activities eliminated

The analysis and continuous modeling of business processes and the composition of their activities provides management with a better foundation for information used in strategic decision making when using formats based on the reporting model examples.

Segmenting customer work activities to the individual customer level can extend the capability of the activity cost matrix even further. A sample of customer profitability analysis is presented in Figure 10.6, showing where Model Manufacturing Company sold units of five different products. The example presents variable margin by product and then utilizes activity analysis to create the profit impact of product work activities and customer work activities based on the level of activity for the units of product sold. This shows how the complexity of customer work activity can be tracked to an individual customer or group of customers. Business-sustaining activities are presented as a total expense and not linked to an individual product. There can be different allocation methods of assigning business-sustaining activities, but for this example percentage of total sales is used as an indicator.

PROFIT-FOCUSED ANALYSIS: GETTING TO THE ROOT CAUSE

This is the ability to gain deeper understanding of how the business functions are enhanced by activity-based analysis. This tool is applied to peel away the layers of cost related to product work and customer work level activities, but the tools need to be applied continuously to all of the components of costs to locate all potential opportunities for improvement. The key is to determine the core problems and issues and fix them.

I advocate using the activity analysis model because it forces us to take new views of the business and its processes. Managers tend to forget that it is the processes that ultimately allow cash to flow. Creating focus using the profit-focused accounting and analysis tools clarifies "effect" so that the "cause" can be identified and corrected. Problems surface and continuous improvement teams then can apply effort to the causes by drilling down to the root causes. When problems are solved at their root levels, they can be eliminated.

Visibility creates a basis for action that generates meaningful results in terms of true bottom-line impact. Now we are not just looking at a traditional financial statement view of the business, but quantifying cost drivers. Cost driver analysis allows focus on fixing the 20 percent that achieves the 80 percent bottom-line impact. Lean and Six Sigma programs, without the benefit of root cause focus, made possible by application of activity analysis and continuous improvement programs, will not achieve the same level of results as they will by applying it.

Root cause analysis can lead down different roads with different destinations. Excessive costs and waste lose meaning without the visibility created by using all of the tools. For example, pricing decisions, scrap levels, raw material quality, skilled workers, and other multiple factors impact contribution margins. The root cause of additional expediting activity in quality control and production control might well be pinpointed to late deliveries from vendors. Symptoms of root causes might relate to any number of different factors. Activity-based analysis provides the visibility and the foundation for improving processes.

PROFIT-FOCUSED IMPROVEMENT

The tools for conducting analysis activity and identifying activities in terms of value added and nonvalue added have been provided and explained. Emphasis has been on continuous improvement and getting to the root causes and eliminating them to achieve permanent versus temporary improvement results. There have been a number of improvement programs, and the latest rage has been lean strategies combined with Six Sigma. These initiatives are all directed at improving or innovating business and productive processes. Our profit-focused accounting model utilizes the Theory of Constraints (TOC) to place a bottom-line measurement for all of these programs. The model provides a clear view of the bottom line and applies the analytical tools to measure the effect from cost drivers.

Continuous improvement needs to incorporate a definition of "getting better at what." TOC and its thinking process can aid significantly in creating the level of profit improvement focus needed to get the most from activity-based analysis and related improvement initiatives. Also, the emphasis on making a profit as part of a continuous improvement effort requires that measurement reflect real cash flow from profitability. Continuous improvement programs typically concentrate on making business processes more effective and on reducing activity cost within the process. Operating in a new world of excellence requires better organization and better learning, in addition to better quality and service. Continuous improvement must relate to all of the processes that are driven by the organization, and that should encompass policies and procedures together with commercial processes, in addition to optimization of production and quality. Improvement embraces all elements of the organization including management from the top down.

The determination of what the organization wants to achieve needs to permeate the pursuit of excellence. There is a tendency for too much emphasis on isolated metrics in contrast to the creation of an understanding of how programs cascade down to the bottom line. The linkages created by cost drivers and captured through our model using activity-based analysis in conjunction with throughput accounting provide cause and effect impact on profitability. Our model, utilizing the Pareto rule (80/20), will provide reasonable relevance to what actually is occurring. It is only necessary to maintain one set of books, not two, in order to create a foundation of operationally focused process thinking capable of drilling down to net income. The profit-focused accounting reporting model is effective at clarifying and presenting general ledger data with multiple views and from the perspective of throughput and process activity by product and customer. Activity-based analysis creates useful signals of the efficiency of processes and profitability by product and customer.

It is one thing to have the tools and another to use them effectively. Activity-based analysis provides us with measurement of activities, processes, and how resources are consumed by cost objects whether they are products, services, or other activities. Improvement does not occur until an organization moves from the stage of analysis to taking action and making changes in the way activities and processes function. It is only when changes are implemented that improvements are realized. Target improvements typically attempt to strengthen the effectiveness of primary activities and eliminate or diminish the impact of secondary activities within business processes. Activities that are nonvalue adding are carefully scrutinized for ways to either reduce their cost or to eliminate them.

In many instances, real improvement does not occur until breakthrough solutions are developed and innovations to processes are created, whereby they are completely revamped. A good example is how robust design and design for Six Sigma change the way products are manufactured and services are provided. Continuous improvement programs typically mention tools such as cause and effect diagramming, Pareto analysis, and 5 whys technique. TOC thinking process tools should also be considered since they offer unique ways to achieve organizational buy in that will enable continuous process efforts to make breakthrough improvements at the management level.

All continuous improvement, no matter what it is called, requires mapping business processes. From this starting point, management and business process owners can identify possibilities for making improvements. They then have to decide what to change and what the changes will create. From this point, they must then determine how to best implement the process changes. Activity-based analysis and the other analytical tools will provide the predictive result of the improvements. The next step is to measure and monitor the impact of the continuous programs in terms of real profitability.

MEASURING AND MONITORING IMPROVEMENT

Activity analysis provides visibility and clarity that will not create value unless ongoing effort to improve the effectiveness of business processes is monitored to see how well improvement efforts are progressing. A good example is how doctors monitor blood pressure and other diagnostic data to evaluate a patient's progress. Considerable emphasis has been directed to manufacturing operations with lean and Six Sigma to improve cycle time and quality levels and reduce inventory levels. Just as much, and perhaps more, opportunity exists for improving commercial activities and business processes by using activity analysis tools and applying them to customer-related cost drivers.

Measuring and monitoring improvement requires documentation of a baseline or starting point and then tracking progress at appropriate intervals on a consistent and regular basis. The frequency and detail of measurement and level of monitoring will be different in each organization. It is necessary to take the measurement to the respective activity level to create responsibility at the point where the activity occurs and by the people creating the activity. This may be on the shop floor or in the sales office where they are processing customer orders. It should not be remote measurement by a consultant, but measurement by empowered employees continuously improving their activities and processes. In addition to measurement at the source, it is critical that overall profitability is measured and monitored in a simplistic way that is understandable. It is important that the employees involved with the ongoing improvement efforts be able to monitor the results.

I provided formats for top-level measurement utilizing profit-focused accounting application of throughput accounting and activity-based management analysis. In addition to the financial statement reporting formats, organizations should consider creating a spreadsheet analysis listing each major activity and reconciling the total cost of the activity with the general ledger. This analysis could also show the cost of value activity and the cost of nonvalue activities together with output quantities and the cost per output. This measurement provides a platform for action when a cost is assigned as to what actually occurs. This is when management needs to understand that 80 percent accuracy is okay since 100 percent will not be attainable.

Measurement requires knowing what to measure. I have provided dashboard charts that can be accessed on a desktop computer using Excel which are available for download at www.jrosspub.com. The download templates provide dashboard charts that can be customized for appropriate time intervals and multiple metrics. They can be used as a statistical process control dashboard where actual occurrences are plotted against the upper and lower control limits for the process as well as the target for the process. The dashboards can also be used for monitoring root cause quantities. There are many different graphical presentation options. Those offered in the download templates represent only one of many possibilities.

DYNAMIC OPTIMIZATION: MANAGING CAPACITY

The tools for analyzing activities help organizations to understand the capacity of their business processes together with the activities that occur within them. Analytical models historically have taken many companies so much time and effort that they become obsolete before their true potential can be realized. The key to success in applying the profit-focused accounting model is the realization that a practical approach is needed to measure and manage the capacity of the organization's resources.

Effectiveness does not require 99.9997 percent accuracy because organizations are fluid and the load shifts depending on the types of transactions that occur within the business processes. We need to be sufficiently close to being right and, in realizing this, begin to understand that lengthy reworking of activity models is not required to deliver effectiveness from activity-based analysis. Direct production processes are monitored by the ERP system, as are many of the transactional cost drivers that occur within the commercial processes. By using these data and estimating the practical capacity of resources, it is possible to get a good handle on the unit time required for performing each activity.

Application of time-based activity analysis using the concept of "it is better to be 80 percent right today than 100 percent right tomorrow" allows companies to determine the practical capacity of all their activities. Once capacity is determined, organizations can evaluate their ability to take on increased demands. They are also able to understand the effectiveness of their continuous improvement effort.

A TOC element has been included in our model because of its focus on throughput. The throughput focus requires identification of the constraint, and time-based activity analysis gives an excellent fix on the practical capacity of resources and what they cost. TOC tools combined with Six Sigma programs or lean strategies and continuous programs will change activity cost drivers. It is critical that businesses gain understanding of which products and which customers consume more than their share of unused capacity and which products and consumers need more capacity. Combining the benefits of throughput accounting and activity-based analysis yields information that is critical to managing capacity and focusing it on the right products and on the right customers. Proper use of these tools produces information that management can use to achieve breakthrough profitability relative to competitors.

PROFIT-FOCUSED PROCESSES

The key to realizing the full benefit from profit-focused accounting lies in the speed and simplicity of creating models. Having a trend format model that allows tracking of volume and contribution is one of the ways that focus is directed at processes and production capacity. Contribution by product and customers is more readily accessible to the managers who need this information. By creating more agile models of activities and processes in standby, we are in a much better position to manage up- and downstream from the constraint.

The reporting model offered assumes that the activity-based segmentation of standby expense ties out to the general ledger. We already have nonfinancial metrics, so creating additional situations where profit numbers do not reconcile will diminish the effectiveness of the model. Once a solid and practical standby process and activity model is created, the key is to understand when changes and improvement efforts indicate a need to recalculate activity times and organizational capacity. This should not be a calendar-driven revision, but rather necessary updates should be based on shifts in the capacity and cost of the resources. While resources typically relate to people and their activities and tasks, there are many situations where technology and equipment shift the capacity of the organization. Maximizing throughput from the capacity of the organization is a driving force of TOC where the goal is to improve profitability continuously over both the long and short term.

While I have spent time discussing the need to create simple activity cost models, it is important to comment that this task will be made easier by using project accounting and charging work orders for exactly the amount of resource they consume. We already charge direct labor and material using standard routings and bills of material. Project costing or accounting can be applied to multiple areas to increase the accuracy and meaningfulness of data. Some examples include product development, process development, and marketing projects.

The advent of Six Sigma has created a new awareness of quality and its impact on profitability. This awareness has been further elevated because of the Sarbanes-Oxley Act passed in 2002. Section 404 of the act requires that publicly traded companies will need to increase their emphasis on having solid process controls in place to guard against the cost of warranty returns resulting from poor quality. This will force extra precaution and steps to ensure that solid processes are in place to provide error-free products. Management will require assurance and not just hunches that the figures are accurate. This provides additional support for activity-based analysis to remove root causes to prevent internal and external failure. The Sarbanes-Oxley Act is discussed in Chapter 12; its inclusion underscores the importance of activity and process analysis.

PROCESS-FOCUSED FORECASTING

Process-focused forecasting starts with trend format statements that direct attention to future results based on the latest actual results and best estimate of subsequent months. We have developed the ability to create time-related activity-based models of organizational capacity that have a solid level of practical reliability. Anyone involved with forecasting will always indicate that a forecast is never going to be right. We have at least created a method that will allow us to be predictive, which frequently provides a significant competitive edge. This approach to profit-focused accounting is to significantly expand on the proven tool of sales and operational planning. The new competitive environment requires greater emphasis on planning and executing strategy. Cost management historically has placed excessive emphasis on lag indicators in contrast to lead indicators that provide better feedback about current reality and the future.

Our ERP systems have been further enhanced by CRM (customer relationship management) and APS (advance planning and scheduling) systems. We have better and more current data about customer demands and orders that are being placed. Businesses will be driven by Sarbanes-Oxley to get back to basics regarding the accuracy of routings, inventory quantities, bills of material, customer service, and shop-floor control and performance. APS has the capability to reschedule and processing orders that was never possible from weekly running of material requirements planning. When this flood of current data is fed into reliable systems, businesses can quite easily provide trend format versions of sales and contribution by product and customer. We also will know the status of productive processes, critical constrained resources, and shipping buffers.

One of the real purposes of adding activity-based analysis capability to our reporting and forecasting model is because of its predictive potential and the power it provides. By using the effectiveness of predicting the impact of positive and negative fluctuation on commercial and business processes (standby expense), we can now gain improved understanding of change straight to the bottom line. No longer is budgeting necessary because we can apply different strategic scenarios and engage process owners and empowered employees in meaningful continuous profit improvement. Trend format balanced scorecards will be introduced in the next chapter as the concept is expanded to execution of strategy.

The key to activity analysis success is to involve employees. They need to participate in the analysis and to monitor their improvement through self-measurement. When everyone becomes a stakeholder and is knowledgeable regarding the creation of practical and reliable models of activity costs, there is renewed reliability of the definition of true capacity. Employees who have participated in regularly monitoring their improvement efforts will be capable of updating the model for events that might shift or change process capacity dramatically. My views on how to improve the sales and operations planning model is discussed in the final chapter. The key here is to realize that integration of activity-based analysis together with the approach to throughput accounting allows for new possibilities in predictive accounting and continuous process improvement.

11

SIMPLIFYING STRATEGY USING BALANCED SCORECARDS

Focusing profit requires focusing the strategy that drives the economic engine of the organization. Strategy is a critical concept for success, and in too many organizations it is not defined, let alone executed with precision. We have seen many claims by experts espousing their strategic approach to lean strategies, Six Sigma strategy, the Theory of Constraints, and activity-based management. None of these tools work unless they are implemented and the organization is capable of executing the selected action steps toward the goal. The void created by traditional cost measurement led to nonfinancial performance measures. The *Balanced Scorecard* by Robert S. Kaplan and David P. Norton, written in the mid-1990s, brought visibility to this movement and helped many companies fill the void left by traditional cost management and measurement. This tool showed how to create a scorecard containing financial and nonfinancial measurements and ways to build a feedback and learning system. This helped companies translate strategy into action. There was, and still is, work to be done to help organizations understand and embrace the balanced scorecard tools to achieve effective strategic focus.

There are thousands of companies that find that the ability to execute strategy quickly and effectively is imperative for their success and survival. The concept of balanced scorecards was described in Chapter 7 to provide the groundwork for creating a baseline level of understanding. This foundation will be expanded to offer further insight on ways to apply and use this tool. I identify it is one of the *enabler* tools that should be carried in the profit-focused accounting tool kit.

UNDERSTANDING VALUE PROPOSITIONS

Value propositions define the experience that customers will receive from an organization's value delivery system and the ultimate relationship developed with the customer. It could be stated more simply as what a company gets for what it gives. This translates into multiple factors that include product, price, place, or service selection. In strategic and competitive terms, it boils down to why the customers should buy from you and how you satisfy the customer. It is frequently good strategically, but worthless unless the proposition can be implemented effectively.

Organizations must first identify the product or service they offer, who they sell it to, and the effectiveness of their ability to deliver it. This is a three-step approach to segmenting what a company gets for what it gives. Kaplan and Norton state, "75 percent of executive teams do not have a clear consensus around the customer proposition." They define the three steps for segmenting strategy as:

1. Product leadership
2. Customer intimacy
3. Operational excellence

In following a strategy of differentiation, it is critical for organizations to be capable of holding their own in all three of these areas, but they must find a niche by excelling in at least one of the areas. A good example is Dell Computer's attainment of operational excellence while still matching or exceeding competitors in product leadership and customer relationship. This allows Dell to set selling prices that enable it to capture a lion's share of the computer market. This was possible because of its effective supply chain execution, order entry, and quality levels that set it above and beyond the competition.

Understanding the value proposition is critical for all organizations if they are to take advantage of executing strategy by using a balanced scorecard approach. Evaluating and measuring the effectiveness of an organization through some assessment evaluation should be the first step in the strategic process. Unfortunately, we see too many companies plodding along preferring to do it wrong, rather than make the effort and apply the resources required to do it right. The assessment or self-evaluation should carefully consider the product and service attributes of value proposition and an equation that should include price, time, effort, quality, functionality, and selection. The equation should also include consideration of brand recognition and product superiority.

SEGMENTING THE VALUE CHAIN

When conducting the assessment, an organization should consider its value chain and its composition. *The Strategy Focused Organization,* by Robert S. Kaplan and David P. Norton, segmented the value chain into the following four internal business processes:

- Innovative processes
- Customer management processes
- Operational processes
- Regulatory and environmental processes

Another way of looking at segmentation might be materials (procurement and supplier relations), research and development, manufacturing, marketing, distribution, and service. The strategy of an organization will require these processes to execute it. Strategy measurement is dependent on understanding the focus of where an organization wants to establish differentiation. Product leadership is dependent on the speed at which new products or services are developed and how fast they are introduced to market. If operational excellence is the strategy focus, as in Dell's instance, then effective production scheduling, quality, and cost management will be the strategy drivers. Each organization will have a different focus.

Creating a value proposition that changes the competitive landscape of the playing field of an organization and shifts the rules in its favor is the objective of strategy. Whatever choices an organization makes or does not make with respect to its activities builds the processes within the value chain. In the previous chapter, we saw how activities consumed resources and produced cost objects, either services or products. These outputs are measurable, as were the costs of the activities and processes. We need to identify the strategic drivers within the value chain and the component processes that feed them. Lead and lag indicators within this framework will provide the measures of the strategy mapped out by an organization.

MAPPING AND MEASURING STRATEGY

The concept of balanced scorecards is to capture the strategy and provide a blueprint of the steps an organization needs to take to execute its vision. The

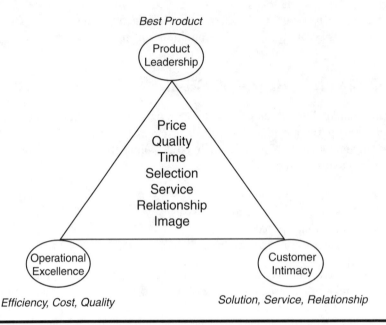

Figure 11.1. Profile of the Value Proposition.

strategy execution steps represent how the organization will turn the vision into reality. The best way to understand this concept is in simple terms as shown in Figure 11.1, which presents the strategic direction of the vision and profile of the value proposition. The value proposition envisioned by the organization must define its products, its customers, its market segments, and its geographic market. The blueprint, which we will call the strategy map, must respond to the question of what are the right things the organization needs to do and how to do these things right. The strategy map will document how to balance the emphasis of the value proposition among the three sectors of excellence aligned with processes comprising the value chain. Building the strategy map helps not only to provide clarity of the organization's strategy, but also identifies the cause and effect relationship associated with executing the strategy.

For the most part, determining the strategy at a higher level is not the problem as the CEO may have identified but not articulated it. Communication of the strategy throughout the organization and having all the oars pulled in unison is a frequent problem. I have conducted many operational assessments and when interviewing the executive team and key employees found that they had no idea where the boss really wanted to go. Furthermore, rarely did anyone devote time to working on the business. The time was always spent working

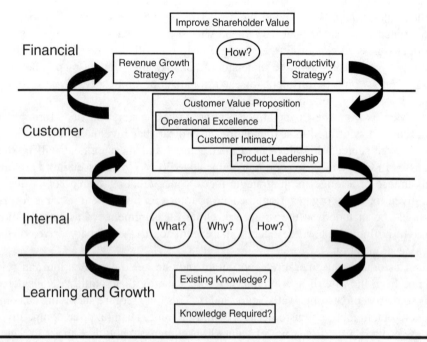

Figure 11.2. The Strategy Map Concept.

in the business. A positive step can be made by any organization by mapping its strategy following the general format outlined and identifying the cause and effect linkage required to accomplish it.

Strategy begins with customers and defining the value proposition. Figure 11.2 provides the key elements from shareholder metrics all the way down to the employees who will ultimately be responsible for turning the strategic vision into reality. The map should paint a picture of what the organization should look like, then drill down to what the respective employees responsible for execution need to do in order to make the picture become a reality. By identifying strategic drivers, the map will include outlining the strategic paths for the trip including checkpoints along the way. The strategic drivers and strategic paths associated with the customer value proposition, internal processes, and employee skill and work environment will provide executable steps to achieve shareholder value.

Balanced scorecards should not become a way to just group financial and nonfinancial key performance measurements, as the real impact of the tool is lost if that is the result. The strategy will become much clearer as the organization team, from top to bottom and from bottom to top, decides how to shape the strategy map. By utilizing the map, strategy becomes everyone's job. The next step is to assign metrics that provide solid feedback at all levels on the effectiveness of executing the strategic vision. I will provide some guidelines on metrics, but it should be understood that, like the strategy maps, the measurements would be different for each organization and especially at different levels of the organization.

Metrics from the financial perspective will be easier, and since throughput accounting is offered as a foundation, it is clear that revenue and profit must be on the scorecard. Value-based management and measurement will be discussed in Chapter 12, so economic value added (EVA™) is essential to provide assurance of a longer term strategic focus. Since creating shareholder value is a given for every organization, measuring return on investment in some format should be included on the scorecard. Other measurements of asset utilization might be important where operational excellence is the primary driver of the value proposition.

Customer value measurements might include customer retention and revenue from the sale of new products. Another metric that should be considered is some sort of customer satisfaction index. This may require surveying customers to obtain input on customer perception of value. Data on price competitiveness provide a hard measure of value. Every attempt should be made to determine how your nearest competitor's prices compare to yours. Prompt delivery time may be an important factor in impacting the customer's perception of value. It is also a measure of the effectiveness of your organization's ability to execute and achieve the desired level of operational excellence. Any analysis of the competitive situation should include estimates of the market and your company's share of it.

I have discussed measurements of excellence in the chapters on lean manufacturing and Six Sigma. Chapter 13 is completely focused on performance measurements and how to determine them. However, I should emphasize that cycle time, quality, rework, and on-time delivery could be critical scorecard measures. In the previous chapter, a range of activity-based cost driver metrics were discussed that could be incorporated into the scorecard. They can include production work-level activities as well as customer work-level activities. Their selection will depend on the strategy that the organizational team selects and in what industry the organization operates.

Frequently, strategy will involve the transformation of intangible or knowledge assets as a key component of the strategy. The strategy team will need to assess the inventory of skills and knowledge of its workforce and identify metrics that correlate to transferring these assets into tangible results. Some of the information might necessitate determining the technological capability of

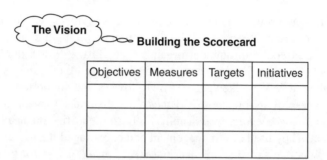

Figure 11.3. The Strategy Scorecard.

the organization, such as the effectiveness of the enterprise resource planning system and the quality of people running it, in addition to the accuracy of data within the system. Serious deficiencies in utilizing the system might require a major retraining effort of existing employees or hiring new personnel who have the required level of knowledge.

The key to mapping strategy is to simplify it so everybody understands what enables effective execution. Once the strategy is understood and mapped in clear terms, then matching measurements should be a fairly easy next step. Figure 11.3 provides a format for building the scorecard. In reviewing some of the approaches taken in many of the balanced scorecard case studies offered, the most successful initiatives met the simplicity test. Employees understood the strategy and further understood how the scorecards should be used to keep on track and maintain momentum. The strategy map templates that I offer contain the key elements using a simpler approach and drilling down to the components, which will make it easier to understand how the pieces fit and flow together.

A LEAN SIX SIGMA STRATEGIC FOCUS

In earlier chapters, we looked at lean manufacturing and saw how it has become a strategy of its own. It is customer focused and applies continuous improvement to increase the effectiveness of operational processes. Six Sigma has been touted as a breakthrough management strategy. Activity-based costing, while not a strategic thrust, has consumed and continues to take a significant effort in order to be effective throughout organizations. In the 1980s, the Theory of Constraints (TOC) entered the management playing field, offering its own strategic drumbeat. EVA™, likewise, has its followers and supporters who praise the effectiveness of its impact. *Relevance Lost* (Thomas Johnson and Robert Kaplan) and *Relevance Regained* (Thomas Johnson) clarified the need for better measurement. They used cost management and encouraged the use of nonfinancial metrics that we saw documented in *The Balanced Scorecard* by Robert S. Kaplan and David P. Norton. What is evolving is a growing tool kit overflowing with capability that can lead to questions and skepticism about what to do, what to use, and what we should do. Each organization will have to make its decisions on what is best for it. Based on my experience, and research of learning and understanding of how all these initiatives fit, I have developed some clear thoughts about what and what not to do.

Lean Six Sigma strategy is grouped together because it has impact on creating a strategic focus in similar ways. I characterize lean more in achieving operational excellence in the customer proposition than with customer intimacy and product leadership. Driving out waste from all facets of organizational processes supports operational excellence within the internal perspective segment of the scorecard. While much of the lean effort is undertaken from a customer orientation, it probably is not a strategy, but more a tactical component of a strategy.

I suggest using the balanced scorecard approach to executing strategy and make lean manufacturing part of the strategy. By including lean manufacturing as an element of the operational excellence component of the customer proposition, it will create a platform for buy in from the entire organization. The lean program would be part of the scorecard measures under the internal perspective segment of the strategy map. Including lean as part of an organization-wide strategy execution program provides assurance that all the critical steps associated with lean programs receive the necessary attention. Lean programs generate a lot of excitement in the area of manufacturing flow, but process control, metrics, and logistics tend not to receive adequate attention.

Six Sigma as a strategy received a lot of press because of Motorola, Allied Signal, GE, and other visible corporations. Again, there are components of Six Sigma that are critical tactical elements of the strategic vision, but organizationally they will not guarantee execution of strategy. The Six Sigma argument, that it is a strategy, is that reduction of defects in industrial and commercial processes provides companies with a competitive edge. Again, Six Sigma should be considered under the concept of strategy execution provided by the scorecard methodology for the same logic offered for lean manufacturing initiatives. Since Six Sigma provides process control, I would urge that these same types of controls be applied in conjunction with lean manufacturing.

Six Sigma provides direction on how to develop breakthrough ideas for processes as well as the development of new products. Six Sigma projects can contribute to all three components of the value proposition, but it is not a complete answer for mapping the entire strategy. Again, having Six Sigma scorecards will help to integrate the initiative and ensure overall execution of the organizational strategic vision. Some smaller organizations might find that the proportional amount of training prescribed may not be cost justified. A balanced scorecard approach to the inclusion of a Six Sigma approach to control lean initiatives could clearly work where the strategy was embedded from top to bottom and vice versa.

While my ideas on how to use balanced scorecards are applicable to organizations of all sizes, they may be of greater assistance to smaller companies that might either not know about this method of focusing strategy or think it only works for larger companies. The basis for this hypothesis rests on the strategic competencies and technological strength of smaller organizations. Frequently, their competitive survival hinges on leveraging a differentiated strategy, and they may lack the organizational understanding and resources to employ lean Six Sigma tools and lack the sophistication to think and execute them strategically. Once they understand the balanced scorecard approach, they can use it to maximize their existing knowledge assets and internal competencies and to articulate their value proposition and strategy. From this understanding, they can then develop an awareness of the additional tools needed to execute the value proposition and strategy. Since smaller organizations are not as likely to address the strategic issues, they will need to align and communicate the call to action in order to achieve more effective strategic execution than larger competitors. The balanced scorecard umbrella will allow these smaller companies to take advantage of the lean and Six Sigma tool kits and techniques because they can utilize the learning capability more fully at all levels of the organization. Cultural shifts are difficult in any organization, but I believe it will be easier to achieve the level of motivation and alignment of the workforce in a smaller and less complex structure. Applying the framework of a strategy-focused organization can leverage the speed and agility afforded smaller companies. Applying the TOC concepts and principles can further accelerate this leverage. It is my hypothesis that when these components are combined with the development of a value proposition and application of lean Six Sigma, breakthrough achievements that are capable of producing spectacular financial performance should be possible.

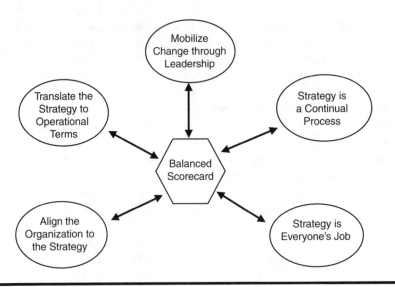

Figure 11.4.   Strategic Alignment.

LINKAGE AND ALIGNMENT

It is one thing for organizations to settle on a strategy and yet another to put it into action successfully. The strategic process needs to identify what resources will be required to execute the strategy and who will consume those resources. This step of the process is strategic alignment and can be visualized by reviewing Figure 11.4 to see where the key components needed for execution of the strategy are focused around the central theme of the strategy.

"Alignment" is putting the components together so they can be coordinated to work toward the accomplishment of the strategic objectives. The balanced scorecard provides focus to the organization's strategy. Imagine looking through the lens of a camera and then bringing that lens into focus to create a crystal-clear picture of the future. It is a lot like using activity-based analysis to look at the general ledger data from a process perspective. When the entire organization has a clear and accurate understanding, it becomes significantly easier to hit the target. When the scorecard approach is combined with the profit-focused accounting model that offers greater clarity, an organization gains better understanding of its profit target and how to align the resources required to achieve it.

If alignment is creating focus of all an organization's resources needed for strategic success, then linkage is how the organization determine who needs to do what. Linkage of all the strategic themes across multiple business units is a challenge. The scorecard becomes a powerful framework for bringing together all the required components for more effective organizational focus. Linkage extends further than just being architecture for complex multiunit corporate structures; it is crucial in every organization.

Organizational architecture is a good way to view the scorecard. Strategies require a foundation for achieving common understanding among all the functional areas, departments, and employees to execute the strategy effectively. The scorecard linkages can be mapped to join together the causes and effects of the strategic themes and the metrics that provide the required feedback to achieve breakthrough results. Each organization needs to create the linkage connections best suited to fit its culture and strategy.

ORGANIZATIONAL ALIGNMENT

Achieving organizational alignment is a critical step in building strategic focus and making it work. A good example of what organizational alignment entails is similar to mapping business processes in an "as is" state and then understanding ways they can be improved by creating a "to be" map. This represents how the scorecards can be used to connect the resource components to be employed to the strategic vision developed from the value proposition. After the resources are aligned with strategy, the next stage of alignment is to link to the people who will consume resources to execute the value proposition. The scorecards become a mapping process by tracking the resource consumption for all of the four levels of perspective to build a strategic foundation that becomes a comprehensive plan.

The strategic foundation will contain many different building blocks that comprise the functional and support units of the business. By linking and mapping this web of building blocks using a communication and planning process, it will be possible to identify the critical resources that will be needed for strategic success. This is a step that links the strategic priorities through a top-down and bottom-up process and then aligns them into a format to create the visibility and synergy required to achieve the strategic vision. Evaluation of the strategic priorities determines what knowledge skills are needed, the necessary technology and equipment and where it needs to be applied, and who will be responsible for the logistics, management, and execution of the plan. This step of aligning the strategic priorities with resources and linking them together will then provide a basis for selecting the scorecard metrics best suited for creating and successfully maintaining strategic focus for the organization.

CAPTURING STRATEGY

In *The Strategy-Focused Organization,* Kaplan and Norton stated, "less than 5 percent of the typical workforce understands their organization's strategy." My observations from operational assessments conducted over the years support their statement. In today's economic environment, businesses must find ways to improve communication so that employees know where they are going and why they are going there. Employees represent the most valuable asset in the organization and they are not even reflected on the balance sheet. Until these assets have a way of understanding the strategic priorities of the organization, the returns earned will be significantly lower than comparative organizations that have strategically empowered their employees. The scorecard process provides an effective tool for organizations to capture their strategy so employees have an understanding of where they are going and how to monitor their progress.

The learning and growth component is where much of the real benefits of balanced scorecards are achieved and what allows employees to gain the necessary understanding required for breakthrough achievement. The first thing that needs to be instituted is an effective communication program so employees, at all levels, understand the strategic priorities. When understanding is enabled, then buy in to the strategy becomes a possibility. We will enhance the commonly known tools for achieving buy in through the application of TOC and the thinking process. Also, the continuous improvement achieved through activity-based costing and management employs powerful tools that can greatly leverage the impact of a balanced scorecard program.

The real key to capturing strategy is when it is executed effectively. This is where balanced scorecard measurement sends regular feedback to all levels of the organization that results are being achieved. Measurements that best fit the strategy are selected for each component of the strategic foundation, making strategy an ongoing component of how the business is run on a daily basis. Strategy becomes real and understandable in contrast to a corporate vision that never has left the boardroom. When addressing the issues of many smaller companies that never have conducted any sort of strategic planning initiative, the balanced scorecard tools can provide a very powerful framework for achievement that they have never experienced before.

When employees understand the concept of capturing the organization's strategy at all levels, then creation and development of a strategy map becomes an exciting process. A sample strategy map outline is shown in Figure 11.2. While this is a hypothetical illustration, it provides a simple outline showing how to connect the strategic priorities and themes within each of the four

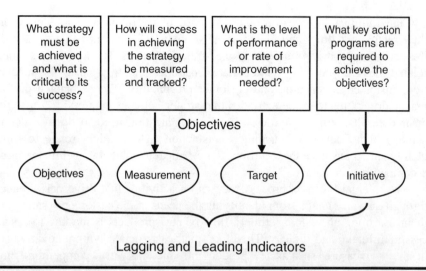

Figure 11.5. The Strategy Map: Cause and Effect Relationships.

perspectives. It demonstrates how the measurements might be selected at the four different levels.

MEASURING LEAD AND LAG

Lead and lag relates to whether a measurement is associated with the cause or the effect of an outcome. Outcomes are reported by lag metrics and are frequently financial measures. In a strategic sense, as defined by Michael Porter, "it means deliberately choosing a different set of activities to deliver a unique mix of value." This means that the strategic success depends on how effectively the mix of activities is executed. The organization determines the mix by making choices that become articulated in the plan as to the desired outcome and how it will be accomplished. Lag indicators such as revenue, profit, and return on investment will measure the outcome. Lead indicators will be associated with the activities responsible for creating the outcome. Lag indicators are outcome measures and lead indicators are performance drivers. The flow of the cause and effect of factors influencing these performance drivers is presented in Figure 11.5.

The typical core outcome indicators relate to profitability, market share, customer satisfaction, customer retention, and employee skills. Financial metrics deal with outcomes such as revenue, cost reduction, and asset utilization. Strategy must ultimately focus on outcome, particularly financial outcomes. From the strategic outcomes and mapping the strategy, it is then possible to identify the performance drivers unique to the strategic themes developed. Customer-related metrics would be market share, customer retention, customer acquisition, customer satisfaction, and customer profitability. The associated performance drivers relate to the activities that strategically are required to cause the desired results. What activities does the organization need to do in order to achieve higher levels of customer satisfaction? These might relate to time, quality, and price since these attributes are critical to achieving and maintaining a competitive advantage.

The internal business process focuses on activities that drive performance through the value chain, from identifying the needs of the customer to satisfying them. Ensuring an ongoing, timely flow of new products is the key to a successful differentiated strategy. Therefore, metrics associated with innovation are desired — measures such as new product introductions versus competitors, time to develop new products, and number of projects categorized as designed for Six Sigma. Hewlett-Packard uses BET (breakeven time) to measure breakeven on research and development projects in addition to monitoring the time to recover the investment using time to market and how long it takes to break even on the project after products are released to manufacturing. Other internal process measures include cycle time and product quality in terms of defects. Measurements of the efficiency and effectiveness of customer service might be candidates for the scorecard depending on the strategy.

Measurements for financial, customer, and internal processes are somewhat easier to understand and develop. Determining what employees need to do in order to execute the strategic priorities is more challenging. Yet if an organization is to be successful, it needs to understand what level of strategic knowledge employees possess, if deficiencies or shortfalls exist, and determine what and how much training is required. It is a process of measuring skills, capabilities, and knowledge at all levels of the organization. Some measurements include hours of training, strategic competency availability indexes, employee attitude surveys, and number of suggestions per employee. Other challenges include developing compensation programs such as gain sharing and employee stock ownership plans. In some instances, employees develop personal balanced scorecards to ensure buy in and communication as well as strategic alignment.

Finding the proper performance drivers or lead indicators is integral to strategic success. Chapter 13 is devoted to performance measurements, how to determine and interpret them. The answers do not lie in finding the twenty metrics and filling in four categories of different perspectives. Finding the right balance of measurements relative to the organization's strategy and getting everyone in the game is the objective.

TOC-ENABLED SCORECARDS

The balanced scorecard is applied to create a strategy-focused organization, and its methodology evolved from the failure of traditional cost management and activity-based costing to fill all the gaps. The use of nonfinancial metrics combined with financial measures came together on a series of scorecards. They are used to drive strategic performance through a process of strategic thinking communicated throughout the organization. Since the objective of this book is to make use of the best management tools available, I have assembled them to achieve better understanding and performance execution at all levels of the organization. After evaluating all the management philosophies and methodologies, there seemed to be an opportunity that had not been exploited. One of the best tools I have seen is TOC, yet even its own disciples have been frustrated with its lack of acceptance in much of the corporate world. Conversely, while *The Balanced Scorecard* and *The Strategy-Focused Organization* have made inroads and achieved success, there are untold numbers of companies that are totally unaware of how to communicate and execute their strategic vision.

The strategic thinking processes of TOC were designed and developed to help management create and implement strategic-level breakthrough solutions. Balanced scorecards are tackling the same issues. It is my thought that when the two concepts are merged, more effective understanding and acceptance will be achieved. Both philosophies and methodologies utilize the value proposition as a key component for addressing strategic issues, and the simplicity of the throughput concept will help for faster and more effective implementation of strategic solutions.

The Jonah process focuses on effective ways to identify and solve strategic dilemmas and offers tools that gain the buy in across functional levels of an organization. One of the areas where the scorecard processes break down is in learning and growth. The Jonah process allows individuals to achieve the clarity and focus in common-sense application that achieves buy in and understanding. The Jonah process also provides for construction of implementation plans that can work well using the scorecards as tools and feedback mechanisms.

The second level of the strategic thinking process is the ability to facilitate cross-functional organizational agreement at multiple levels. The silo structure that permeates business organizations gets bogged down with regularity, and

TOC provides effective tools that can create consensus and commitment for solving problems and executing solutions. This is also the objective of balanced scorecards, yet organizations find progress slowed or stopped because they could not fully harness the power of their tools. When TOC tools are applied in conjunction with balanced scorecards, then breakthrough solutions to functional dilemmas can become even more powerful. Conversely, where balanced scorecards have gained management acceptance, it only stands to reason that effective demonstration of the TOC constraints process will add visibility and momentum for better acceptance of both concepts.

Finally, when we consider that strategy is all about choices directed to how to best accomplish the organization's goals, then combining strategy execution with the external constraints process should represent a win-win opportunity. TOC provides better tools for addressing complex situations to resolve core conflicts by creating more effective value propositions for both parties, either partners or customers. Overcoming external constraints is exactly what the scorecard approach is attempting. In my opinion, adding scorecards to TOC and vice versa is like putting high-octane fuel in the tank to achieve greater leverage and much better performance. TOC gains the use of the scorecard approach, plus expands its own potential for success without having to reinvent the wheel. It is no different than vastly improving the effectiveness of throughput accounting with activity-based analysis.

THE CASCADE EFFECT

The cascade effect might be better called the awareness effect. Because of the tendency of organizations to have unawareness of strategy and what it means, communication is critical. This is especially true for programs that are designed to execute the strategy. If the organizational team knows what the strategy is and its role in making it a reality, then the chances for successful execution improve dramatically. Knowing and understanding is only the first step of a long process. The creation of a cascade effect is like water flowing down from the top of a mountain. Scorecards and the signals they convey represent a vehicle to help employees understand what they need to do to fulfill their respective missions.

If the scorecards are developed in alignment with the strategy map and the value proposition, they provide a framework for the organization to understand the strategy. That is the first hurdle, and just because the corporate vision is posted in the lobby does not mean that all the appropriate players have received and understood the message. The scorecard approach is unique in that the measurements convey a message because when people think they might be held accountable for results, they pay more attention to the instructions associated with what needs to be done. Since the scorecards are categorized by perspective and tailored to fit specific performance drivers, they offer an approach more likely to achieve understanding than the more traditional approaches organizations have used to communicate strategy.

When employees understand the message, it is more likely that they will buy in to the strategic message being conveyed. The thinking processes of TOC represent an excellent tool for educating key players and having them buy in to the solution. Moreover, these processes will afford them opportunities to provide feedback about the strategy. Frequently, lower level employees will have better solutions than top management. When the process becomes a two-way street using effective tools such as the scorecard and TOC, success becomes more probable. The feedback mechanism cascading back up the mountain, overcoming gravity so to speak, is when strategic competitive advantage really takes hold and breakthrough results become a reality. This is when employees talk and management listens.

CONTINUOUS STRATEGIC IMPROVEMENT

Most strategic planning efforts are infrequently held retreats when top management teams gather to develop a vision for the future. Sometimes these are bottom-up processes where no one plans himself or herself out of existence. These types of plans are simply how to fix what we are already doing. A plan gets crafted and sits on top management's bookshelves until it is time for the next exercise. Today's economic environment does not lend itself to achieving success with this feeble attempt at strategic planning. Strategic planning must become a continuous way of thinking throughout the organization.

The balanced scorecard approach has demonstrated real potential for creating complete involvement on a continuous basis. Communication using the scorecards and providing measurement of leading indicators of performance will provide incentive for more regular strategic involvement on a continuous basis. This is a critical point since differentiated strategies will demand more focus and attention because the pace and speed of innovation are much faster. Involvement on a continuous basis is accelerated when more employees understand the measurements and the scorecard process.

The continuous strategic process is better suited to taking advantage of knowledge assets and fully utilizing the capability of an organization. The scorecards assist in providing the alignment of knowledge capability within an organization by providing the measurements and scorecards for tracking its success. Since the speed of change has accelerated, it is now more critical that organizations be ready for change. The learning and growth component of the scorecard creates the focus and leverage needed by creating more focused ways to motivate the team and reward effective strategic execution.

A PROFIT-FOCUSED TREND APPROACH

In finding ways to simplify and increase the effectiveness of balanced scorekeeping, we applied our concept of trend format reporting to the scorecard. The scorecard is unique in its approach to presenting metrics using the current forecast in addition to actual data, providing the capability of capturing the trend right on the scorecard. By presenting data for each month, year to date, and full year, team members can monitor how they are progressing in addition to evaluating the best estimate of future results. This offers a more powerful framework when monitoring and working with predictive lead indicators.

The scorecards can be layered within each of the four perspectives and by measurement under each of the four categories. Additional layering is possible by business unit or department. Customization allowing personal or partner scorecards is also a possibility depending on the needs of the organization. The selection of metrics based on strategy might be either financial or nonfinancial. I think that the trend format scorecards provide a dynamic feedback tool that can be adapted to present daily or weekly data in addition to the monthly presentation scorecard presentation. The ability to visualize a full year compared to plan and last year offers capability that makes understanding, acceptance, and buy in easier.

The trend format model facilitates my concept of continuous forecasting and application of strategy. My formula for maintaining two years of current forecast data eliminates the need for formal budgeting. By driving the strategy themes and priorities through the scorecard, strategic thinking and development becomes a continuous and ongoing process. The latest innovation and change to the strategy are always there, and the scorecards and forecast projections are updated every single month or more frequently if required. The strategic model is maintained and updated as necessary.

CREATING CHANGE AND IMPACTING CULTURE

Improvement requires change, and every methodology discussed is focused on bringing about better change. There are three types of change:

1. Anticipatory
2. Reactive
3. Crisis

Having been involved with, and exposed to, significant changes over the years, I have observed very little tendency to change on an anticipatory basis. Most change falls into the crisis category. There is very little reactive change and even less anticipatory change. No one really wants their cheese moved, and it is no different with organizations. Leadership understands the need to create change, but accomplishing it, even in smaller organizations, is like trying to turn a battleship. It is not that easy. Balanced scorecards represent a new evolution of tools and techniques for organizations to focus on strategy and turn their choices into competitive realty.

Changing strategy or the organizational structure will only achieve a limited amount of success. If management and employees do not buy in to the strategic change being pursued, then not much happens. The scorecards get real because they can communicate the desired results and provide a measure of their achievement. By utilizing performance drivers that represent future results, the scorecards provide a strategic road map for all levels of the organization.

Strategy is a continuous process of change, and the scorecard empowers change through its ability to create a framework for understanding and tracking progress. My belief is that the process of continuous improvement is most effective when the employees are empowered to act on making strategy a reality.

MAKING IT WORK

Balanced scorecards represent a powerful tool for helping organizations guide their future. The dynamics of the executive team can be communicated more effectively and understood by all levels of the organization because they help to articulate the desired results. When linked and aligned with innovative strategic choices, it becomes a tool for communicating performance. Measuring strategy is very difficult, but it is easier when the proper blend of financial and nonfinancial metrics is employed. Leveraging and strategically focusing the knowledge value within an organization is very difficult. However, the scorecard is well suited to meet this challenge. When this tool together with TOC and other methodologies are utilized, organizations can experience breakthrough results never before imagined.

12

CREATING, MANAGING, AND MEASURING VALUE

Value can be a fleeting thing as many shareholders discovered when the tech bubble burst and corporate governance slid downhill. Market capitalization of retirement portfolios dropped to the depths from which most will never recover. The world changed so fast that it became a blur in the vision of most observers and will likely never be the way people remembered how they lived and worked for most of their lives. At the center of this storm were the CPAs and financial executives responsible for creating the mess and the corporations and CEOs to whom they reported or were accountable. While it is easy to blame these people, a good share of this load has to be carried by the shareholders and the gullible public who looked for a quick buck. From this tangle evolved the Sarbanes-Oxley legislation in 2002 and a business world that has seen productivity improve. This has brought heightened attention to corporate performance management and the reliability of accounting data. I am going to add my profit-focused accounting ideas to this stew and offer some recipes that will provide direction for how to improve the effectiveness of creating, managing, and measuring value.

A SHORT OR LONG VIEW

My choice for a financial reporting format is simplicity because it builds better understanding. Achieving success, in the complexity of today's global business environment, depends on the ability to innovate and to execute. Achieving agility and responsiveness requires that employees understand the measurement of results and the strategy for the future. They also need to understand the business processes they utilize to achieve strategic competitiveness today and for the future. I offer a combination of throughput accounting, activity-based analysis, and balanced scorecards to accomplish this objective. This recipe, when used effectively, allows managers to have their cake and eat it too.

The short view has been entrenched because of the continued fixation on earnings per share (EPS) and a current quarter versus last quarter perspective of net income. The EPS mentality evolved from generally accepted accounting principles (GAAP), which have been the traditional measure of corporate performance and stock market value. GAAP comprises the rules that govern how and what accountants measure. These rules specify the inclusion of overhead in inventory values to increase earnings and interest expense as reduction from income. These are just a few simple examples that enter into the determination of EPS. The stock market continuously adjusts to a price earnings multiple based on EPS, which in turn drives a company's share value.

One of the most notable examples of EPS manipulation is Enron's use of special purpose entities where it made material investments in low-return ventures. Enron borrowed heavily to invest in off-balance-sheet investments and at the same time avoided raising common stock to avoid any dilution to its shares, which increased EPS and inflated the share price. By fabricating earnings, inflating revenue, and hiding the financial risk in off-balance-sheet limited partnerships, Enron was able to stay within the rules of GAAP. The Financial Accounting Standards Board has now taken away the loophole associated with special purpose entities and off-balance-sheet guarantees. However, the treatment of allowing the free use of retained earnings and the EPS mentality still has not been addressed. In my opinion, the value of earnings should be determined over the long haul using a short-term view as a checkpoint on the progress being made in achieving the strategic vision. Value must be determined by its ability to generate future cash flow on a going-concern basis, providing a foundation and framework for employees and shareholders to understand the meaning and measurement of value. Value should not be determined based on the ability of corporations to hit their earnings target. Value should be based on building factual trends using cash-based earnings. Value should give consideration to the importance of intangible knowledge-based assets. These assets are critical to create and build a solid foundation of continuing future value.

THE ACCOUNTING MODEL VERSUS ECONOMIC MODEL

The short view versus the long view provides a good launch into the debate of whether the accounting model needs to be overhauled and what key components of the new engine are. Accountants trying to maintain their balance on a slippery slope have repeatedly manipulated the EPS accounting-driven model created by GAAP. Accounting measurements need to address the hard cold facts of economic reality.

When investors make contributions to capital, it is with cash. At the end of the day, they want their investment paid back in cash plus a fair return as compensation for their risk. They do not want smoke and mirrors; they want results they can put in the bank or reinvest. Banks charge interest on their loans and loans are shown as a liability on the balance sheet. Vendors that extend credit for goods and services want to be paid back, and the purchase price paid for those goods and services should include an amount representing their profit. Shareholders, or the owners and investors in a company, expect to earn a rate of return at least equal to or greater than what they would receive from investing funds elsewhere. The accounting rules allow for interest charges for the use of funds and yet do not consider the associated cost of capital provided by the investors.

The economic model can be explained as what is left after the taxes are paid. Employees are paid cash wages based on the hours worked. Unless the land and buildings are purchased with cash, it will be necessary to pay rent in cash. Goods and services are paid for in cash. The economic model basically says that profit is what is left over out of revenue after everyone has been paid. The economic model is driven by the sources and uses of cash.

Accounting profit is determined using accrual accounting and a vast array of complex rules and principles designed to match revenue and expenses appropriately and categorize what represents assets, liabilities, and shareholders' investment. The GAAP rules provide for including overhead expenses in the valuation of inventory. These rules also require that investment in research and development (R&D) be expensed when incurred and not amortized over the period of time when the benefit will occur. As long as GAAP provides for the current rules used to embellish EPS, that is what will drive stock share prices.

Stock prices will not reflect value since accounting profit will not reflect value. Managers within the corporate ranks may be capable of adjusting for economic reality, but until the accounting profession and the investment community face reality, confusion over interpretation of results will continue, as will the potential for fraudulent manipulation of accounting records. Bonuses are tied to bottom-line accounting measurement, not economic measurement representing an additional issue relative to traditional accounting measurement. This paradox greases the already slippery slope even further, compounding an already difficult problem.

In recognition of the economic model, I used the measurement of earnings before interest, taxes, depreciation, and amortization (EBITDA) in the profit-focused accounting format for reasons of simplicity. Managers at the operating level frequently have difficulty understanding the complexities of financing decisions and how depreciation figures are determined. Accordingly, I provided a bottom-line number over which they exercised greater control by eliminating interest, taxes, depreciation, and amortization. Another reason for EBITDA is its use in performing business valuations and approximation to cash earnings where a multiple is applied to the result for the purpose of projecting a market value. Since these factors must be included in calculating net income and retained earnings, a reconciliation adjustment is made to arrive at net income and for the purpose of calculating returns and turnover ratios. The intent is to focus business unit managers on a measurement that is understandable and yet difficult to manipulate. In addition, managers also need to understand and be held accountable for the effectiveness of asset investments. We will see that by adding factors such as financing and the cost of capital, managers can be measured on the impact of their actions and decisions affecting inventory and fixed assets.

ECONOMIC VALUE ADDED (EVA™): A METRIC WITH MEANING

EVA™, a trademarked symbol of Stern, Stewart & Co., is a metric that adopts the economic value–based model to measure performance and offers a way out of the accounting measurement mess. EVA™ holds businesses accountable for the cost of capital they use and determines whether or not real value has been created for the shareholders. EVA™ is determined by subtracting a charge for the full cost of capital, equity as well as debt, from operating earnings after taxes and adjusts for accounting distortions such as intangibles. By including the EVA™ concept in the profit-focused accounting model, there is better measurement of value creation to provide an incentive for encouraging growth from new products, particularly equipment and manufacturing facilities. EVA™ holds business units responsible for driving value and is a good measurement for determining compensation awards based on value creation rather than accounting-based measurement.

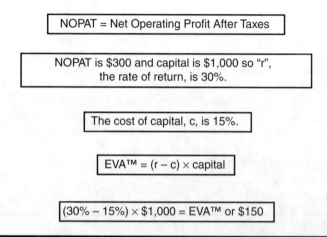

Figure 12.1. Simple Example of EVA™.

If EVA™ is a better measurement of value creation, why is it better? The underlying principle of any business activity is the same as provided by the Theory of Constraints. The business must not only provide a profit, it must also earn enough to justify the cost of capital used in its business pursuits. In other words, a business must create a surplus of profits after covering all of its costs, including capital costs. Until a business has earned an economic profit, it has not really generated a profit. When the net economic profit of the business exceeds its cost of capital employed, positive EVA™ results and value is created. If net economic profit is zero or negative, then value is lost.

Before going further, let us understand how EVA™ is calculated and determined. The chart shown in Figure 12.1 provides an overview of the calculation. We see that net operating profit after taxes (NOPAT) is reduced by the cost of capital times the amount of capital, and the result is either a positive or negative EVA™. In its simplest sense, there are only three ways to increase EVA™:

1. Increase operating efficiency
2. Undertake value-adding new investments
3. Withdraw capital from uneconomic activities

The focus provided by understanding this measurement provides management and investors with a much better grasp of how value is or is not being created. This is much different than the EPS model followed by Wall Street and prescribed by GAAP.

Add to Capital

- Deferred tax reserve
- LIFO reserve
- Cumulative goodwillamortization
- Unrecorded goodwill
- (Net) Capitalized intangibles
- Full cost reserve
- Cumulative unusual loss after tax
- Bad debt reserve
- Inventory obsolescence reserve
- Warranty reserve
- Deferred income reserve

Add to NOPAT

- Increase in deferred tax reserve
- Increase in LIFO reserve
- Goodwill amortization
- Increase in (net) capitalizedintangibles
- Increase in full cost reserve
- Unusual loss (gain) after tax
- Increase in other reserves

Figure 12.2. EVA™ Equity Equivalent Adjustments.

The EVA™ model makes several reconciling adjustments to convert GAAP financial statements by eliminating accounting and financing distortions. NOPAT represents a firm's net operating profits after taxes. Capital is equivalent to all the cash invested in the firm's net assets over its life without regard to its business purpose or how it was financed. The only noncash charge deduction from NOPAT is depreciation because it is deemed to represent a true economic expense. Figure 12.2 shows a table computing EVA™ that presents and takes into consideration the major reconciliation adjustments typically included in the calculation. The premier source for understanding EVA™ and its complexities is *The Quest for Value* written by G. Bennett Stewart III of Stern Stewart & Co.

The first step in calculating EVA™ is to determine NOPAT from the accounting version of net income. Each business will have a different set of adjustments to make in arriving at NOPAT. When making an adjustment, there are four considerations to determine the requirement for making it:

1. Does it materially impact the EVA™ calculation?
2. Can managers manipulate the outcome?
3. Will operating people understand the adjustment?
4. Are the data readily available?

For NOPAT, the objective is to adjust accounting net income and the asset and liability balances affected to arrive at free cash flow. Free cash flow is that cash which is net of cash originally invested for business growth. Some of the typical adjustments are listed in Figure 12.2 and include deferred taxes, increase in LIFO (last in/first out), amortization of goodwill, and capitalization of R&D expense. Other adjustments might be unusual gains or losses after taxes.

Capital adjustments represent adjustments required to convert a firm's accounting book value into "economic" book value. This represents the cash investors have at risk in the company and on which they expect to earn a return for their risk. Typical adjustments include deferred taxes, LIFO reserve, bad debt reserve, inventory obsolescence, warranty, and deferred income. The balance sheet adjustment might additionally include the net present value recognition of operating leases that could have been considered an asset. All future lease payments are considered a debt.

The cost of capital represents an enormous factor in making EVA™ calculations. It will vary depending on the size of a company, its position, and financial history. It should represent the minimum acceptable rate of return on investments made by the firm. Accordingly, the cost of capital becomes the hurdle rate for accepting new projects, i.e., Six Sigma projects. The rate is used for calculating EVA™ and assessing rates of return on capital employed. *The Quest for Value* defines the rate as "one that is equal to the total return that a company's investors could expect to earn by investing in a portfolio of stocks and bonds of comparable risk." The more risk, the higher the rate.

There are four costs of capital to consider. As mentioned previously, the cost will vary depending on the company and industry.

1. Cost for business risk
2. Cost of borrowing (after tax at firm's marginal tax rate)
3. Cost of equity on which an investor expects to be rewarded
4. Weighted average cost of capital, which is the blended cost of a firm's debt and equity (available for download at www.jrosspub.com)

The cost of capital for calculating EVA™ is the weighted average cost. Again, I refer you to *The Quest for Value* for almost 800 pages of complete and detailed discussion. In today's business environment, the cost of capital might be 7 percent at the low end of risk to 12 percent for a higher risk business.

The elements and theory of determining EVA™ have been described to provide a basic understanding, in addition to sources for learning about the concept in greater depth. My purpose is to offer the metric as an alternative to the traditional accounting measurement of net income and EPS. Figure 12.3 illustrates a more complex computation of EVA™ that considers the typical components entering into its determination and calculation.

EVA™: A STRATEGIC TOOL

EVA™ offers many opportunities to leverage and measure the strategic decisions and capability of a company. The concept of throughput and its vision

Calculating NOPAT		
Sales	$	800
Cost of Goods Sold		500
Contribution		300
Operating Expense		100
Taxes at 40%		80
NOPAT		120
Increase in LIFO Reserve		10
NOPAT	$	130

Adjustments to Capital		
Cash	$	20
Accounts Receivable		100
Inventory		300
LIFO Reserve		50
Accounts Payable		(200)
Net Working Capital		270
Fixed Assets		530
Total Capital Employed	$	800
Cost of Capital		12.00%
Capital Employed Charge	$	96
NOPAT	$	130
EVA™	$	34

Figure 12.3.   An Example of Calculating EVA™.

is to provide direction and insight relative to simplifying and focusing on earning a profit. EVA™ aids in understanding how well assets are being managed. If EVA™ is positive, then the business is doing something more than just owning assets. This is an attribute that measurements, such as return on assets and return on equity, fail to provide. EVA™ brings all the measurements together at a top level. Throughput accounting and profit-focused accounting provide a short-term profit focus and EVA™ provides an even broader global perspective.

One of the ways that EVA™ can be used motivationally is as a basis for incentive compensation. The measurement is not as subject to manipulation as many programs that are grounded in accounting net income and return on investment. Since EVA™ drives value, the use of the measurement to determine managerial bonuses gets managers to think more about their decisions and how they will impact future results in contrast to the quarter-to-quarter mentality. Managers are forced to consider levels of inventory, receivables, and the realization of results from spending money on new equipment. Moreover, they are forced to look continually at unused capacity and underperforming assets. There are multiple scenarios for applying EVA™ to determine incentive awards and how they are paid.

EVA™ represents an excellent indicator of the strategic potential value of a company. Companies with heavy investments in knowledge assets in contrast to capital-intensive companies offer much greater opportunity for value creation. A good example is Microsoft, which is a high-return, high-growth company, in contrast to GE, which has generated lower returns and lower growth.

Much of this relates to the composition of the dependency on the use of knowledge assets in contrast to capital assets. The other strategic opportunity for EVA™ is the evaluation of potential acquisitions. It helps to align corporate interests with shareholders when considering strategic priorities and further helps to align salaried employees by linking incentive compensation to creation of value as measured by EVA™.

MEASURING LEAN SIX SIGMA PROJECTS

A common continuing question is whether lean Six Sigma projects are paying off and how much better the bottom line is. All too frequently, these projects and initiatives are measured locally and yet the expected benefit fails to appear on the profit-and-loss statement. A large reason for these measurement issues is due to how the initiatives are managed and measured within an organization. The answer is to attain buy in throughout the organization from all the key players in order to build architecture for effective communication. By understanding what and how to measure lean Six Sigma, the problems will disappear, resulting in more successful and profitable results. The element of smoke and mirrors associated with measurements will disappear when EVA™ metric concepts and principles are correctly applied.

Selecting the correct projects is the first step in the application of EVA™ measurement. This requires documenting and detailing the expected cost of the initiative and making appropriate determinations of expected profit improvement. All too often, initiatives will show savings locally that do not roll forward because they created capacity that was either not utilized or sold. EVA™ measurements using the guideline of accepting only returns that exceed the firm's cost of capital help to prevent burning energy and resources on projects with poor potential. The evaluation process should consider whether the project and initiative results generate throughput from increased revenue, reduced investment in assets, or cost reductions. The estimated savings, from the selected projects, should be capable of producing a return that exceeds the organization's return on capital by 5 percent or better. The application of this guideline will help to ensure that initiatives selected will produce real bottom-line results.

Project selection is critical. Value-based management principles need to be applied to project selection on the front end. This means that the leadership of the organization has to be involved in project selection to determine if lean Six Sigma projects meet the criteria of strategic priorities. Project selection was discussed in Chapter 8, and the need to apply focus using the Pareto rule of 20 percent to yield 80 percent of the benefit is worth repeating. After the best

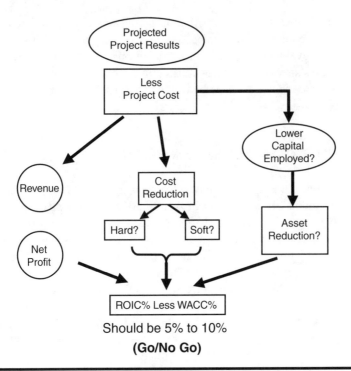

Figure 12.4. Value Management Measurement of Project Impact.

projects have been selected, the projected results should be measured to calculate the projected return on invested capital. If the return is not at least 5 to 10 percent greater than the weighted average cost of capital, then the project should be rejected. Figure 12.4 shows the criteria that project results should achieve using the value management tools.

The value management criteria for measuring lean Six Sigma should be extended to measuring the net income of organizations globally to ensure that real value is being returned to the shareholders. Too many initiatives produce apparent savings that fail to produce real value because the savings created capacity that could not be converted into throughput because of market constraints. This fork in the road is where the Theory of Constraints and value-based management provide a direction more organizations need to follow. Lean Six Sigma is too frequently applied to nonconstrained resources where there is little payback in terms of real profit improvement. This is when productivity improvements fail to translate into shareholder value. I am not suggesting that productivity be stifled, but it is critical that a value proposition be developed together with a resulting strategy that increases throughput. If that is not possible, then the assets need to be either diverted or sold in order to produce returns that exceed the cost of capital.

VALUE MANAGEMENT IMPLICATIONS OF SARBANES-OXLEY

The Sarbanes-Oxley Act of 2002 was enacted in response to accounting scandals and fraudulent reporting with the purpose of refocusing the managements of publicly traded companies on shareholder interests. It is my belief that this legislation will ripple through accounting firms and companies with widespread implications that will be felt for years to come. Value management is at the very core of not only providing better information to management and shareholders, but in the creation of value. My statement is based on the reality that all companies will gravitate to building a reliable foundation of internal controls, businesses processes, and good governance. The legislation might have started the movement, but public and competitive pressure will drive companies to adopt a back-to-basics approach to create a rock solid foundation for financial and strategic survival.

Compliance with the Sarbanes-Oxley Act applies to companies listed with the Securities and Exchange Commission (SEC), and the new rules require compliance for fiscal years ending on or after November 15, 2004. Company CEOs and CFOs are required to certify that financial statements contain no untrue statements or omissions of material fact under the provisions of Section 302. They are also responsible for establishing and maintaining an adequate internal control structure and procedures for financial reporting. They are further required to report that they have made an assessment of the internal control structure as of the end of each fiscal year as to the effectiveness of the internal control structure and procedures for financial reporting. Section 404 requires an attestation of the assessment by the company's external auditor. Section 409 of the act will necessitate companies to report material changes in their financial conditions "on a rapid and current basis." The first phase of compliance is for larger companies with revenue in excess of $75 million, and smaller companies must be in compliance by July 15, 2005. The act makes the CEOs and CFOs explicitly responsible for establishing, monitoring, and evaluating the effectiveness of internal control over financial reporting and disclosure, backing it up with stiff fines and imprisonment for violators. The legislation provided for the Public Company Accounting Oversight Board (PCAOB), charged with ensuring the preparation of informative, accurate, and independent audit reports. While the Sarbanes-Oxley Act has no direct effect on private companies, since they are not required to register with the SEC, it will have an impact on accounting and auditing standards by setting a tone that will cause many privately held companies to fall in step with the spirit of the established requirements and standards.

Having laid out the overview of the legislation, let us look at what it really means and the impact it will have on value management and measurement. The intent is to improve the accuracy and reliability of corporate reporting and disclosure. The heart of the issue is the ability to have, or the lack of, visibility into what drives earnings and the factors that can create operational and financial surprises. The investment market demands systems capable of providing real-time answers to financial questions that will cause companies to dig into the processes and systems supporting the infrastructure that produces financial data. The problem associated with this challenge is that an overwhelming number of companies have underlying data sources feeding business intelligence infrastructures and financial reporting that are not supported with good fundamental basic business processes and accurate data. Furthermore, these companies implemented enterprise resource planning (ERP) systems in a rush to comply with Y2K, but never properly trained their employees how to effectively manage and use these systems. There is a high risk of making more mistakes faster because of poor inventory records, inaccurate routing, erroneous bills of material, and a failure to identify and map business processes. Many CPAs who will have the responsibility of providing attestation on the reliability of internal controls and systems will require additional training on the complexities of operational issues and supply chain management. Needless to say, financial managers and CPAs will need to become oriented and more involved with operations.

The ramification of Sarbanes-Oxley is not just financial legislation, but extends to the basis for the very source of financial statements and the standards used to build the foundation on which the confidence of investors relies. It is actually the foundation companies use to ensure their economic survival. CEOs, CFOs, and CPAs really need to ask themselves about the quality of the infrastructure, the integrity of transactions, and the business processes containing the activities that are responsive to the drivers that impact financial results. Rapid improvements in technology will not overcome the shortcomings of outdated and undocumented processes that many companies utilize. Companies will need to discard the manual outdated concepts widely used in so many businesses and upgrade them with continuous improvement and lean thinking. The Sarbanes-Oxley Act is already putting the spotlight on issues like customer satisfaction, brand recognition, and knowledge assets that are not measurable by financial metrics. Companies will have to consider balanced scorecard solutions to match their strategy execution with nonfinancial measures.

Some consulting firms and software vendors offer "return to basics" advice that includes greater focus on many of the issues already discussed in this book. In fact, the business model I recommend embraces all of the basic solutions such as forecasting and integrated business planning rolled into a simpler and speedier model that does not become burdened with excessive complexity. Sales and operational planning has been offered as a step toward plugging the dike with something that companies can employ to assure them of avoiding possible risks. While it is a good step forward, it does not extend far enough. The profit-focused planning process discussed in Chapter 15 brings everything together in a formula that addresses these concerns.

Sarbanes-Oxley is here and will become a bigger concern for all companies. It is not something a software program or new technology is going to fix. The heart of the solution is with the business processes and they will need to be fixed from the bottom up. An additional component of the problem rests with the model accountants use to determine and measure net income. That model needs to be changed. There are also problems with the quality of training and education that go to the heart of the learning and growth component of the balanced scorecard. Businesses need to recognize the need to devote greater effort to develop multidimensional employees. Financial managers need to gain a better understanding of sales and operations. Likewise, sales and operations managers need a better understanding of financial and accounting measurement.

KNOWLEDGE MANAGEMENT

Any discussion of value management must include knowledge management and its impact on profitability and the creation of value. Innovative strategies are driven by the knowledge and information required to provide the input required by new products, services, and processes. Rapid responsiveness of global customers, changing markets, and information-based society places increased demands on the ability of companies to keep pace and maintain a competitive edge. Knowledge management is the ability to manage the critical components of information for the purpose of processing it to create and produce innovative products, services, and business processes. Knowledge is the unrecorded asset on the balance sheets of many companies, which provides them with their strategic and competitive advantage.

Effective management of knowledge requires that organizations share the knowledge existing within their workforce and then leverage it to create and convert it into desired results. David J. Skyrme, a recognized expert on knowledge management, identifies seven areas or types of knowledge:

1. Customer knowledge
2. Product knowledge
3. People knowledge
4. Process knowledge
5. Knowledge retention (organizational memory)
6. Relationship knowledge
7. Asset knowledge (intellectual capital)

The ability to effectively measure knowledge assets in financial statements is nonexistent. Much of the management of knowledge falls into the soft areas such as leadership, organizational culture, brand image, technology, and skill capability within or accessible by companies. The balanced scorecard is one of the more effective models we have seen for identifying the learning and growth component of an organization and can have a profound impact on how effectively strategy is converted into profit and value creation.

While the balanced scorecard approach is a step in the right direction, it still falls short of providing organizations with a clear direction for effectively managing all of the components of knowledge to achieve a sustainable advantage. There is a great deal of work to be accomplished in the area of achieving sustainable results through people and knowledge management. I clearly do not have all the answers, but I have observed some excellent examples that are worth sharing. *Profit Beyond Measure* by H. Thomas Johnson and Anders Bröms describes how Toyota and Scania have utilized a "managing by means" approach to achieve sustainable profit and growth. These companies captured the essence of knowledge management and offer a blueprint for and insight on how knowledge management can be part of an organization's strategic culture.

A KNOWLEDGE SCORECARD

Traditional financial statements fail to provide help with the measurement and management of knowledge based-assets. The GAAP rules require that expenditures for R&D, brand awareness, and productivity improvements be expensed rather than reflected as intangible assets on the balance sheet. Since there is no indication of value on the traditional balance sheet, it is necessary to look to other tools to find some indication of value. EVA™ is a measurement discussed earlier that takes some recognition of these factors into consideration. Because of the recognized significance and importance of knowledge-related assets, there have been greater efforts to create focus on measurement of these factors.

Baruch Lev, an accounting and finance professor at New York University, has developed and patented a method of quantifying intangible values. Application of these formulas includes a discounted value calculation and represents an estimate of the amount of value attributable to knowledge or intangible assets. This value, termed "knowledge capital," is used to quantify intellectual, human, customer, and supplier capital. It represents the sum of the intangible factors that enable a company to earn a higher than average return on its GAAP-valued asset base. The knowledge capital calculation clearly reflects the significant impact of intangible assets as evidenced by the share valuations of companies within the software, biotechnology, and pharmaceutical industries. The difficulty with this approach is that it is a lag measurement when the speed of innovation requires a better lead indicator for measuring invisible assets.

INTELLECTUAL CAPITAL

While they may not be visible, knowledge assets are clearly drivers for the creation of value. The gap between the market value of knowledge-based companies continues to widen with no letup in sight. The adage "you can manage what you can measure" does not always apply in the age of innovation and knowledge assets. Intellectual capital is intangible, in contrast to hard, tangible, cash-related assets. It requires activities and processes to transfer it into future value, monitored using nonfinancial predictive lead indicators of value.

Intellectual capital can consist of a variety of things such as technology, processes, people skills, supplier relationships, and customer relationships supported by the financial and investment structure of an organization. While intellectual capital is not readily quantifiable, nonfinancial metrics help to provide some direction. The balanced scorecard measures of learning and development skills represent some indication for the potential of human capital. The information technology capacity of organizations, together with enhanced business processes and systems, provides structural capital. Intellectual property such as brands, trademarks, and patents provides another dimension of value creation. The key to utilizing these capital components fully rests on the ability of an organization to align its strategy and unique value proposition properly to achieve the best utilization of these invisible assets. If the strategy cannot be executed, the assets will be of little value.

MANAGING CUSTOMER RELATIONS

Customer relationship management (CRM) has become a focal point as companies have tried to capture more information and knowledge in order to delight the customer. Customer capital perhaps should have been included in the previous discussion on intellectual capital. One of the big advances in CRM has been technology and software to provide better data. The problem with these systems has been system integration and streamlining the business processes that support this critical element of the value proposition.

I included CRM because the customer has been the focal, underlying theme in one way or another with all of the business philosophies and methodologies presented. It may be profit-focused accounting, but there will be no profit if there is no customer. CRM is not restricted to just companies that employ a customer-intimacy value proposition. Dell utilizes a value proposition of operational excellence and then links its strategy to accessing and managing customers on a one-on-one basis.

CRM provides critical information required to develop accurate current forecasts of sales and is a key component of our trend format for predictive financial reporting. The value chain begins with the customer and identifies the needs, then ends with servicing and satisfying the customer. The real-time requirement of performance management is driven by the ability to monitor and manage the latest up-to-date information flowing from the value chain. When the components of customer demands are known, then it is possible to feed data through business intelligence systems and into our revenue and cost models to build and create meaningful forecasts and shift to the needs of the marketplace.

BUSINESS INTELLIGENCE

The advances in technology combined with the requirement for more reliable data that can be translated into knowledge have evolved into what is known as business intelligence (BI) systems. These systems take data from operational ERP and other systems (including CRM systems) and organize them into formats that provide a foundation for analysis, planning, and execution. These systems typically utilize database analytical tools such as query, reporting, OLAP (On-Line Analytical Processing), and data mining to rapidly access and analyze data. The analysis process identifies trends, patterns, and exceptions within databases that provide knowledge to user organizations. This knowledge is then applied to rules, decision-making formulas, and for creating forecasts based on changing market conditions.

BI systems are not transactional systems, but are used to gather transactional data, market information, and customer trends from CRM and then use the data in analytical ways to make better business decisions. They support decision making and help to anticipate future events. BI systems help to create understanding of why things happened and predict what will happen. In many instances, BI systems are used to monitor what happened by creating dashboards and decision engines. This information is used to support strategic, tactical, and operational analysis. CRM systems feed BI to increase customer value and satisfaction that drives increased revenue.

In the section on Sarbanes-Oxley, the case was made for making sure that the underlying processes were solid to ensure accurate data. BI systems are only as good as the data they are fed and the soundness of the rules used to perform analytics. Another problem with BI systems is training and the inability of users to achieve the true capability of their power. Even if these factors do not exist, then failure to correctly align strategic priorities with the technology tools produces frustrating results. These tools will be slow to reach their potential because people need to be trained and good data will not follow until users have been properly trained. Just trying to comply with Sarbanes-Oxley may hinder the progress needed to achieve effective performance management reporting systems.

THE PROFIT-FOCUSED ACCOUNTING VALUE MODEL

The profit-focused accounting value-creation model is intended to provide a framework since each organization will have its own specific issues and situations. The first component is to employ EVA™ as a means for measuring project activities and business unit net income. Project measurement should be applied to knowledge-related projects that can be captured through work order accounting to avoid unnecessary allocations. The projected return on capital employed computations should be applied to potential projects during the process project selection.

The second step of the model is to assess the organization's knowledge capability and create a knowledge strategy map that is aligned and linked with the organization's value proposition and strategy. Knowledge strategy will be a theme that is a component of other strategic themes, and the map becomes the vehicle for breaking down and labeling the knowledge components of the organization. The following components should be identified for use with balanced scorecard strategy management:

1. Sharing of knowledge
2. Creation of knowledge
3. Learning

Appropriate knowledge indicators should be developed for each organization. The different types of knowledge that I indicated should be used to develop meaningful indicators and measures. While the measures will not quantify the value of knowledge, they will provide leading indicators that will provide the potential benefits based on cause and effect relationships. By linking knowledge measurement to balanced scorecards, organizations will be taking a step in the right direction. The added dimension to scorecard measurement will help to focus the knowledge emphasis to customers, processes, and better financial results.

Ultimately, the value of the organization will increase due to the interconnectivity of human capital, relationship capital, and structural capital through linkage with strategic and business processes. The objective is the achievement of ongoing sustainable growth and creation of value on the bottom line. While management may not result from measurement, knowledge leadership through action and just doing it will be the driver that counts the most.

WAV   Web
Added
Value™

This book has free materials available for download from the
Web Added Value™ Resource Center at www.jrosspub.com.

13

SCOREKEEPING TOOLS: METRICS AND METHODS

Most people are familiar with the saying "if you can measure it, you can manage it" and yet in the previous chapter we learned that you have to manage it, but that measuring it might not be that easy. We also saw where accounting net income and earnings per share do not necessarily add up to value. The recent trend in reporting has been to produce reams of data that confuse and overwhelm even the savviest of financial specialists. If we are to achieve a profit focus with accounting and reporting, we need a starting point and it must align with the organization's strategic value proposition.

WHAT TO MEASURE

What to measure starts with assessment and a clear sense of where the organization is going. Additional questions follow as to why we are going there and how will we get there. The Theory of Constraints (TOC) and balanced scorecard tools provide companies with the framework for gathering the answers to these questions. From this foundation, each organization can develop its unique profile regarding what needs to be measured. A sample performance measurement profile checklist is presented in Figure 13.1 and will provide a guide to the key issues that should be evaluated in determining what should be measured.

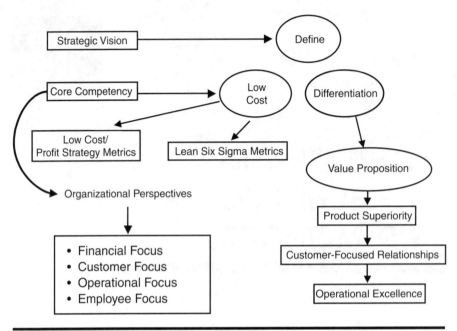

Figure 13.1. Performance Measurement Profile.

One of the reasons for measuring is to provide a mechanism for knowing if we are on track. Organizations need to determine who needs to know and what they need to know. From this platform we can determine:

- What to measure
- Who will monitor it
- How to show it

Another consideration in developing performance measurements is setting priorities. The organization must understand what it is monitoring and why. There is little point in measuring and reporting on areas that have a low priority. Nonconstrained resources represent an example where constant measurement would not be needed or desired. A good barometer is to measure the vital few factors to gain the maximum benefit. It is critical to know what is working and how well it is working. Six Sigma guidelines can be applied even if an organization does not have a formal program. The techniques and concepts are still valid. Knowing if processes are under control and if improvements are required will be reviewed as we progress through the scorekeeping tools and applications, all the way from the cost of quality to continuous improvement programs.

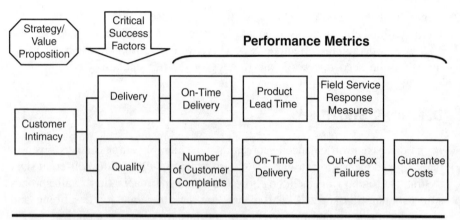

Figure 13.2.   A Framework for Measurement.

A FRAMEWORK FOR MEASUREMENT

After creating a measurement profile, it is important to establish a framework for measurement. A sample measurement framework is illustrated in Figure 13.2. The framework requires identification of the organizational strategy. The predominant strategy themes will be explained together with the metrics that typically are associated with them. After specifying the strategic theme or themes, an organization should determine its critical success factors (CSFs). Based on the CSF selections, appropriate and aligned measures can be selected.

During the process of selecting measurements, a gap assessment may be necessary. Figure 13.3 illustrates this concept. Measuring the alignment between strategies and factors driving the CSFs should be performed for all three

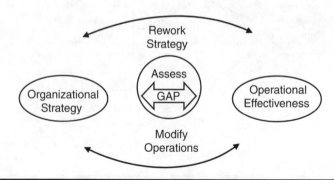

Figure 13.3.   Measuring Strategic Alignment.

elements of the value proposition so that a gap assessment can be developed for operational effectiveness, product innovation, and customer intimacy. Figure 13.3 uses operational effectiveness, whereby a determination can be made regarding the need to rework the strategy or modify operations or both.

DEFINING STRATEGY

In the discussion on balanced scorecards, considerable emphasis was given to mapping and measuring strategy. Defining strategy will provide a different slant to strategic components including how and where an organization's value proposition should be executed. This discussion sets the tone for describing and explaining the common measurements and how to compute them.

In Figure 13.4, we see how different strategies drive the need for different metrics. The illustration begins by showing a flow from core competency to three different strategic themes. Core competency requires consistent, time-tested measurements that are prerequisites needed to execute any strategy. These

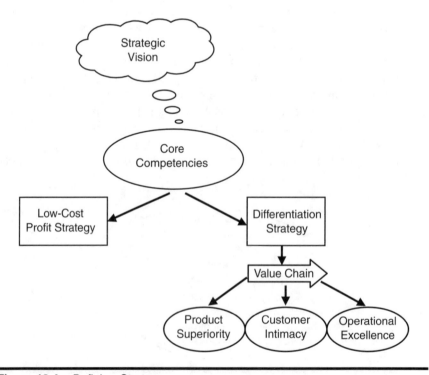

Figure 13.4. Defining Strategy.

measurements will be identified and explained. Low-cost profit strategies include those metrics that concentrate on maximizing short and intermediate profit levels and maintaining a strategy focused on being the low-cost producer in the market. Differentiation strategies seek to be unique in their market. These strategies focus on attributes that include customer relationships, superior products and service, or operational excellence. The three niche strategies all have unique performance measurement requirements and are defined with an explanation of how to calculate them. Metrics for each of the strategies are described, including how to calculate them, why they are important, and how to interpret the data.

CORE COMPETENCY METRICS

This category represents the basic measurements essential to understand the health of any enterprise regardless of its strategy. Some of the measures were discussed earlier in the book, but will be included again as a reference point. The only way these metrics will be helpful is to track them and analyze the trends. They should also be benchmarked against competitors and industry trends. The profit-focused accounting trend format provides for projecting the best estimate of full-year results so that expected results can be compared against the original plan and last year. This approach gives greater meaning to interim data that traditional formats fail to provide.

Economic Value Added (EVA™) — It is a measure of financial performance that combines the concept of residual income with corporate finance, which says that capital has a cost and that earning more than the cost of capital creates value for shareholders. EVA™ is computed by taking the difference between the return on net assets employed (NOPAT/capital) after the necessary adjustment (see Chapter 12) and the cost of capital. Another view is (RONA less the cost of capital) times capital employed. For greater detail and explanation, refer to Chapter 12 and the appropriate templates (available for download at www.jrosspub.com).

Return on Net Assets (RONA) — This is the ratio of net income (EVA™ less NOPAT) divided by net assets. Net assets are equal to total assets less total liabilities or the equivalent of shareholders' equity.

Return on Assets (ROA) — This is the ratio of net income divided by average total assets. This metric provides an indication of how effectively current capacity is being utilized and also a measure of the productivity of assets.

Working Capital Employed — This measurement indicates a company's liquidity as it is determined by deducting current liabilities (accounts payable, current notes payable, and accrued liabilities) from current assets (cash, accounts receivable, and inventory). It is an indication of the portion of a company's balance sheet that is readily convertible into cash. In-depth analysis will assess how quickly accounts payable and accounts receivable are being turned over, usually expressed in days outstanding.

Inventory Turns — This is a key metric that indicates how much money is tied up in raw material (RM), work in process (WIP), and finished goods (FG) and how long it takes to convert it into sales and profit. The calculation is determined by dividing average inventory, beginning and ending, for the year into total cost of goods sold. The higher number of inventory turns is an indication of the effectiveness of a company's scheduling and using its capabilities to convert material into customer orders. WIP turnover levels can indicate bottlenecks and other manufacturing problems. RM levels are an indication of the effectiveness of procurement, use of supplier relationships, and warehouse utilization. FG turnover indicates the level of effectiveness in integration of sales and operational planning. These issues will be further discussed in the later section on the cost of inventory.

Absenteeism — This measurement is determined by the number of employee hours absent from the facility divided by the total available employee hours within a single month. Each monthly total is accumulated and divided by 12 for the annual percentage. This metric can indicate morale issues or a need for "flex time" or family-related benefits.

Employee Turnover — Turnover of employees is usually expressed as a percentage where the number of employees that leave each month is divided by the total employees to yield a percentage. Employee turnover is an indication of employee satisfaction that must be analyzed to determine morale levels, high stress, and the root causes for the turnover.

Absenteeism and turnover are hard measures of employee satisfaction and usually are tracked on a monthly basis.

LOW-COST PROFIT STRATEGY METRICS

A low-cost profit strategy includes measurements that will also be attributable to any organization attempting to achieve operational excellence. Companies pursuing lean Six Sigma programs fall into this definition. A separate section is provided to explain the measurements typically indicative of attributes specific to lean Six Sigma initiatives.

The profit-focused accounting terms and definitions are used in addition to common traditional accounting terminology. This will provide information for companies that do not want to utilize a throughput accounting approach. The correlation of terms and their meaning will also aid companies that do want to consider a transition to throughput accounting. This will hopefully help to avoid confusion and make this book a more effective reference tool.

Sales/Revenue — This measurement should reflect the net value of orders or services provided to customers. It is used as a base for determining percentage relationships of costs and margins and net income to sales. Net sales per employee are considered a traditional benchmark of profitability. A good analytical comparison is to calculate the difference between the average net sales per total employees and production employees to show the accumulated cost of support within a manufacturing facility. When benchmarking with other companies, consideration should be given to make sure that you are comparing similar types of manufacturing companies since job-shop metrics will not be the same as a repetitive manufacturer.

Material Cost — This measurement, also called direct material, is the same whether using throughput accounting or traditional accounting. A typical measurement is the percentage of material used in the final product compared to total manufacturing costs. I like to look at material as a percentage of sales. The amount of outsourcing and vertical integration will affect the percentage of material relative to total costs, as will scrap and waste generated by the production process. Relationships with suppliers will impact quality heavily, as discussed under the cost of quality.

Labor Cost — Included in labor costs are all direct full-time, part-time, temporary, and subcontracted workforce labor dollars including fringe benefit costs. The labor cost percentage is the percentage of this total divided by the total manufacturing cost. The profit-focused accounting approach does not include overhead dollars in total manufacturing cost in contrast to traditional generally accepted accounting principles. However, for benchmarking and competitive analysis, overhead should be included for comparative purposes. I like to calculate direct labor as a percentage of sales.

Contribution/Gross Margin — Differences between throughput accounting and traditional accounting occur here specifically in how overhead is handled. Contribution is sales less direct material and direct labor. Gross margin includes manufacturing overhead. Throughput accounting excludes direct labor from the calculation. Contribution as a percent of sales is a key indicator of variable profitability. Increasing sales volume when there is excess capacity will usually increase profit assuming positive contribution. However, caution is urged since individual profitability of products needs to be examined and analyzed relative to critically constrained resources to provide the most profitable mix of products.

Standby/Overhead/Operating Expense — Included in standby expense are all other expenses with the exception of interest, depreciation, amortization, and taxes. The traditional accounting model would include interest, depreciation, and amortization in the determination of overhead expense. The throughput accounting model includes all other expenses in operating expense. This category of expense has grown in significance and requires careful analysis to understand the impact on profitability and execution of strategy. Calculating the percentage of overhead attributable to total manufacturing costs is a meaningful metric for benchmarking purposes.

EBITDA — This measurement is representative of *earnings before interest, taxes, depreciation, and amortization* and is used to measure earnings separately from the impact of financing decisions and variable depreciation and amortization policies that can be distorting. Frequently, some multiple determined by the level of risk will be applied to this measure to calculate market value of a company. In our reporting model, we used this measure as being more understandable at localized levels than net income.

EBIT — *Earnings before interest and taxes* is used to eliminate distortions associated with a company's capital structure and is the basis for presenting the basic earning power of the business irrespective of how it is financed. Return on invested capital (ROIC) is calculated by EBIT (1 less t) divided by capital. The marginal tax rate is designated by t.

EBT — *Earnings before taxes* is an important measure for many companies and usually is expressed as a percentage of sales.

Effective Tax Rate (Income Lost) — The "effective" tax rate represents income taxes as a percent of net sales. There are many factors that can influence taxes, such as accelerated depreciation, the corporate structure, and use of R&D and other tax credits. Cost segregation studies can also impact how facilities are classified in different asset categories (building versus equipment) as well as the determination of depreciation lives for book and tax purposes.

Net Income — Net income after taxes as a percentage of net sales is a common measure of profitability. Net income per the average number of outstanding common shares of stock is known as earnings per share (EPS), which Wall Street commonly uses to determine market value.

Obsolete Inventory — Obsolete inventory is the value of any inventory deemed to be unusable due to eliminated product lines or engineering changes. Slow-moving inventory is an inventory component or raw material that has a very slow rate of usage. A ratio for benchmarking purposes is determined by dividing the sum of obsolete and slow-moving inventory by net sales.

LEAN SIX SIGMA

The measurements presented as lean Six Sigma, while typically applied in waste elimination and process controls, apply to any strategy and organization striving to achieve operational excellence. The list is not all-inclusive, but is geared to measurements focused on productivity and profitability. Each metric is described as how to calculate it and where it should be applied.

Cycle Time/Cycle Time Efficiency — Cycle time for an operation is the amount of time, including lead time, required to complete one full complete cycle. Processes contain multiple operations. Cycle time represents the amount of time to complete a full cycle for the overall process. A complete cycle contains time waiting, or lead time, and actual value-added time, which add up to total cycle time. Cycle efficiency can be defined as the ratio or percentage of added-value time divided by lead time. This metric can be determined for all processes throughout the organization and lean efforts to improve the efficiency can be monitored. The amount of cycle time is also frequently tracked using different charts and dashboards. Cycle time is a critical measurement for lean Six Sigma initiatives and the attainment of operational excellence.

Setup Time — This measurement is determined as the average time required for a specific machine, resource, work center, or line to convert from the production of the last good unit of batch A to the first good piece of batch B. It is critical to record, chart, and communicate the time required to change over a machine or a production line. Every minute of setup time reduction allows manufacturers to reclaim a minute of productive time, resulting in increased profitability. Lean Six Sigma specialists will usually streamline setups by separating internal and external setups (internal when the machine is shut down and external when the machine is operating). Converting internal setups to external setups and then streamlining the internal setups to the shortest time possible is how lean specialists accomplish a reduction in the overall setup time.

Engineering Change Notice (ECN) — ECNs have a significant impact on profitability since they roll through the entire production process, reducing margins and creating waste by making inventory obsolete and increasing maintenance and warranty costs. Three effective steps to improving ECN management includes:

1. Clear assignment of responsibility for bill of material accuracy
2. Easy accessibility to bill of material files
3. Clear audit trails, configuration control, to trace the history of the bill of material from initial introduction to final obsolescence

Bill of Material (BOM) Accuracy — The accuracy of the bill of material should be tracked and related to changes in ECNs. The percentage of accuracy is critical for achieving any semblance of operational excellence and should be 97.5 percent or higher. The accuracy impacts both the accuracy of routing and inventories that flow through to the enterprise resource planning (ERP) system and the integration of all other data that are dependent on the reliability of these data. This information is the backbone of inventory planning and production scheduling. Erroneous data lead to waste and excess investment in assets, people, equipment, and working capital.

Routing Accuracy — Routings contain the detailed method of how a product is manufactured including the sequence of each operation and the time standards for production runs and setups. This information is contained in the item master of the ERP system and includes specifications on tooling, operator skills, inspection, and testing for every part produced in the production facility. Accuracy of routing information correlates directly to accuracy on the shop floor. Routings are used to determine the load on the plant and produce accurate schedules. Measuring and tracking routing accuracy are critical especially since the level of accuracy correlates directly to all of the production processes.

Inventory Accuracy — This measurement generally refers to the level of accuracy associated with either physical or cycle count variations. Most companies with operational excellence strategies will utilize perpetual inventories and not just rely on an annual physical inventory count. The reliability of the perpetual inventory system drives the level of accuracy related to production schedules and meeting customer delivery dates. The minimum level of accepted accuracy is 95 percent. Accordingly, the cycle count variations should be tracked and applied utilizing an ABC inventory methodology. This methodology refers to breaking the inventory into A, B, and C categories. A class is equivalent to 10 to 20 percent by number of items and 50 to 70 percent based on dollar volume. B class items will equate to 20 percent of the number of items and 20 percent of the dollar volume. C class items will represent 60 to 70 percent of the items and between 10 to 30 percent of the dollar volume.

First Pass Ratio — This measurement represents the percentage of product passing all quality requirements without rework, indicating that a process is in control and thus minimizing the cost associated with rework. By identifying and removing quality defects as early as possible in the manufacturing process, companies increase their agility on the shop floor with a resulting increase in profitability. The production people maintain this metric and charts are updated daily, thereby initiating ownership and process improvement at the shop-floor level. Zero defects equate to zero waste.

Average Line/Cell Downtime — Monitoring the amount of time that a line or cell is shut down will provide an excellent indicator of potential problems. This is where total preventive maintenance programs are effective in contributing to higher profitability by avoiding surprise and unnecessary shutdowns and disruption. These unscheduled interruptions ripple through the entire production facility creating waste and excessive inventory. A good way to view downtime is to measure uptime since it is not desirable to be making product unless it is immediately required. This is a good measure of the consistency of production.

Guaranty and Warranty Costs — The cost of making guarantees in product quality or cost of warranties typically is measured as a percentage of sales revenue. These potentially high costs represent an excellent reason for utilizing Six Sigma and eliminating the possibility of latent product defects. In addition to the cost of the direct guarantee, additional costs to service complaints, shipping, and providing replacement products can all have a significant impact on profitability.

Customer Return Rate — Companies typically will show the actual amount of credits issued for returned products; however, this should be tracked in detail to determine root causes and what products are being returned and for what reasons.

Delivery Performance — Measuring the delivery performance is tracking the ability to meet the customer's originally negotiated delivery date on time. Performance can be expressed as a percentage based on the number of orders, line items, or dollar volume shipped on time. This is a critical measurement in evaluating the ability of a company to compete at a basic level and as a qualifier to obtain additional orders. The importance of just-in-time (JIT) performance can be a strategic competitive advantage even as to the time of day when a package is delivered. This the method used by Airborne Express and others to differentiate themselves to selected customers. This metric is a two-way street as it is also used to track vendor performance.

Process Lead Time — Overall process lead time is the cumulative time to procure raw materials and manufacture all components and subassemblies of the final product. Delivery lead time is the amount of time given to customers for delivery from the time an order is placed. Customers continually place pressure on manufacturers to reduce these lead times. This factor has led to deployment of design for manufacturing and configured order entry to meet or exceed customer expectations. In addition to measuring the amount of lead time, many companies also use the D:P ratio. This is the ratio of delivery lead time to production lead time. This ratio links customer requirements with the manufacturing process.

Defects per Thousand or Million Units — This is a standard quality control measurement. It is used to determine if processes are in control utilizing statistical process control (SPC) charts. These charts and measures were part of the earlier discussion regarding tracking continuous improvement efforts.

Travel Distance — Measuring the distance material has to travel is critical to lean programs since greater distances require more time and handling. This leads to wasted time, which frequently results in inventory buildup to offset the added distance and has a direct relationship on profit margins.

Space Utilization — All space represents a cost, so every effort to utilize warehouse and plant facilities fully should be made to eliminate the need for additional investment. This factor will also create focus on travel distance and produce shorter lead times and delivery times. This metric also forces good housekeeping, a critical component of lean thinking.

Sales per Employee — Net sales per employee is not only a measure of profitability but also a gauge of productivity and is determined by dividing annual sales by the total number of employees.

DIFFERENTIATION: PRODUCT SUPERIORITY

Measurements associated with differentiated strategies such as product superiority and product development correlate directly with an organization's ability to innovate. Product development and R&D activities are key drivers for maintaining a continuous flow of new ideas and concepts. Project evaluation is also covered.

Product Development Lead Time — The lead time for product development is very similar to production lead time and represents the amount of time required to develop new products from conception to final design. A second component for this metric is the amount of time required to take the newly developed product from final design to introduction to the market. The measurements here might be weeks or months.

Production Innovation — This can be measured by tracking the number of saleable new products that have been introduced. A typical time period might be annually and would be determined using the price list or product catalog. In addition to first mover advantage to gain market penetration, new introductions provide pricing leverage, which will provide higher margins in the early stages. This in effect provides "double gain" higher sales volume as well as higher profit margin.

Amount of R&D Expense — This ratio is determined by dividing a company's total expenditures for creating new products and processes by total annual sales. Higher percentages are indicative of the amount of commitment a firm devotes to product innovation.

Product Life Cycle — Products have a limited life and they pass through distinct stages from introduction, growth, maturity, decline, and then to obsolescence. Tracking products by sales and profitability over time will reflect various shifts and movement as they evolve. It is particularly important to track these trends, as innovative product concepts are crucial to maintaining a competitive advantage in today's economy. Percentage of sales from new products and revenue from new products are also key metrics to monitor.

Employee Competency Index — Product innovation is dependent on the knowledge and intellectual capabilities of employees. Developing an index unique to the organization that is based on patents received, innovation-related awards, competency levels of employees, and Baldrige assessment scores can be a good indicator.

ROIC % – Process/Product Improvements — This measure refers to the return on invested capital (net assets employed) earned by process and product improvements annually. A later section explains in detail how to use this measure to analyze and justify prospective projects.

Number of DFSS Projects — Tracking the number of design for Six Sigma projects on a trend basis will provide insight as to effort being applied to customer-driven ideas for new product or process projects.

DIFFERENTIATION: CUSTOMER INTIMACY

Metrics offered here apply to customer-driven strategies, but can also be tracked even when they are not the primary value proposition. Again, just because a measurement is listed does not mean it should be tracked. Organizations need to select the metrics that best fit their strategy and situation.

For marketing-focused strategies, it might be a good idea to develop a marketing scorecard of key measurements that provides management feedback on the effectiveness of customer-driven efforts.

Delivery Performance — Measuring on-time delivery is crucial for any customer-driven strategy and was described in detail in the section on lean Six Sigma metrics.

Field Service Response Time — The growing emphasis on customer service makes this measurement an important element of a differentiation strategy. It is determined by monitoring the average number of hours required to respond to a customer service call. Lengthy and numerous field visits are indicative of problems that may require attention. Many companies have increased their focus on service by establishing Internet sites and user communities to allow on-demand access for time-efficient self-diagnostic information. In addition, firms may want to track the average cost of making service calls.

Market Share Percentage — This measurement will indicate a firm's sales as a percentage of sales in its target market. Other indicators might include monitoring market growth compared to a firm's sales growth to provide clearer focus on the rate of progress.

Changes in Customer Master File — The customer master file in the ERP system contains all the key information about customers, including increases and removals. Monitoring changes will provide indicators about customer retention and new customers.

Sales Orders — Tracking sales orders by number, type, and dollar volume is something that should be done daily and weekly to provide the latest update on trends and forecasts.

Customer Satisfaction Index — Every firm will have a different set of standards and methods for building a customer index. Some factors to consider in building an index are customer retention, revenue from existing customers, market share, satisfaction surveys, complaints, and returns. Companies may also want to evaluate product quality, service quality, and sales of new products.

Number of Past-Due Orders — Measuring the number of past-due orders and the relative amount of tardiness should be tracked on an ongoing basis using trend charts.

Lost Sales Analysis — There are many ways to determine the amount of sales lost. Service and sales order people can track how frequently customer inquires were received and failed to order due to stock-outs or other reasons. Quotations submitted and lost can also be tallied. Salespeople can offer intelligence that will provide data and insight. Customer relationship management systems can also provide data regarding lost phone calls and other key data about customer inquiries. Gathering these data is important and will yield abundant information relative to the effectiveness of an organization's execution of strategy.

Lifetime Value of Customer Analysis — Developing customers into long-term loyal relationships will build into continued repeat business that can extend to multiple products as evidenced by Harley-Davidson's theme of "customer lifestyle." Gaining insight on the potential value of ongoing relationships produces understanding and insight into the value of each customer and how that tracks to the strategic value proposition.

DIFFERENTIATION: OPERATIONAL EXCELLENCE

All of the measurements described can relate to operational excellence, and most of them were covered in the lean Six Sigma section. However, there are a few more that did not apply to the other categories, which have been added in this section. Every company needs to decide what drives its level of operational excellence and it further needs to benchmark itself against other companies to determine where and how it compares.

Capital Investment as a Percentage of Sales — This metric is determined by dividing additions to fixed assets as well as disposals by net sales. Analysis of where money is spent will yield insight on programs for process improvements, capacity, and new products versus administrative or technology integration. Likewise, it will indicate the sale of unneeded productive capacity that has been created.

Lost Time Accidents — This measurement typically is tracked on an ongoing basis to reflect the safety focus of a plant facility. Safety is critical, not only to ensure public and environmental responsibility but also as a good indication of many production disruptions that are resulting from the failure to provide safe and orderly facilities.

Vendor Reliability — Reference was made to tracking on-time delivery by vendors in an earlier metric dealing with on-time delivery. Quality also correlates to reliability as companies aspire to achieve zero defects throughout the production process from receipt of material to delivery to the customer. Programs such as vendor-managed inventory and electronic data interchange transfer of funds, orders, and invoices utilizing paperless systems are also components of vendor reliability.

REPORTING CONCEPTS AND TOOLS

After providing guidance on what to measure, what the measurements mean, and how to determine them, it is important to consider the variety of ways they can be used. A good place to start is: Who needs information, what do they need, and why do they need it? Our discussion will cover a wide area of issues and ideas. The new reporting model will be applied to a range of scenarios that also fits more traditional situations.

Speed combined with reliability is a critical issue in transmitting information in the current economic environment, and some level of reporting is needed on a daily basis. By issuing what I call a "flash report" daily, an organization can stay on top of critical information. Each organization will differ, but a starting point might be sales, orders, cash, and some indication of production compared to the planned schedule on a daily basis. If management stays on top of the critical elements on a daily basis, then the potential for surprises is reduced. For weekly reporting, I suggest expanding the amount of data for managers to look at and show more metrics as fits the organization. One of the problems with data and reporting is that there is a tendency to have more information disseminated than can be used and acted on logically. Every effort should be made to keep the number of measures down to *the few that really matter*. Shop-floor and operations people have their own key data that they track, so from a financial standpoint, it is important not to create any overloads. If anything, it is better for financial and operations people to spend time working on identifying root causes of problems and solving them in contrast to generating a haystack of meaningless data and reports that are never looked at.

Before going further with reporting formats, it is important to point out that current levels of technology make it possible to generate data on demand and in almost any scorecard format plus digital dashboards, charts, and graphical illustrations. While all this is possible, we need to remember, and never forget, that if we feed in bad data, we are just setting ourselves up to make more mistakes faster. The flash reports should focus only on the data needed, so that managers focus only on what is important to help them stay on track. In discussing reporting concepts and tools, identification of how to present the right metrics is critical, as is providing a framework of how the data are presented. History provides a reference as to where we have been and needs to be part of the framework. Measuring the impact of what happened using lag indicators falls short in providing guidance in executing strategic themes. Nonfinancial metrics and a balanced scorecard need to be part of the reporting foundation in order to provide lead indicators of performance. The use and application of trend formats indicative of future performance provide management with tools that lead performance toward desired results. Once the structure for the daily and weekly trend format flash reports is in place, companies can distribute the information through a company portal over the Internet to increase speed and accessibility. A desirable objective is to create a structure for developing a rapid exchange of current forecast data for use with the trend format approach.

There are many links of responsibility and levels of reporting requirements that need to be considered in building a flow of data. Our focus is primarily from shareholders downward. If the foundation is solid, there will not be problems meeting the requirements of stakeholders, banks, government, and suppliers. From this point, I will take the flow downward for ease of illustration and with the realization that the critical areas for building a solid foundation are at the bottom of the pyramid. I constructed a reporting pyramid portrayed in Figure 13.5 and show how it is built up from activities and processes at the bottom, rising to shareholders at the peak. Linkages are connected to other users of the data lying outside the perimeter of the organization. The frequency of options for reporting information is shown in Figure 13.6. Every organization needs to build its own model for reporting frequency.

KNOWLEDGE MEASUREMENT AND MAPPING

The reality of understanding and measuring knowledge represents a difficult task. Having said this, we must understand how vitally important knowledge management and measurement are to any organization. Elements of knowledge management were covered in the previous chapter because of its significant impact on value and value management. There will be no single answer on valuation methods that will be satisfactory, least of all to accountants. In this

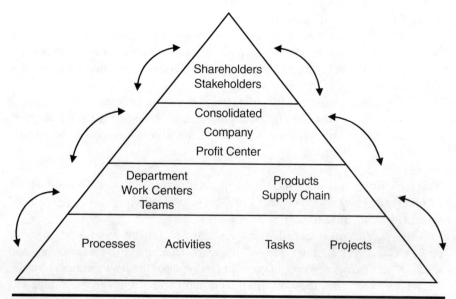

Figure 13.5. The Pyramid of Information Flow.

* Real time
* Hourly
* Daily
* Weekly
* Monthly
* Quarterly
* Annually
* Multiyear history

Figure 13.6. Reporting Frequency Options.

instance, the financial people are going to have to accept some nonlinear concepts and measures.

Knowledge, while it defies measurement, is the key strategic component to creating and sustaining value. There have been four primary tools for measuring intangibles and knowledge that include:

1. Direct intellectual capital (DIC) — Methods where the value is estimated using assessment methods and placing a dollar value on the components.

2. Market capitalization methods (MCM) — Equivalent to the difference between a company's market capitalization value and shareholders' value.
3. Return on assets (ROA) methods — Discussed under the knowledge scorecard technique in Chapter 12 and also the other value-based metrics that have been previously described.
4. Scorecard method — Identifies the various components and is measured through indexes and graphical presentations based on using a composite index of some type, but without placing a dollar value on the amount of intangible assets.

There will not be a clear method that will satisfy every question. The best advice I can offer is what you have already seen presented, which are EVA™, balanced scorecards, and Baldrige assessment scores.

One other area associated with knowledge is gaining an understanding of how it is converted into value. Mapping is a technique for identifying and tracking the sources of knowledge within an organization to a business process. Figure 13.7 identifies the flow from tacit and explicit knowledge to business

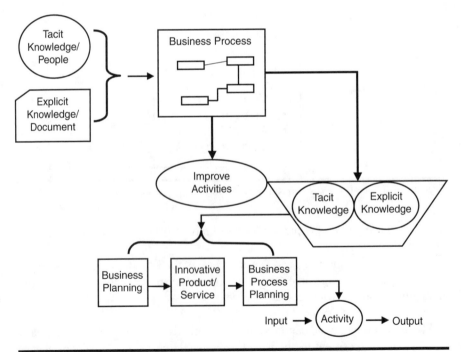

Figure 13.7. Concept of Process-Based Knowledge Mapping.

planning, innovation, and business process improvement. This is intended to be a brief introduction to the possibilities for linking knowledge management with business processes and scorecards to help identify and link knowledge that has strategic or business process impact for innovation and improvement. This topic goes far beyond the scope of this book, but it has implications for my future work on dealing with how to improve the profit focus of business processes and execution of strategic themes.

The underlying concept is to create a map identifying and showing the sources of knowledge and connect them to business processes and activities to assist organizations to improve the processes and effectiveness of strategy. The application is applied to people (or tacit knowledge) as well as explicit knowledge in the form of documented content. A multiphase approach consisting of mapping knowledge and sources of knowledge is then followed by analysis and application to create a framework for action and execution. This approach will only work when definitive documentation of business strategies has been developed and then combined with development of strategy maps. The potential for using this tool to improve the effective return on knowledge assets is significant when applied to the right situations.

COST OF QUALITY

Cost of quality could consume this entire book, so we must realize that if we touch on the basics, our objective has been achieved. Managers need to at least understand the two key concepts of quality cost: the cost of failure and the cost to control quality. Identifying and measuring these costs are not easily extracted from traditional accounting systems, and for this reason I suggest using activity-based analysis and Six Sigma tools to identify process costs and control them. This approach is based on providing the costs associated with each of these two concepts and applying the mix of methodologies to track and manage them.

The cost of failure, or nonconformance, is split into internal failure and external failure, as shown in Figure 13.8. The primary cost of internal failure is cost incurred while product is still in the production facility. Also shown are typical reasons for costs relating to external failure due to problems occurring after products have been delivered to the customer. Factors and issues related to prevention and deterrence of quality are identified in addition to the costs of appraisal.

The activities presented in the four charts can be analyzed and the cost of quality developed using activity-based analysis data. This analysis will provide a fairly accurate picture of the cost associated with defects and programs designed to eliminate them. In addition to the cost of quality, consideration should

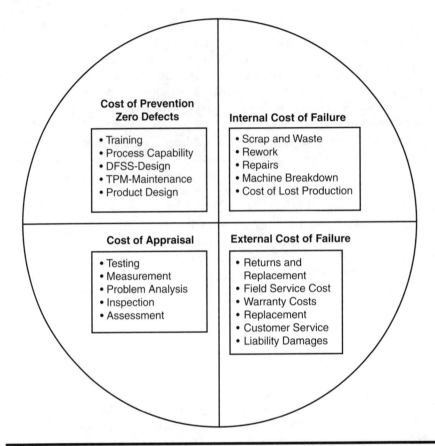

Figure 13.8. Cost of Quality Circle.

be given to techniques for continuous improvement and Six Sigma initiatives. The matter of inventory accuracy also relates to quality and its cost, so measuring inventory accuracy, accuracy of bills of material, and routings needs to be factored into the impact of quality costs.

COST OF INVENTORY

A chapter on measurement would not be complete without addressing the issue of determining the cost of inventory. Lean and TOC initiatives focus on reducing inventory and the savings it can generate. The question of how much inventory reduction programs save in real profit dollars is asked on a regular basis. Even though the savings are significant, it is not easy to understand the basis for the computation and the impact does not always show up immediately.

While inventory is an asset for accounting purposes, it is in many ways a liability and is the most difficult asset on the balance sheet to control. The object should be to only carry the amount of inventory necessary to buffer critically constrained resources and to ensure timely delivery to the customer.

The composition of inventory carrying costs includes three primary factors:

1. Capital costs relating to the cost of money invested in inventory and not available for other investment and opportunities. Minimally, this represents interest lost by not having to borrow at the going rate to fund the inventory investment. Based on the EVA™ model advocated, the capital cost should be a company's cost of capital (see Chapter 12).
2. Storage costs represent a charge for space, workers, and equipment.
3. Risk costs include:
   - Obsolescence, the loss of product value associated with changes in a model or style or technological development.
   - Damage associated with inventory being held or moved.
   - Pilferage representing goods that are lost, strayed, or stolen.
   - Deterioration relating to inventory that rots or dissipates in storage or whose shelf life is limited.

The cost of carrying inventory will vary from industry to industry and between companies because of the variability in the cost of capital and investment opportunities. Chapter 12 provided an outline for determining the cost of capital. The rate to be applied should be the weighted average cost of capital for the company in calculating carrying costs. Storage costs will vary with location and the type of storage needed. Risk costs also vary from very low to close to 100 percent for perishable goods.

A common guideline offered is to use a rate ranging between 20 and 30 percent as a cost for carrying inventory and an example might be:

- Cost of capital, 10 percent
- Storage costs, 8 percent
- Risk costs, 6 percent
- Total cost, 24 percent

The rate of 24 percent is a reasonable indicator on a pretax basis and breaks down to 2 percent per month. Assuming a 24 percent rate, an inventory reduction of $100,000 for an entire year would theoretically produce savings of $24,000 of income before taxes.

Every company should develop its own model because of the differences mentioned earlier. In addition to these factors, there are issues that will influence profitability because of removing unnecessary inventory such as improved production velocity due to reduced cycle times and other lean factors. In the discussion of EVA™, I cautioned about the danger of freeing up space and creating excess capacity that would not translate into savings unless it is utilized or sold. Likewise, savings in handling costs will not drop unless there is additional volume to replace it or the cost is eliminated. The savings from inventory reduction, while it might be lower, will likely be higher, perhaps as high as 40 to 50 percent. Whether the savings are 24 percent or 50 percent, it still is a significant saving that represents both a challenge and a huge opportunity.

PROJECT JUSTIFICATION

The details of financially justifying capital additions and setting priorities for projects have become somewhat of a lost art. My thoughts on measurements and methods for justification and setting project priorities are included to provide guidelines for making these calculations and decisions.

All potential projects associated with lean, Six Sigma, TOC, and capital appropriations should be identified and selected using common criteria applied consistently across the board. The common criteria have to be based on a set of financial guidelines that are consistent with the strategic vision of a company using measurements that will ensure the generation of economic value that exceeds the cost of capital. Earlier instructions were provided for calculating the weighted average cost of capital. This is suggested as representing a baseline return and that prospective projects should generate returns in excess of this minimum level.

The financial analysis should provide clear guidelines for minimum cost-reduction projects and rules for how the savings are calculated. The guidelines should factor in the amount of time required for implementation since this correlates to the speed that the savings will flow to profitability. In addition to savings, the proposed projects should indicate the length of time estimated to produce the calculated savings. Some projects will generate hard savings such as inventory reductions, faster cycle times, and setup reductions. Other savings will be "soft savings" relating to increased revenue, increased capacity, and new product innovations that have high risk. Other product innovations may be designed for Six Sigma specifically based on customer requests and have little or reduced risk. All of these issues should be spelled out and deal specifically with issues related to an organization's industry.

Justifying a project's potential will be more focused if follow-up audit and measurement of results are clearly spelled out. The audit procedures should specify the time period for tracking and the criteria for measurement. The evaluation process needs to include global guidelines for ensuring that projected savings end up on the bottom line. Savings associated with creating excess capacity must provide for how the excess will be utilized. It is recommended that a work order accounting procedure be established for accumulating costs associated with each project to avoid the necessity of allocations.

LINKING STRATEGY TO VALUE

In concluding, it seems appropriate to provide focus on creating the blend of measurements that will link the voice of the customer, the value chain, and the strategic themes so they will correlate to both physical and people assets. Figure 13.9 presents a strategic value loop that combines the ingredients of our discussion. The creation of scorecards should document and help execute the strategy. Customer satisfaction is supported by execution of the operational

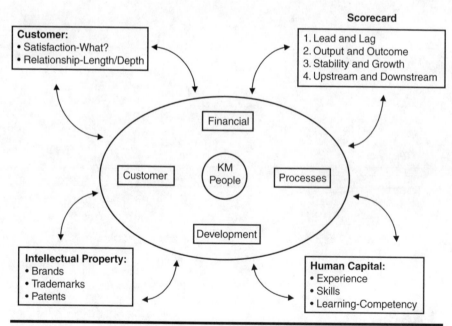

Figure 13.9. Strategy Value Measurement Loop.

processes and employee learning and growth activity that create real value to the shareholders.

The contributing factors in the strategic loop should help to guide the creation of the scorecards and selection of measures that will enable the senior leadership team, the organization, and its partners achieve their objectives. Clear understanding of the measures in addition to linkage, alignment, and relationships all need to be coordinated to keep the strategic vision on track.

This book has free materials available for download from the
Web Added Value™ Resource Center at www.jrosspub.com.

14

LEADERSHIP FOCUS, DISCIPLINE, AND DETERMINATION

All organizations require people to provide the creativity that builds value. However, the ingredient that provides the focus and discipline to convert knowledge and intellectual capital into value is leadership. This chapter is a necessary component for applying all the tools and measurements to produce effective bottom-line results. Without leadership and the passion of a vision, people and organizations will not become all that they can be.

This chapter brings together the discussion and concepts that represent my vision for this book. I will touch on issues of leadership and teachings of others in concrete ways that will make sense and help to bring together the tools and methodologies into useful and practical application. I needed a reference that provides a good explanation of all the management tools being offered as "the best answer and solution" to business problems. After conducting research and working with all the different methodologies and concepts, I have reached the conclusion that there is *no single best solution.*

There is a great deal of confusion in organizations, at all levels, as to how to use the various tools and how to measure results. Company management is frequently confused about what to do. In many situations, those in management think they know what they are doing, when in reality they have no clue. Conducting countless operational assessments, consulting engagements, and sitting in meetings with executives at all organizational levels leaves me with the conclusion that many businesses make money in spite of themselves. They could really create value if they had better training and better processes. One of my sayings is "management doesn't know what it doesn't know."

In my career, I also have been fortunate to work for, and be trained by, some of the best leaders and consultants in the business. From this foundation, I realized that a critical component for applying all the tools and concepts to create lasting value requires leadership and execution of strategy. The two best sources of guidance that I have found are Jim Collins' book *Good to Great* and *Execution* by Larry Bossidy and Ram Charan. These resources will be used to underscore some of the key lessons and examples that will be helpful and are needed in pulling it together and putting it to use for creating real value.

KNOWLEDGE MANAGEMENT BEGINS WITH PEOPLE

The invisible asset is knowledge and, as we learned, it will not generate any value unless somebody does something with it. In *Good to Great,* Jim Collins provides wonderful guidelines for defining leadership. Collins created a hierarchy consisting of five levels of leadership with "Level 5" at the top of the pyramid. Not that every leader can become a Level 5, but it is a model worth replicating since the potential value and benefits far outweigh not making the effort. The work ethics and ideals of how they are pursued provide a model that fits perfectly with our concept of value-based management and measurement.

The Level 5 approach emphasizes how critical it is to find the right people before attempting to find the right strategy. All the balanced scorecards in the world will be a waste of time if the right people are not on the bus and in the right seats. Getting the right people on the bus will first determine what additional people and knowledge are needed before embarking on the pursuit of strategy.

Getting the right people on the bus was a formula followed by AT&T Universal Card Services and it gave the company a significant competitive edge. This case study was detailed in *The Discipline of Market Leaders* by Michael Tracy and Fred Wiersema and describes the method used to hire team members. Universal Card Services used an approach of hiring "eager people with a lot of potential" and screening potential candidates that fit the attributes for performing routine work in a high-attitude manner and being adaptable to working on cross-functional teams focused on quality and continuous improvement of operational processes. The company took the time to hire the right candidates and then provided them with extensive training. The result was the application of a simple strategy based on operational excellence and continuous improvement utilizing empowered employees to capture a huge share of a competitive credit-card market that competitors took years to understand. I am not sure that

Paul Kahn, the CEO of Universal Card Services, was a Level 5, but if he was not, it sure seemed like he was a high Level 4. One further point: when Universal Card Services initially benchmarked itself against the Baldrige template it scored poorly, but after three years of applying its formula, it won the award. So getting the right people on the bus and focusing on who first produces results rather than focusing on "what" strategy was a clear winner in this instance.

PATIENCE, FOCUS, AND DISCIPLINE

Three effective guiding principles to follow in life and in business are:

1. Patience
2. Focus
3. Discipline

Impatience is a tendency to want too much too fast, and we see this weakness appear frequently on many fronts. Patience is the perseverance to stay on course to get the job done to achieve objectives. It represents the courage to do what needs to be done. Patience is easier when things are kept simple. The simpler we can keep things, the better. Jim Collins articulated what he calls "the hedgehog concept" using the story of Isaiah Berlin's "The Hedgehog and The Fox" to illustrate that hedgehogs take complex issues and make them simple and understandable. This is what I have attempted to do with the concept of profit-focused accounting, simplify it. The "hedgehog concept" was used by Collins to describe how great companies used one simple concept and stuck to it.

Focus brings clear and distinct sharpness to the target of attention. Whether the target of attention is a strategic theme, a problem, or a conflict, focus is the lens that provides clarity to narrow issues and choices. When choices are simplified, it becomes easier to focus the lens. Collins uses focus to illustrate how great companies apply the "hedgehog concept" by using three circles that intersect to gain deeper understanding and a framework for referencing their strategic choices. The concept provides a focused blueprint for how great companies apply the following three concepts:

1. What can you be the best in the world at?
2. What drives your economic engine?
3. What are you deeply passionate about?

Consistent application of this wonderful concept in conjunction with the tools I have presented is something every organization needs to utilize.

Discipline is my third principle. There are many good ideas and good strategies. Jim Collins conducted research that indicated that organizations with a high level of discipline achieve great results by focusing on achieving predictive results, whereas those with low discipline place their focus on measuring where they have been with lag indicators. Another example of discipline is execution, which Larry Bossidy and Ram Charan define as "the difference between promises and results."

THE FOCUS OF VALUE CREATION

Creating sustaining value requires that organizations and people place trust in their core capability and apply it with purpose. In the discussion of performance measurements, I described the core components organizations should monitor and the metrics that linked to specific strategies. Measuring for the sake of measuring, without a careful examination of the critical elements that represent the basic core of capability and culture aligned to goals and strategy, is a waste time and effort. Unfortunately, there are not enough companies that have taken the time and made the effort to apply the hedgehog concept and evaluate the results. This is not something I can do for organizations, but if they expect to create value by utilizing the tools I describe in this book, it is something they must do.

In Jim Collins' first book, *Built to Last*, co-authored with Jerry Porras, they pointed out that the "authenticity" of an organization to achieve "alignment" with core values and its culture was more important than the content of its "ideology." Core values represent the guiding principles of the organization. The organization's reason for existence can be called its purpose and provides the guidance that, when combined with core values, provides the foundation for its culture. Core values and purpose are presented by the leadership of an organization and provide the backbone of its culture and direction to the people striving to execute the vision and strategies. When all these fibers are aligned and woven together, then measurement on the scorecard takes on real meaning and the creation of value becomes possible.

Overcoming the lost relevance not only of traditional accounting but also of lost governance represents a major challenge for business leaders. The challenge we face today is that there are way too many foxes that we need to convert to hedgehogs. Actually, my experience is that the foxes are not as cunning as they thought and many of them need to spend a lot of time becoming involved and learning the basics. Managers need to go through a period of self-discovery or awareness to achieve authenticity as pointed out by Bossidy and Charan.

Figure 14.1. The Three Circles of Value Creation.

When they know themselves, managers with fox-like tendencies are able to make the transition to hedgehog thinking. This is a process of personal mastery that provides the ability to produce results when combined together with principles supporting the way results are achieved.

The "three circles of the hedgehog concept" brings a critical component that both individuals and organizations need to apply as they weigh the possibilities of values and purpose together with economic reality. In the context of the purpose of this book, I carefully considered each of the three circles and then applied my own thoughts as presented in Figure 14.1. The first step should be passion of purpose. Since we need to be successful, I think strategic superiority fits the second step. For the third step, I selected economic value. This seems to be a good fit for the concept of value creation.

SUSTAINING MOMENTUM

The creation of value is not a sudden event, but rather continued cumulative results achieved consistently over time. The entire concept of value-based management utilizing economic value added as a measurement was combined with the throughput accounting (profit-focused accounting) approach to overcome any tendency toward short-term profitability versus lasting benefit. It is fitting that Jim Collins used the "flywheel effect" to demonstrate that the power of continuous improvement applied consistently produced the great companies in contrast to the just good companies. The "flywheel" is described as "a massive metal disk mounted horizontally on an axle, about 30 feet in diameter, 2 feet thick, and weighing about 5,000 pounds." The key to the story of the flywheel is that once you get it going, after a great deal of initial effort, it just keeps on going. It takes a while, but when the things are working and initial results are achieved, continued results flow much easier. Many of the methodologies presented and described offer the promise of breakthrough results, but in reality the flywheel represents the best opportunity for breakthrough results.

This section is called "sustaining momentum" because real value can only be created through the sustained effort of people turning the flywheel to achieve the momentum of their efforts. The combined efforts of empowered people who are capable of working in multifunctional disciplines seem to represent the so-called "Holy Grail" that businesses search for but rarely find. The Toyota story emerged in Chapter 1 and several times since as a shining example of what it takes to achieve cumulative real value. Toyota, utilizing the training and concepts of W. Edwards Deming, is the best example of the flywheel I have seen.

When Jim Collins talked about the flywheel effect, he described the simplicity and focus of leaders to gain commitment and achieve alignment. Collins' examples, like Toyota, just did it and continued doing it. In the discussion relative to knowledge management and intangible assets, it was clear that no value emerged from these assets until something was done. Toyota represents one of the best examples of utilizing knowledge management as evidenced by the way its people communicate with each other, share information, and solve problems. Like the flywheel effect, it just happens on a continuous basis.

The balanced scorecard technique of measuring and executing strategy is really dependent on the flywheel effect for any success it generates. The scorecards represent a very effective enabling tool when organizations are instilled with the hedgehog concept and the flywheel principle. In other words, it will take more than just the scorecard to achieve success. Scorecards and other breakthrough methodologies such as Six Sigma will not achieve anywhere near the same results until they are used in conjunction with organizations employing value-based management founded on the principles of sustained momentum provided by the flywheel principle.

MAKING IT HAPPEN

Larry Bossidy and Ram Charan describe execution as "the difference between promises and results." Making it happen is getting things done. *Execution* provides some very direct and practical advice for getting things done and reinforces the concepts offered by Jim Collins in *Good to Great*. When the two points of view are combined, executives are provided with an exceptional set of guidelines for taking the management tools that have been discussed and achieving breakthrough results. Educating and converting the foxes so they can operate like hedgehogs becomes an achievable mission when employing the advice and tools offered by these authors.

Bossidy and Charan offer seven key concepts that will convert the foxes:

1. Know your people.
2. Insist on realism.
3. Set clear goals and priorities.
4. Follow through.
5. Reward the doers.
6. Expand people's capabilities.
7. Know yourself.

It is better to read *Execution* than for me to attempt to describe this excellent manuscript. During my career, I was fortunate to work for a man who was as tough and talented as Bossidy. From my perspective, I will highlight some key messages.

A key principle is to be in touch with the business. I learned to walk the floor and understand what was happening and this put me in touch with the people. Asking tough questions and creating a dialogue can connect executives with the reality of the business. By being authentic, executives put themselves into a hedgehog state and this removes the ego. Not every executive will reach a Level 5, but leaving one's ego in the closet, as they say, enables and provides the basis for the effective dialogues so necessary for solving problems. I have a friend who was an executive for a Fortune 100 company who frequently reminds me how he relied on his staff to get things done and feed him information because he did not have time to get involved. Every time I hear this story, it makes me shudder. Bossidy told the story of how Jack Welch would take the time to find out the facts and the details. More managers should take the time to leave the tower and go get the facts. If you do not do it, you will never be connected to the business and the people who make it successful, including the customers.

CULTURE AND CHANGE

Culture is much like business processes that evolve over time from the people responsible for creating them and working with them. It is a collection of mental models that get set into place, and making changes in the culture is a tough proposition. Level 5 leaders define culture by the power of adhering to the flywheel effect. One Level 5 leader said, "We tried to bring our plan to successful conclusion, step by step so that people would gain confidence from the successes." This is just the way they do it, and when people see where they can go, it turns out not to be a big deal.

Bossidy and Charan state it a little differently, but with the same meaning. They indicate, "Cultural change gets real when the aim is execution. You don't need a lot of complex theories or employee surveys to use this framework." The concept is based on continued coaching and rewarding performance. It becomes a continuous process of coaching and improvement until the desired changes are implemented. The process is constantly measured combined with feedback and reinforcement. The technique is predicated on maintaining an informal and authentic atmosphere using continuous dialogue. This is what Collins calls the concept of "confronting the brutal facts," and Bossidy and Charan call it the "unvarnished truth."

Changes will be required if improvements are to occur. Change and its implementation represent a topic for another book, but clearly the need and the challenge for change are present. My experience has been that an approach of "seeing the light" will probably not have the same impact and results as "feeling the heat." While change is tough, Collins, Bossidy, and Charan offer excellent advice on facing current reality.

GOVERNANCE

The topic of compliance with Sarbanes-Oxley and its requirements was discussed in Chapter 12 and correlated to value-based management. The principles I am espousing here go beyond legislation to the foundation of what will make governance occur. My sense is that no Level 5 ever experienced difficulty with understanding ethics and cooking the books would never be an option. The creation and building of true value will emerge without any fuss and fanfare.

This chapter is not required reading for organizations that already practice what I have preached, but is for those leaders looking for a good road map. The power of the concepts offered by Jim Collins, Larry Bossidy, and Ram Charan should be convincing proof of the road to follow and the forks to take. One of these men has researched the good and the great; the other two have lived the journey.

One element of governance does need to be expanded on; that is having the foundation for providing understandable and reliable financial information that is trustworthy. Lean, Six Sigma, activity-based analysis, and balanced scorecards — when applied together with an effective and simplified accounting and reporting system utilizing value-based measurement — will provide a rock solid foundation. People need to understand the possibilities, the effort, and the time required to build a good foundation. The answer is not in the methodologies, but in the people.

LINKING STRATEGY WITH PEOPLE

I was fortunate to be able to attend a week-long accountant's boot camp that was a workshop designed to help CPAs become effective business advisors. One of the primary themes voiced again and again was FTI. FTI is an acronym for "failure to implement." There are no shortages of ideas and strategies, but they are worth nothing if they are not implemented. Ideas and strategies do not implement themselves; they require people to implement them.

Effectiveness begins with putting the right people in the right spot combined with the necessary motivation to get the job done. Good leaders get to know their people and know what is required to implement and execute the strategy. Jim Collins, Larry Bossidy, and Ram Charan send a clear message about finding and placing the right people on the bus. Then if you give them a balanced scorecard to map the strategy, they will take the bus to the destination, maybe utilizing some routes we did not know about.

After the right people are on board, they then need the coaching and training combined with the right tools to get the job done. I have provided the basic knowledge regarding a wide variety of tools. Both the people selected to execute the strategies as well as the leadership of the organization need to be aware of the tools and their own capacity to execute strategy. Good leadership, good people when they have the right tools, and measurements have a significant capacity to do a great job executing an average strategy in contrast to a great strategy that cannot be executed.

MASTERING CHANGE

One of the events that provided new direction to me occurred during a stint with a national CPA and consulting firm. The firm sent me to a unique management-development program established for both clients and its own staff. One of the team members suggested that I read *The Fifth Discipline* by Peter Senge and *Mastery* by George Leonard as guides for achieving self-mastery. One of my friends, a sports psychologist who works with PGA tour players, helped me gain more understanding of the process of mastery and its relationship to leadership.

There is nothing more difficult than making changes, especially in business organizations. However, the process of focusing on what, why, and how will start to make the mountain of change easier to climb. The more that leaders and employees can grasp the process of self-mastery, the easier it will be to make the climb. This is a much better alternative than trying to cope with crisis change. Leaders who guide the way for the right people driving the bus are more likely to build and create lasting value.

A FEW SMALL DETAILS

The message of this chapter has been to provide direction on how the great organizations become "great" by not accepting just "good." Leadership is a key component of the formula because leaders need to select the right people and then help them understand how to use the right tools for the job.

The ability to get the job done defines the discipline of executing strategy, not making strategy. Discipline is having the focus and patience to apply the hedgehog concept and the flywheel effect to concentrate on the vital few details that really matter. By applying self-mastery and understanding people, I hope that the leaders (together with the aspiring leaders who read this) will gain some understanding about how to use the tool kit. I think the process between leaders and employees is a two-way street and the ideas can go up the ladder as well as down the chain.

WAV Web Added Value™

This book has free materials available for download from the Web Added Value™ Resource Center at www.jrosspub.com.

15

MEETING THE MEASUREMENT CHALLENGE

Management methodologies emerged continuously up until about the year 2000 and then the bubble burst, sending everyone into a hunker-down mode. Enron, WorldCom, Tyco, and other scandals have put us into a governance mentality. While Sarbanes-Oxley is applicable to firms regulated by the Securities and Exchange Commission, there will be a cascade effect that will set a standard for all organizations to measure against. This dose of reality is a good thing because it will start making companies go back to the basic essentials necessary to create value. Lasting value will become the accepted norm in contrast to quarter-to-quarter short-term results that provide an incentive for bad decision making.

By forcing management back to basics, the methodologies and tools I have been explaining then need to be applied in the proper situations and with understanding of how to use them. For me, this book represents the start of an ongoing procession of teaching and training tools that can be used to build on this effort. This chapter brings together all the tools and provides direction and expectations for focusing them on generating profit and creating value.

My objective was to educate business owners, managers at all levels of the organization, accountants, and educators on how to effectively use the best management philosophies and methodologies with a simplified approach to accounting and performance measurement. Accounting gets to the bottom line, so by evolving from simplified accounting back through the management concepts, it will create better understanding.

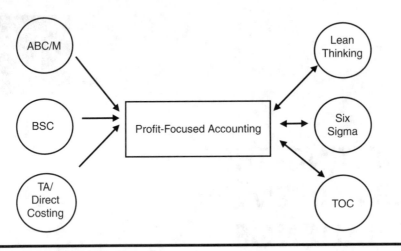

Figure 15.1.   Where We Have Been.

WHERE WE HAVE BEEN

Understanding where we have been can be best illustrated by referring to Figure 15.1 to see the interrelationships of how the variety of tools flow together. The underlying premise was to make management accounting relevant by providing a model based on throughput accounting and the Theory of Constraints (TOC). This model is called profit-focused accounting. These concepts were discussed in Chapters 4, 6, and 9. By overcoming some of the objections that the traditional accountants and CPAs associated with throughput accounting, it will provide more opportunities for TOC as a management philosophy to be utilized and understood by organizational management at all levels. It is a good tool; therefore, why shouldn't it be used?

Because of the shift of organizational expenses to overhead from direct labor and variable costs, it is important to utilize activity-based analysis to gain understanding of what drives these costs and activities. Therefore, activity-based analysis needs to be in the tool kit. It was not my intent to integrate activity-based costing with the accounting system, but rather to utilize a simple time-based model to direct overhead to products and customers. The objective was to achieve at least 80 percent accuracy in contrast to searching for a perfect answer. Process analysis and continuous improvement are essential for any business, and traditional cost management and throughput accounting did not always provide the needed focus. While it is management's job to execute strategy, a map and a scorecard become essential tools for getting the job done. The balanced scorecard is not the last word in strategy execution, but it sure can help.

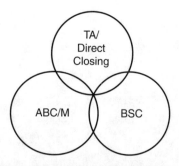

Figure 15.2. The Three Circles of Profit-Focused Accounting.

The balanced scorecard was added to the model since lead indicators provide better insight than traditional financial lag indicators. Understanding the intangible assets and knowledge assets contained within the organization is often the difference between success and failure in pursuing innovative differentiated strategies. I did not view the balanced scorecard as a method for tracking nonfinancial key performance indicators, but as a critical component in aiding organizational leaders to track their performance pursuing strategies and to help keep them on target. Balanced scorecards complete the model that I call the three circles of profit-focused accounting as shown in Figure 15.2.

Actually, the book started with a summarized description of the lean enterprise after the initial history lesson in Chapter 1. There is no one who will argue that eliminating waste throughout an organization is a bad idea. What we did learn is that companies that pursue lean are not necessarily applying Six Sigma to control processes after they have been streamlined. On the contrary, there are organizations pursuing Six Sigma that have not utilized lean. In fact, there frequently is confusion between the two methodologies. A third philosophy, called TOC, is being utilized by a number of practitioners to the extent that APICS added TOC to its body of knowledge and offers a wide range of educational material. TOC practitioners utilize both lean and Six Sigma concepts. TOC has many tools and attributes that should be used to leverage and accelerate lean and Six Sigma programs. By utilizing them together, management will achieve much more than by isolated application. The three circles of management philosophy are presented in Figure 15.3. TOC was strategically placed in the top circle since it links to the concept of profit-focused accounting and has a wider reach than lean and Six Sigma because of its ability to achieve buy in and provide multiple management solutions not provided by the other philosophies. By moving from left to right, lean should be implemented before Six Sigma since it is easier to implement conceptually and it does not make sense to try to control processes before they have been accelerated and the waste

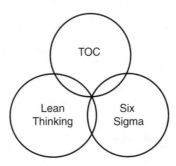

Figure 15.3. Three Circles of Management Philosophy.

removed. The project management capability of TOC represents a significant benefit to improving the effectiveness of Six Sigma, which is a project-driven methodology.

The remainder of the discussions focused on the principles of value-based management and creating true long-term value. It is important to realize the difference between the accounting model and the economic model. Application of the economic model that employs the concepts of economic value added (EVA™) is very important in applying the profit-focused accounting approach. Consistent with EVA™, we need to look beyond the compliance issues of the Sarbanes-Oxley Act to fix and stabilize the reporting process and underlying business processes. This will provide shareholders with the trust that financial results have a solid foundation.

None of the concepts and methodologies are worth a plugged nickel without leadership. Management needs a lighthouse founded on the concepts of the hedgehog and application of the flywheel of effective execution. This sets the stage for how we can best apply these concepts and get the wheels turning.

THE PROFIT-FOCUSED ACCOUNTING MODEL

Throughput accounting is a key component of TOC, a management philosophy that is still searching for its true potential and acceptance. One of the reasons why it has not arrived is the failure of its accounting component to be embraced by traditionally trained business managers. Actually, accountants like the concept of direct costing and the simplicity it offers. The shortfall lies in the complexities of the global supply chain, as its informational requirements have not been adequately addressed. The model of throughput (sales less material) less operating expense was not capable of providing enough detail. This lack

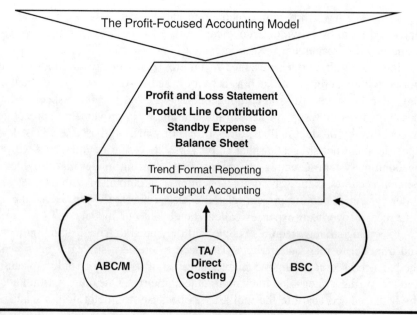

Figure 15.4.   The Profit-Focused Accounting Model.

of flexibility, when combined with terminology that did not fit the traditional understanding, took away from the initial appeal created by *The Goal* (Goldratt). Accountants like *The Goal*. From the training workshops I conduct, it seems to be one of the most recognized business books even though it is almost twenty years old. Based on the need for something better than generally accepted accounting principles (GAAP) and the lack of relevance provided by traditional accounting, I decided to "fix what was broke" and provide a better model as presented in Figure 15.4.

The core concept of the accounting model is throughput accounting because it provides the simplicity and speed required to meet the demands of business conditions. Recall that throughput accounting was doctored up by adding back direct labor even though the case was made in *The Goal* that it really was not a variable cost. Most enterprise resource planning (ERP) systems utilize the quantity of time measured by labor equivalents to drive their planning modules. This, combined with long-term acceptance and immateriality, led me to modify the throughput model without giving up much (if anything) and perhaps gaining some new understanding from the "traditional" camp. The profit-focused accounting model employs trend format reporting that lends itself to continuous forecasting and evaluating full-year data in contrast to focusing on quarterly numbers. We have throughput accounting and all the TOC benefits and have enhanced them by providing added capability of *enabling tools* and predictive value-based management measurement.

In viewing the model presented in Figure 15.4, I make sure that it is supported with enabling tools such as activity-based costing and management and the balanced scorecard. The components of overhead and the respective business processes they support needed the continuous improvement approach and traceability by product and customer offered by activity-based analysis. I was specific about not suggesting that activity-based costing be integrated with the accounting system. Creating an activity-based costing model that provides 80 percent accuracy is the way to go. This approach, combined with using a work order system to capture project-related costs, is necessary because of the significance of overhead expenses called standby in our model.

Executing strategy requires people, but they need to have leading indicators and a model to map out strategy. The need to create a strategic focus makes the balanced scorecard a good enabler because of its ability to aid in executing and measuring strategy and track nonfinancial metrics. One other reason I added the balanced scorecard to the tool kit was because it is helpful with managing knowledge assets and intellectual capital.

Before I leave the profit-focused model, I need to underscore the importance of viewing the results of operations through a direct costing lens. The direct costing/throughput model creates understanding of how volume and pricing impact profitability that is not provided by the traditional costing presentation. By adding balanced scorecard and activity-based analysis, managers gain a multidimensional picture of the strategic possibilities that is not offered using traditional accounting.

BARRIERS TO PROGRESS

Perhaps the biggest obstacle to adopting a profit-focused accounting model predicated on TOC is resistance to giving up the traditional model even if it is not relevant and is flawed. Traditionally trained managers frequently have difficulty making a change even when they realize that what they are doing is not working. It is like trying to get cigarette smokers to stop even when they know it is bad for their health. One of the additional roadblocks is that direct costing is not supported by GAAP because of the requirement to include overhead as a component of valuing inventory assets. This may shift as the economic accounting model becomes more popular. The leaner our thinking when combined with faster inventory turnover, the less significant the overhead component becomes. The key is to convince and show accountants how they can bridge the gap from direct costing to GAAP. It is really a pretty easy crossing.

The biggest challenge is the time and effort to train entire management teams on how to make the transition and prove to them that the bottom line will get better by making the change. I think that the impact of the Sarbanes-Oxley Act will provide motivation as it takes hold and shifts down to privately held companies because of the cascade effect. Corporate reporting systems are currently not providing reliable data, and as these processes get fixed, by law, we will see more activity toward new concepts because managers will start seeing the advantages associated with them. Like the flywheel effect described, once the wheel starts turning, the greater will be its momentum. Management may not like the cost of education and the cost to fix processes, but after years of neglect will finally not have much choice.

I cannot discuss barriers to progress and not comment on the problems related to organizational silos and turf mentality. People are people, and when they create their pockets of power, it is tough to get them to let go. This was a problem that sales and operational planning addressed. This concept needs to be pushed beyond the sales and operational levels; it needs to encompass the entire organization. Again, Sarbanes-Oxley is resurrecting sales and operational planning as a "back-to-basics" approach.

Before we will gain much ground in launching a new initiative, we have to gain support from senior management. This again goes back to education. The educational mission needs to drive senior managers to become committed and involved with a focused direction. We will not always succeed in placing Level 5 leaders into every organization, but the more these types of leadership qualities become the norm, the more success we will see in achieving a shift to a new accounting and reporting model that utilizes all the tools.

RELIABLE REAL-TIME REPORTING

Real-time reporting is being expected of corporations, as investors increasingly demand more information, both financial and nonfinancial. The trend is to future-driven information that is indicative of tomorrow's bottom line for next year and beyond. Because of available technology, it is possible to provide financial data almost as it occurs by using the Web and XML and XBRL. The question is: How good are the data and can we trust them? When we start providing financial information on a real-time basis, then it is critical that organizations make sure there is a solid foundation of business processes feeding the technology. While the technology and integration systems may be capable, the same cannot be said of the underlying business processes. Organizations have done a poor job of documenting and employing reliable business processes and internal control systems. These weaknesses can be found in ERP systems that were poorly implemented and where users were not adequately trained to use them. These systems often fail to provide reliable data and are certainly not ready for real-time reporting.

The more simplicity provided in the accounting model, the easier it becomes to support a real-time reporting system that is reliable. One of the key components to real-time reporting will be the use of predictive process-based reporting systems to provide the financial and nonfinancial data frequently demanded by investors and management. It is true that we have a knowledge-based economy, but it takes trained people and time to provide a reliable process framework capable of supporting meaningful data that can be trusted.

The profit-focused accounting model provides the capability of moving to a real-time reporting system. Combined with the predictive trend reporting format, this lends itself to meeting these new demands. Adding an activity-based analysis feature to throughput accounting represents a big step forward to achieving continuous process improvement so that business processes will gradually become more reliable. Organizations will have to move in this direction or go out of business because they cannot compete.

BUILDING VALUE-BASED PROFITABILITY

Sustained profitability is essential to building and creating value. A simplified reporting model makes understanding easier and allows for acceleration in providing the key data that managers need to generate sustained profits utilizing an economic model. The economic model that employs EVA™ to monitor the effectiveness of sustained profitability represents a departure from the accounting model driven by earnings per share. The combination of a longer term emphasis such as EVA™ measurement with a throughput focus offered by profit-focused accounting provides the measurement formula necessary for value-based profitability.

In a knowledge-based economy, it will take more than measurement to generate and build value-based profits. Figure 15.5 illustrates the components of some key additional elements on which organizations will need to focus. The strategy is knowledge, and knowledge will create the strategy and innovation necessary for survival by helping to build a foundation of profit and value creation. In effect, the knowledge matrix and map is a scorecard that organizations need to create. The elements suggested should, as a minimum, include

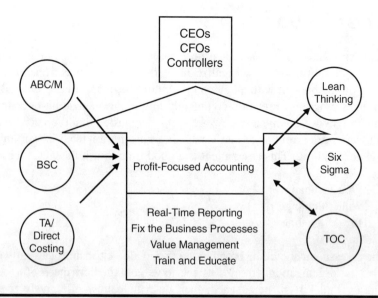

Figure 15.5.   The Components of Value-Based Profitability.

employees, intangibles, customers, and processes. Employees represent the source of knowledge, and too frequently organizations are not aware of the knowledge and skills their employees possess. You have to understand what you have before you can make any determination of what the organization needs. A similar inventory should be conducted of intangibles which would include patents, brands, image recognition, and other types of assets that will not be recorded on the balance sheet. Information should be gathered regarding customer preferences, satisfaction indexes, and other soft information about what customers expect.

The key information regarding all of an organization's business processes should be inventoried. This step should include mapping both production and commercial processes. Activity-based costing will provide information as to process costs and reliability of process controls. Process information will yield data that will help generate predictive forecasts and create models for simulation to provide a competitive advantage.

Linkage relates to the effectiveness of how the processes flow relative to knowledge that needs to be employed. By knowing where knowledge is located and how processes are linked, it is possible to create alignment to build and create value-based profitability. Mapping knowledge together with business processes becomes a key component and driver of sustained profitability and innovation.

HOLY GRAILS DO NOT EXIST

The concepts and models that have been discussed will not suddenly produce instant profitability. When we realize how the flywheel effect operates, then focusing on the present with an eye on the future begins to make sense. Before launching a program to revamp completely how the organization operates and plug in an array of completely new tools, it is suggested that the very first step be to assess the current state and establish a baseline of what is working and what is not working. This assessment is a good time to ask the TOC questions:

1. What to change
2. What to change to
3. How to change

The assessment should be broad based and evaluate the tools currently being used by the organization. If some of the tools contained in the profit-focused accounting tool kit are being used, then determine how effectively they are utilized and where improvements can be implemented. If some of the tools I suggest, as *enablers,* are not used, ask why they are not being used. When conducting this assessment, remember the three questions that represent a key component of TOC. It is very difficult to argue against employing the TOC logic and tools. The Sarbanes-Oxley Act is a good reason to take stock and evaluate, even if your company is not publicly traded. Faster, more reliable information represents a competitive advantage, and now is not the time to wait and see what everybody else is doing.

In the discussion of creating and building value-based profitability, I was explicit about the importance of business processes. A thorough review of the effectiveness of an organization's business processes should be a key element of any assessment. All segments of the organization should be assessed from the perspective of strategy, leadership, learning and growth, sales and markets, and product innovation. Nothing should be omitted. If processes are out of control, then perhaps Six Sigma should be a consideration. If your organization feels that such an approach is too costly, then consider using the Six Sigma tools to the extent they are affordable and effective.

Not all the tools will work for every organization. My purpose was to offer a new TOC accounting and reporting model that I knew would work based on proven results. Even though the exact reporting model might not fit, I suggest that the basic concepts I have presented are on the minds of many financial executives who are under pressure to provide accurate financial results faster. Even though balanced scorecards might not be right for every company, the underlying concepts of how to employ nonfinancial metrics and to cope with knowledge management represent opportunities. However, by conducting an assessment and evaluating the possibilities, organizations at least have stopped to realize the possibilities and the potential of the tools that are available and can understand their application.

Do not expect miracles and instant results. I suggest selecting and trying the tools that will do the best job for each situation. Perhaps lean is a tool that can work well with TOC, and if Six Sigma is needed to develop a robust product design or design a process for Six Sigma control, then it makes senses to take this approach. Think about how the thinking process of TOC might achieve buy in and melt down the functional barriers to progress and profitability. Common sense should prevail. There is no shortage of tools. We need to go back to basics and apply them to increase profitability and create value.

Many of the problems we are attempting to solve did not occur overnight. They represent a buildup that occurred over a period of time. Therefore, why do we expect to resolve these issues by sprinkling twinkle dust on them to create solutions? I offer TOC because it has a broad range of capability that will function well with the other tools. Activity-based costing and management is grounded on continuous improvement, which will be needed to identify and eliminate the root causes. Continuous improvement only goes so far and it does not drive innovation of products and services. So why not use this tool for its intended use? When used in conjunction with TOC, root causes will be eliminated and the TOC tools will help keep organizations focused on continuous development of value propositions that can produce breakthrough results. I will offer my vision of how all of these tools flow together and a replacement for the sales and operational planning model.

THE PROFIT-FOCUSED PLANNING PROCESS

This model evolved as I wrote the book, and more evolution will be required to adjust and tweak these original concepts. Since a picture is worth a thousand words, a model, called the profit-focused planning process, is presented in Figure 15.6. Similar to sales and operations planning, the model or planning process begins with the customer. Information beginning with assimilation of knowledge-based data from the customer flows to the organization linked in cross-functional teams within the functional structure in real-time format. The cross-function buy in is facilitated utilizing the TOC thinking process and marketing concepts based on achieving maximum throughput. Information is disseminated to teams to coordinate and feed the business intelligence analysis that is grounded on solid business processes that employ all three elements of the profit-focused accounting model. The balanced scorecard is a key element

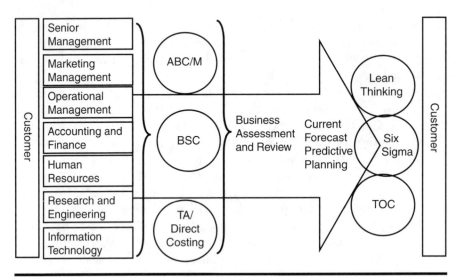

Figure 15.6. The Profit-Focused Planning Process.

of the communication flow to process information to key knowledge components that are mapped and linked with the strategic theme of the organization. The speed of throughput accounting and time-based activity analysis is then used to assist with a continuous business assessment and review to produce a process-based current forecast and a predictive planning simulation model. A model of continuous process planning similar to how advanced planning and scheduling systems operate would replace the concept of a rolling forecast. The entire profit-focused planning process is based on a solid foundation of reliable business processes and a reliable real-time financial reporting system. The vision is to have knowledge management models that process data from customers to create reliable and predictive forecasts. This process is pervasive across the entire organization in real time that extends beyond the scope and capability of sales and operational planning.

The technology to provide information in the fashion described is available. Making the model workable and effective depends on simpler concepts to handle the acceleration without giving up accuracy and key data. By creating and building a process-based throughput accounting model, the planning concept then becomes a practical and attainable vision. The TOC thinking process and methodologies combined with a strategy execution scorecard and mapping tool will be required to link and align the cross-functional organizational teams. The predictive forecasts then flow through lean thinking, Six Sigma, and TOC to provide the customer with the organization's unique value proposition. Perhaps traditional accountants would call this a pipe dream, I would call it a competitive necessity in a global knowledge-based economy.

LEADERSHIP

The success of achieving real progress in building and implementing reliable profit-focused accounting models that will be relevant requires leadership. Since I referred to the Level 1 through 5 model provided by Jim Collins, I would suggest that the humility, will, and determination of Level 5 have to be the goal. As we have seen, evidenced by the continuing scandals, it would be nice to see more unwavering resolve to do what must be done combined with the ability to look in the mirror and take the blame. Good leaders give credit to their team because a single person can only do so much. When team members are rewarded and given credit, they will make sure that the leader hears what he or she needs to hear.

THE RIGHT PEOPLE

The right people are more important than the right strategy and having a scorecard to execute it. Having the right scorecard with the wrong people will not get you out of the driveway, so making a highway trip is out of the question. Many times, the right people exist within the organization, but they need to understand the potential of what is possible and have the right tools available so they can apply them. I have conducted countless operational and strategic assessments and have come to the conclusion that many times all that was required was training and education. The learning and growth component is overlooked too frequently and given a lower priority as leadership searches for a silver bullet.

When the right people are on the bus and understand the tools and how to use them, the potential for breakthrough results exists. When shareholders want to create value, it is important for organizational leadership to learn the value of the right tools and make the effort to learn about them so they can be deployed within the organization. Part of the education process for senior leadership is to come to grips with the time and effort required to make effective use of the wide range of tools and applications described in this book. CEOs are not going to take time they do not have to read the countless manuals describing all the methodologies that have been presented. However, by gaining a sense of what has been provided, they will be in a position to grasp the underlying concepts and be realistic regarding the needs of their supporting teams. They will gain a sense of the vast potential of philosophies such as TOC and use it to capture the benefits to build profit-based value.

I provided the leadership component in this book because the tools will be *ineffective* without *it*. When leaders understand the hedgehog concept and fly-wheel effect, they will realize the importance of finding the right people and removing the wrong people. The right people will know where to take the bus and what maps to use to chart the trip. Educate and empower the right people and there is no limit as to what might be possible.

CONFRONTING REALITY

The profit-focused accounting approach is based on acceleration of simplified data that employs the concept of always viewing the latest forecast of full-year results. This approach only works when managers confront current reality and employ the best factual data. Forecast data need to be as realistic as possible based on solid actual data and reliable processes that provide the predictive forecasts. Frequently, this means listening to what the customer actually says and not what you would like customers to say.

The effectiveness of the profit-focused planning process requires creating a climate where people communicate facts and not hunches and hearing the brutal truth is okay. The atmosphere created by the teams of the right people will encourage a culture of questions and not just answers. Teams are encouraged to pursue root causes and conduct probing analysis without blame and retribution. The profit-focused accounting model should trigger warning flags that convert information into action. My hope is that Dr. Deming's advice regarding the elimination of fear will prevail.

DISCIPLINE, CLARITY, AND FOLLOW-THROUGH

A key component of the training is to create a culture of discipline. TOC offers a wonderful concept called critical-chain buffer management that is grounded in the principle of avoiding multitasking. This requires disciplined people exercising disciplined thought to produce disciplined action. Discipline is a term that is the foundation for *Good to Great* based on Jim Collins' results of researching the ingredients it takes to be great. This was also the conclusion presented in *Execution* by Larry Bossidy and Ram Charan.

Along with discipline, it is important to create and communicate clear priorities and goals. Organizations and the people within them have to make disciplined choices. That means paring the wide range of options down to the few simple and clear priorities that really count. Clarity is achieved through the process of taking a multitude of complex data and choices down to the simplest level possible in order to gain increased understanding. There will no doubt be many critics who might say that simplified financial reporting as I suggest it will never work. I would counter by commenting that we have not succeeded in fifty years in making management accounting relevant, so why not take a simplified proven approach that does work. I have taken some slight liberties with the original Goldratt concept of throughput accounting and have added the enhancement of enablers where they might apply, but the foundation is the simplicity and focus that were originally intended.

The simplicity of the profit-focused accounting approach facilitates follow-through. Because of its ease of understanding and readability, we avoid chances for not following through. The presentations and approach are designed to concentrate accountability that will be understood. When applied in a culture of commitment and discipline, procrastination is eliminated as a possibility.

A PROFIT-FOCUSED CONCEPT FOR ACTION

This book was based on the hypothesis that more and better information should be provided in a single source about all of the management philosophies and methodologies that are being touted as cures for all business ailments. I was trained in contribution accounting, and knew that TOC-based throughput accounting could be enhanced, thereby giving it greater acceptance. There is only so much you can present when the objective is to provide improved understanding on a wide range of topics, each with its own level of complexity. Certainly, more refinements are possible and will occur as use expands.

In providing an educational foundation about different methodologies, it became clear that the accounting and measurement tools could work together as *enablers* to provide better information for better decisions. Traditional management accounting started to lose relevance back in the early 1960s and after the bubble economy. My recommendation is to return to simple basics using direct costing and to employ value-based management and valuation concepts to drive real value creation. The basics of throughput accounting are a solid tool that should be utilized by more companies, along with activity-based analysis and balanced scorecards. I have seen too many companies that fly blind and are making bad decisions just because they do not know better. This becomes an educational and training challenge to lift CPAs and traditionally trained accountants and management to a new era of enlightenment. This is where I feel the Sarbanes-Oxley Act may be a blessing in disguise because it will shift some paradigms.

The development of this book and my research allowed me to gain an understanding of what could be possible if organizations would come to understand how TOC, lean thinking, and Six Sigma could *enable* each other for much greater impact. I saw some indication where the three methodologies were being employed together, but for the most part were islands unto themselves. If senior management realized the potential impact it could achieve by putting all three horses in the harness, it would be astounded. This is especially true when you put TOC in the lead harness to assist guiding the way and *enabling* lean and Six Sigma. The reasons for this conclusion are that TOC provides the capability for buy in, marketing, measurement, project management, and for operational scheduling. When value management is included, the flywheel can really turn.

The profit-focused planning process will not work unless the business processes are fixed. My assessments and observations provide indications that the underlying "back-to-basics" processes have not been mapped and improved to run ERP systems let alone real-time reporting systems. The desire and the technology may be there, but the underlying structure still has a way to go. Companies are restating financial results because of errors associated with installing ERP systems and the failure to train employees properly on how to use them. This might be a blessing created by Sarbanes-Oxley since CEOs and CFOs have to assess and certify that their reporting systems are reliable under penalty of fines and imprisonment.

Real-time reporting provides a competitive advantage to companies. Not only does it yield a market advantage, but it affords managers with faster access to information the ability to jump ahead of their competitors. Real-time reporting will become a reality; it is just a question of time. The simplicity of the reporting model offered by profit-focused accounting and its enabling supporting tools represents a great opportunity for organizations to achieve this objective with the least amount of investment and the greatest opportunity for increased bottom-line impact.

This formula is not a blueprint that will fit all organizations. However, every organization can apply these concepts to enhance its management, financial reporting, and performance measurement. It will take leadership, education, and training combined with the discipline to execute the concepts that will work most effectively for each organization. You now have a tool kit and basic knowledge of where and how to use it. I encourage you to open your mind to the possibilities of building a foundation of profit-focused value.

This book has free materials available for download from the
Web Added Value™ Resource Center at www.jrosspub.com.

REFERENCES

Arnold, J.R. Tony, *Introduction to Materials Management*, Prentice Hall, Englewood Cliffs, NJ, 1998, pp. 420–421.

Bartley, Robert L., Economic profit vs. accounting profit, *Wall Street Journal*, June 2, 2003.

Bossidy, Larry and Charan, Ram, *Execution*, Crown Business, New York, 2002.

Brown, Mark Graham, *Keeping Score*, Productivity Inc., Shelton, CT, 1996.

Cashman, Kevin, *Leadership from the Inside Out*, Executive Excellence Publishing, Provo, UT, 1998.

Cokins, Gary, *Activity-Based Cost Management: Making It Work: A Manager's Guide to Implementing and Sustaining an Effective ABC System*, McGraw-Hill, New York, 1996.

Cokins, Gary, *Activity-Based Cost Management: An Executive's Guide*, John Wiley & Sons, New York, 2001.

Collins, James C., *Good to Great*, HarperCollins, New York, 2001.

Collins, James C. and Porras, Jerry I., *Built to Last*, HarperCollins, New York, 1994.

Corbett, Thomas, *Throughput Accounting*, North River Press, Great Barrington, MA, 1998.

Corporate Renaissance, *The Underflow of Knowledge* (www.destinationkm.com), January 25, 2001.

Crosby, Philip, *Quality Is Free: The Act of Making Quality Certain*, McGraw-Hill, New York, 1979.

Cunningham, Jean E., Fiume, Orest J., with Adams, Emily, *Real Numbers: Management Accounting in a Lean Organization*, Managing Times Press, Durham, NC, 2003.

Deming, W. Edwards, *Out of the Crisis*, Massachusetts Institute of Technology, Cambridge, 1986.

Feld, William M., *Lean Manufacturing, Tools, Techniques, and How to Use Them*, St. Lucie Press, Boca Raton, FL, 2001.

George, Michael L., *Lean Six Sigma*, McGraw-Hill, New York, 2002

Goldratt, Eliyahu M., *The Haystack Syndrome*, North River Press, Great Barrington, MA, 1990.

Goldratt, Eliyahu M., *The Goal*, 2nd rev. ed., North River Press, Great Barrington, MA, 1992.

Goldratt, Eliyahu M., *The Critical Chain*, North River Press, Great Barrington, MA, 1997.

Goldratt, Eliyahu M. and Fox, Robert E., *The Race*, North River Press, Great Barrington, MA, 1986.

Harry, Mikel and Schroeder, Richard, *Six Sigma*, Doubleday, New York, 2000.

Hobbs, Dennis P., *Lean Manufacturing Implementation,* J. Ross Publishing, Boca Raton, FL, 2003.

Jacob, Dee Bradbury and McClelland, William T., Jr., *White Paper: Theory of Constraints Project Management*, Avraham Y. Goldratt Institute, New Haven, CT, 2001.

Johnson, H. Thomas, *Relevance Regained*, The Free Press, New York, 1992.

Johnson, H. Thomas and Bröms, Anders, *Profit Beyond Measure*, The Free Press, New York, 2000.

Johnson, H. Thomas and Kaplan, Robert S., *Relevance Lost: The Rise and Fall of Management Accounting*, The Free Press, New York, 1987.

Juran, Joseph M., *Juran on Quality by Design*, The Free Press, New York, 1992.

Kaplan, Robert S. and Anderson, Steven R., *Drive Growth with Customer Profitability Management*, Acorn Systems (www.acornsys.com), Houston, TX, April 7, 2003.

Kaplan, Robert S. and Norton, David P., *The Balanced Scorecard*, Harvard Business School Press, Boston, 1996.

Kaplan, Robert S. and Norton, David P., *The Strategy Focused Organization*, Harvard Business School Press, Boston, 2001.

Leonard, George, *Mastery*, Plume Books, New York, 1992.

Lev, Baruch, *Intangibles — Management, Measurement, and Reporting*, Brookings Institute Press, Washington, D.C., 2001.

Maskell, Brian H., *Performance Measurement for World Class Manufacturing*, Productivity Press, Portland, OR, 1991.

Miller, Jeffrey G. and Vollmann, Thomas E., The hidden factory, *Harvard Business Review,* pp. 143–146, September-October 1985.

Noreen, Eric, Smith, Debra, and Mackey, James T., *The Theory of Constraints and Its Implications for Management Accounting*, North River Press, Great Barrington, MA, 1995.

Osterland, Andrew, CFO's third annual knowledge capital scorecard, *CFO Magazine*, April 1, 2001 (www.cfo.com).

Patrick, Francis S., *Program Management*, Focused Performance (www.focused performance.com), 1998.

Plumley, Deborah, *Process-Based Knowledge Mapping*, Knowledge Management (www.destinationkm.com), March 3, 2003.

Porter, Michael E., *Competitive Advantage*, The Free Press, New York, 1985.

Porter, Michael E., *On Competition*, Harvard Business School Press, Boston, 1998.

Pryor, Tom, *Using Activity Based Management for Continuous Improvement*, ICMS, Arlington, TX, 2000.

Ryans, Adrian, More, Roger, Barclay, Donald, and Deutscher, Terry, *Winning Market Leadership*, John Wiley & Sons, Toronto, 2000.

Schonberger, Richard J., *World Class Manufacturing: Lessons of Simplicity Applied*, The Free Press, New York, 1986.

Schonberger, Richard J., *World Class Manufacturing: The Next Decade*, The Free Press, New York, 1996.

Senge, Peter M., *The Fifth Discipline*, Bantam Doubleday, New York, 1994.

Shank, John K. and Govindarajan, Vijay, *Strategic Cost Management*, The Free Press, New York, 1993.

Shook, John Y., Bringing the Toyota production system to the United States: a personal perspective, in *Becoming Lean*, Liker, Jeffery K., Ed., Productivity Press, Shelton, CT, 1998, p. 57.

Skyrme, David J., www.skyrme.com, 1996.

Smith, Debra, *The Measurement Nightmare*, St. Lucie Press, Boca Raton, FL, 2000.

Spendolini, Michael J., *The Benchmarking Book*, American Management Association, New York, 1992.

Stewart, G. Bennett, III, *The Quest for Value: The EVA™ Management Guide*, HarperCollins, New York, 1991.

Sveiby, Erik, *Methods for Measuring Intangible Assets* (www.sveiby.com), April 2001, May 2002, October 2002.

Tomas, Sam, *What Is Motorola's Six Sigma Product Quality?*, APICS Reprints, 1997, pp. 118–120.

Tracey, Michael and Wiersema, Fred D., *The Discipline of Market Leaders*, Perseus Book Group, New York, 1995.

Walton, Mary, *The Deming Management Method*, Putnam Publishing Group, New York, 1986, p. 35.

Womack, James P. and Jones, Daniel T., *Lean Thinking*, Simon & Schuster, New York, 1996.

Womack, James P., Jones, Daniel T., and Roos, Daniel, *The Machine That Changed the World: The Story of Lean Production*, HarperCollins, New York, 1991.

INDEX